THE

KNUMPTYWAGEN

JOURNALS

—

Travels and Travails In A Motorhome
Through The UK & Europe

—

Andy Paterson

First published in Great Britain by On-and-on-media.com
an imprint of Knumptytravel.com

A catalogue record for this book might be available from the
British Library but don't hold your breath.

ISBN: 978-1-0683511-0-5

Typeset in crispy clean and legible Verdana
then sustainably printed and bound by
Bookpublishinguk.com in Peterborough, UK.

Cover design, illustration and artwork
by the author
with the ever-patient assistance of
Kate Slater at
kateslaterillustration.com

"There's real life for you, embodied in that little cart. The open road, the dusty highway, the heath, the common, the hedgerows, the rolling downs! Camps, villages, towns, cities! Here today, up and off to somewhere else tomorrow! Travel, change, interest, excitement! The whole world before you, and a horizon that's always changing! And mind! This is the very finest cart of its sort that was ever built, without any exception. Come inside and look at the arrangements."

The Wind In the Willows
Kenneth Grahame

CONTENTS

PART ONE

Knumpties

Almost a decade ago, the Oxford English Dictionary appealed to the public to find a printed record of the word 'numpty'.

A similar word 'numpy' was duly found in a spoof playbill dating from 1785. The imaginary farce featured a character named Numpy the Third, a teasing term at the time for a cuckolded husband. It's thought that the 't' was added later due to the influence of the nursery rhyme, Humpty Dumpty.

Both versions of the word derive from 'numps' – a 16th century term for a simpleton.

Source:
Susie Dent, Radio Times Word of the Week
January 2024

The Prologue - Starting Out

Lichfield, Staffordshire, England

So we bought a Motorhome. A compact, pre-loved and very pleasing German-built Knaus Sport Traveller, based on the ever-popular Fiat Ducato chassis.

During our initial shop-around of local dealerships, we were dumbfounded and almost despondently blinded by the plethora of chaotic, migraine-inducing crimson, rust and yellow upholstery patterns, so the subtle grey-blue striped interior, warm beechwood furnishings and cool grey counter-top endeared us to our new acquisition.

Secondly, on an apprehensive test-drive around an oil-slicked truck-yard adjacent to the dealership, we're instructed to turn around on full-lock: 'Turns on a sixpence" encourages our new friend, Bill from the rear lounge seat, as indeed it does, so with no more ado, we hand him our pension-lump-sum deposit and become the proud owners of a newish second home.

In acquiring such a vehicle – and with little in the way of experience of driving such an oversize, lumbering beast - we christen ourselves Knumpties. With Knaus. (Geddit?)

You know the type. We infuriate you as we trundle from place to place, with our overwide bulk rolling from side to side, often at a pace annoyingly just below the speed-limit you're desperately trying to break.

We impede your hurried progress; we saunter; we slow – right – down – going – up – steep – hills . . . then, maddeningly (because we weigh over three tonnes) we gain momentum on the downward slope and speed up – so you still can't get past us.

We stare over hedge tops because we can; we smirk smugly at lowly Caravanners (labelling them

"Tuggers", just for the fun of it) and we brew tea wherever we stop, shunning the expense of roadside cafes and motorway service stations (unless of course it's Tebay or Gloucester, obviously).

We also get into scrapes. Our acquaintance with dry-stone walls; tree-trunks; narky farmers; frightened L drivers; black-ice; aged car-drivers unable to reverse; grown (bearded) men at the wheel of brand-new, bright metallic-orange pick-up trucks paralysed with fear at the prospect of scratching their flared wheel-arches as we ease by; sat-nav induced wrong turnings and . . . well, yes, on a couple of occasions, the Police – these have all increased exponentially as we've piled on the miles knumptying our way around the British Isles and Europe.

Please feel free to clamber aboard and join us on our travels as the miles and the pages unfold before you, dear reader. You hold in your hands a journal of our travels: self-indulgent, semi-instructional and hopefully entertaining & amusing.

Enjoy. We are.

Queen Of The Lakes

Derwentwater, Cumbria, England

Aah, Derwentwater, Queen of the English Lakes. Except I think that may instead be the description more accurately associated with Windermere. Or maybe even Ullswater? No matter.

The point is, Derwentwater will always hold a special place in my heart and memory, as the focal point of many childhood family holidays. Staying on a delightfully hospitable full-board sheep farm in the Newlands Valley, our regular holidays were made even more special by our early discovery of Nichol End Marine, nestled in a fold of topography on the western shore of the lake. Here, in those days, there was nothing more than a peeling, green-painted tin shed, seemingly growing out of the mossy bank on which it was perched and within which could always be found a delightfully chaotic clutter of chandlery – permanently permeated with the head-spinning top notes of creosote and fibreglass resin.

Under the overhanging greenery alongside the timber jetty, we would moor our little inflatable boat with its little outboard motor – and spend many happy hours goading the lowly tourists as they rowed innocently into our domain from the Keswick public landing stages.

As complete beginners, we also fished here with simple float and worm – from the boat and the jetty itself, where several obliging and gallant perch, wearing their comical green-black striped pyjamas and pricking their spiky dorsal fins with indignation at being hauled from their natural habitat, imbued the author with a lifetime's fascination with piscatorial creatures of all shapes, sizes and habitats.

Returning to this childhood haunt has always been an exciting experience and so it was that we journeyed up a typically clogged M6 to return to Keswick in the trusty Knumptywagen. This we manoeuvred into a pre-booked slot at the frighteningly well-run camping site set at the head of 'our' lake. Many benefits accrue from 'camping' here, especially when the slightly inconvenient three-night-minimum-stay comes complete with clear blue skies and solid sunshine, affording such magnificent views down the lake and of the surrounding mountains, that it's no effort at all to imagine yourself in a variety of more exotic locations such as Switzerland or the Italian Alps.

Other benefits of the site include the immediate adjacencies not only of the lapping shallows of Derwentwater itself, but also proximity to a localised upmarket supermarket – the sole aim of which is surely to make another more nationally prolific upmarket supermarket appear downmarket, if you get my drift?

But childhood-revisited wasn't our sole reason for taking up our sunny pitch; plugging in the electrics; rolling out the awning and putting out the reclining chairs. (Can you now see why the word 'camping' appeared above in inverted commas?) We were here to fulfil a longstanding appointment with a doyen of the angling community in the Lakes, the legendary Eric Hope, whose acquaintance we'd been lucky enough to make several years previously when he guided us onto the water for our first thrilling introduction to Esox Lucius, aka the northern pike.

Characterful, humorous, relaxed, hugely knowledgeable of both the lake and its various inhabitants, Eric is the go-to fishing guide in this neck of the woods, which is why we keep – well – go-toing him!

The weather remained glorious for our day-on-the-water as we cruised the bays, islands and drop-offs of the lake. Under our Guide's expert tutelage we boated five very fine and very fit pike, in various sizes, the majority of which were caught (of course) by Her Ladyship, The Chief Navigator and Rt Honourable Pikess of Knumptydom, no less.

Unbelievably, the following day provided yet more clear blue sky and sufficient sunshine to encourage us back onto the lake, now ourselves nothing more than lowly tourists as we disembarked onto Nichol End's landing stage from Keswick's delightful public launch service. From here we could walk to the recently re-opened Lingholm Gardens, where a striking new café and octagonal walled garden had been installed, adding a very stylish and attractive wow-factor to Derwentwater's western shore.

A walk then along the lakeshore amidst bursting greenery splashed with vibrantly coloured azaleas and rhododendrons, then stepping out briskly along the elevated walkways which traverse the marshy southern end of the lake. Our perspicacity allowed a perfectly timed ferry rendezvous at the Lodore jetty, where we had sufficient sailors' insight to sit on the leeward side as – amidst much shock and embarrassed hilarity as breeze-induced waves created a rather incongruous wet-T-shirt competition amidst the open-air windward seating, providing free entertainment for those of us in the leeward dry seats.

Returning to Keswick, we stepped ashore like the intrepid explorers we were and traversed aptly named Crow Park towards the campsite. Our upmarket supermarket beckoned us in for supper supplies which, with the weather still set fair, became a disposable barbecue, subsequently and unfortunately drifting disproportionately embarrassing clouds of smoke across the campsite.

This accidental kippering thankfully didn't seem to upset anyone, as most of our fellow campers had already disappeared inside when dusk fell, leaving a collection of variously sized wheeled 'camping' vehicles scattered around the site like clusters of white corpuscles. From within each of these shiny cells, tiny flickering neon-coloured nuclei could be seen pulsing, as unseen inhabitants tuned their aerials and roof-mounted satellite dishes ('camping'?) to receive their daily dose of passive entertainment.

Being responsible outdoor types, we instead communed with the midges; fed our faces with charcoaled steak sliced over salad; drank some wine; admired Skiddaw; doused our barbecue and followed the example of our fellow Knumptyers by retiring into our corpuscle and powering up our own little nucleus. Night night.

Black Ice

Mawddach, Gwynedd, Wales

From the coastal solidity of the A493, which runs along the southern edge of the inspiringly beautiful Mawddach estuary, and in search of a local campsite for the night, we were encouraged by our trusty Satnav onto a minor road which not only led us inland and upwards but which quickly began to narrow between high, dry stone walls.

This 'road' became steeper and narrower the further we progressed and with no option to turn around we trundled gamely on, passing just one isolated farm where, with hindsight, we should have decided to seize the day and turn back. However, the flickering flame of our pioneering spirit burnt still bright in our newly Knumptied hearts, so we pressed on, with the van's widest point – the exterior rear-view mirrors – soon clipping the dry-stone walls on both sides. It was on one of these narrow stretches, through paying more than careful attention to said mirrors, that I caught sight of a curiously incongruous (and alarming) image – we were being tailed by a police car.

Thankfully we had met no other traffic so far and with the police car now trailing in our wake, we reached a patch of firm-looking grass onto which we pulled to let him pass. As he drew level, windows were mutually wound down to exchange pleasantries. Set against a stunning backdrop featuring an early-February, late-afternoon sunset shimmering on the estuary which lay several crisp, clear miles below us, the incongruity of our situation surfaced in the face of the smiling policeman as he politely enquired if this was "our preferred route, sir?"

Now gently whimpering in a passable imitation of Stan Laurel, we did our very English best to express our interest in the police officers' local knowledge of the area; our grateful astonishment at their timely arrival and the overwhelming sense of reassurance this had brought to our otherwise isolated and idiotic predicament. Our two Officers of The Law seemed to be quietly amused at our situation, expressing surprise and (what we decided later must have been) admiration at our stoic stupidity, as we'd clearly managed to get so far and the worst of the route was now behind us. With a cheery wave, they therefore passed by ahead of us, suggesting rather pointedly that if we didn't emerge in thirty minutes, they'd be happy to call out Mountain Rescue on our behalf.

Well. It's safe to say that neither of us could remember being as scared as we became in those thirty minutes after we waved them off. Although our onward uphill route had widened ever-so-slightly, the road had also become tortuously steep and a section had clearly been washed with an overflowing mountain stream – now sheening under the lowering sun into a slick of black ice which stretched between high-verge-with-dry-stone-wall on the driver's side and soft-verge-with-gully for the passenger to contemplate on theirs. And just for good measure, there also lay malevolently amidships of this darkening sheen, a huge pothole of van-swallowing proportions.

So, everything to go for, then. With a beautiful Welsh dusk threatening to fall; a plummeting temperature and our only source of succour now disappeared over the brow of the next hill, we attempted a first, cautiously low-speed approach onto the ice-slick which, of course, was all set to repel us with its increasingly frictionless surface.

From our tentative and nominally advanced position, we then experienced – with chassis creaking and van contents gently shaking as if in fear – a slow-motion, excruciating, inexorable, bowel-relaxing slide backwards down the ice-slick, our progress being only marginally slowed through frantically spinning wheels and slipping clutch.

As if to add insult to our already injured pride, as we regained dry tarmac and continue rolling backwards, we managed somehow to steer the offside wheels onto the ever-rising grass verge, tipping the whole van slowly sideways to an impossible angle as we inch – creaking on the brakes – further back downhill. Thankfully our offside rear wheel rolled up against a rock which impeded any further backward progress and we came to a silent stop, our pressured whistling breaths uncannily reminiscent of the sound of airbrakes echoing around the cab.

Realising that the van could now thankfully go no further back down the hill, we risked abandoning the cab (yes, alright, still in our 'travelling' slippers) and disembarked to assess the situation at ground level. From here, it became abundantly clear that our only solution lay onwards; that reversing to anywhere was an impossibility and the inevitable requirement for forward motion was going to necessitate a jolly good run-up.

Right then. Repeat after me: We're exceptionally brave. We're really very brave indeed. We may look pale and still have our slippers on – but we are damn-near Superheroes. So, gritting teeth and revving like a dragracer, we spewed mud, verge, sheep-dung, diesel fumes and a few strangulated expletives into the gloaming – all the while forgetting to admire the magnificent view and low-streaming rays of the setting sun. Wheels spun, engine roared and we inched painfully forwards again, off the verge and somehow, through brute ignorance and horsepower, we managed to get all four tyres back onto tarmac, where the handbrake held us poised and creaking as we girded ourselves for our second attempt at the lethal-looking ice-sheet-and-pothole combo which lay ahead.

With screaming revs, alliterative slight-sideways-slithery-skidding and a toe-curling sense of slow-motion we hurtled up the short stretch of dry road and onto the ice where – just as our critical forward momentum began to decay beneath us – our wheels passed either side of the pothole and reached dry tarmac on the other side of the ice. With red faces and regained friction, we cheered ourselves onward beyond our nemesis and up towards the brow of the hill, where we were greeted around the next bend by one of our friendly Welsh constables, casually leaning over an open gate. From here, he was clearly pleased to be able to comment wryly on the smell of burning clutch which "seemed to be prevalent up here at this time of year."

We exchanged further relieved pleasantries and copious thanks before we allowed ourselves sheepishly to be escorted off the mountain (thankfully without the ignominy of blue lights) back down to the coastal A-road – from which we should never have departed in the first place.

Strong sweet tea was brewed in the next lay-by, supped with all the savour and panache of a champagne-cocktail as the crisp winter sun signed itself off through the windscreen. Off went the Satnav, out came the maps and back we trekked around the estuary to the welcoming bosom of Barmouth where we enjoyed a satisfyingly close call with a surprisingly low railway bridge as our Grand Finale.

Finally, and with great relief we parked up for the night on a deserted, gloriously flat, ice-free promenade – where we promptly steadied our frayed nerves through the unmitigated consumption of our entire on-board duty-free allowance for the rest of the trip.

Thank you, Wales. You're always a lot of fun.

The Camper's Friend

Aberaeron, Ceridigion, Wales

Blue roll! Quick, hands up, who knows what I'm on about? If you're motorhoming and have never discovered the huge benefits (along with the massive OCD delights) of Blue Roll, then I can only suggest you get yourselves down to our favourite American-style wholesale warehouse (other suppliers also exist) and avail of a six-pack.

We discovered the benefits of Blue Roll several years before we started our Knumptying activities, when we were abject and avid fans of said wholesale warehouses, an astonishing import to our fair shores – rammed full of fascinating products – all bulk-purchasable and none of which, once you'd witnessed their existence, could you ever do without ever again.

Trips to our nearest outlet became accidentally expensive family days-out, where we'd wander aisles towering with desirable consumer goods, marvelling open-mouthed at the overwhelming array of LCD TVs as well as shelves seemingly teetering under industrial quantities of double A batteries; toothpaste; canoes; buttermilk pancake mix; Worcestershire Sauce; garden furniture; kettles; lobster; Curly-Wurlys; Chateau Neuf du Pape; spanners and stuff even Aladdin would have been hard-pushed to imagine.

Nestling unassumedly in the slightly-less exciting and therefore rarely visited Household Cleaning section were also to be found impenetrable fortresses built from shrink wrapped six packs of huge, fat, absorbent blue paper rolls. These unsung giants of domestic cleaning exist solely to mop up industrial-sized spills of you-name-it and with a young family, they became a cost-effective staple of our home cleaning cupboard, each roll being at least 27 miles long and therefore far more cost-effective (per sheet, of course) than traditional kitchen-roll.

So where am I going with this? Bear with, as tonight, our in-van supper has been more than the usual culinary triumph.

Parked up as we are on the harbourfront at Aberaeron, Ceridigion, Wales and overlooking a windswept, grey and almost autumnal Cardigan Bay, we managed to procure some very fresh fish from The Hive fishmongers in the centre of town. This haul included fresh shell-on mussels, king scallops (complete with those delightful aerofoils of coral-coloured roe) and two hake steaks, cut from the whole fish in front of our eyes and therefore just the right width for our purposes.

Back in the Knumptywagen and juggling the culinary priorities of a three ring gas-stove, the In-Van Map-Reading Fishmongering Chef d'Cuisine set-to and produced a menu to which not one of the professional catering establishments lining the High Street could have held a candle.

Ready? OK, start dribbling at tonight's pop-up menu:

Linguine with fresh shell-on moules cooked in a white wine, shallot and cream sauce served with scallops and hake, pan-fried in black-butter, accompanied by a chilled Marlborough Sauvignon Blanc and a Welsh cheeseboard to follow.

A triumph and a delight! Made more so because clearing up after fish-cookery is always a bit of a mess – and 'camping' wild with an onboard grey-water tank doesn't lend itself to washing up the remains. Which is where this particular tale began. Step into the spotlight, please, Blue Roll, and perform your duties as preliminary wiper-upper of every single item from tonight's extensive fish-based batterie d'cuisine – from cutlery through plates to pans – to ensure nothing untoward enters the waste-water course and instead all goes, very hygienically, into the bin!

Away To Foreign Lands

Rutland Water, Rutland, England

The Knumptywagen is back on the road.

With a cargo of immovable spiders clearly resident in the casings of both oversize wing-mirrors, we are newly road-taxed following a Covid-induced period of SORN, (DVLA's acronym for Statutory Off Road Notice – forgive me if I don't expand on DVLA as well or we'll be here all day) and the Knumptywagen took to the road again at approximately 11:50 hours this morning, Monday 23 August, at which we joyously cried 'Hurrah'!

Foreign lands? Well, inasmuch as we rarely have cause to travel anywhere east of the M1, on this particular post-lockdown trip, we're headed for the coast of Norfolk – and that does entail crossing borders into strange hinterlands previously only rarely explored, and where there may indeed be dragons.

Nevertheless, the sun has shone mightily on our pioneering endeavours and smiled on us as we heaved-to in a grassy camping field alongside Rutland Water, where awning and reclining chairs were quickly deployed, under and on which we promptly fell soundly asleep in appreciated afternoon warmth.

Two new bicycles graced the Knumptywagen's rear-mounted rack, lovingly swaddled in an also-new shiny silver cover (ostensibly to protect them from road-borne grime – and prying eyes) but which more unexpectedly rendered our trusty reversing-camera completely useless – unless we desired to view on our little dashboard screen the shiny silver cover billowing like a spinnaker behind us as we bowled merrily along.

Research undertaken by the Navigating Goddess of Eastern Lands advised that Rutland Water enjoys the benefit of a predominantly flat lake-edge path (designed for the combined use of both cyclists and pedestrians) which circumnavigates its 17-mile perimeter – and you'll be as impressed as my Mother was when I regaled her with the news of our perambulatory triumph. Until of course, you were also made aware that our two new bicycles both featured electric motors, whence the impressed, congratulatory tone may falter a little, as it becomes evident that we hadn't travelled that astonishing distance exclusively under our own motive force.

The sun has now set; the summer-like temperature has plummeted like a dropped anchor; we've re-racked the bikes; beered and dined in-van and are now – as darkness envelops us at just beyond 9:00pm – contemplating further sleep, this time for the night, since tomorrow awaits, as does a further tale of two nearby towns, the names of which (somewhat mysteriously) both start with the letter 'S'.

A Tale Of Two Esses

Spalding & Stamford, Lincolnshire, England

In order to make some contextual sense of the seemingly mis-spelt title, I must ask you, gentle reader, to rewind with your humble author a good few years (and probably many more – memory tends to telescope with increasing maturity, I find) to a previous Knumptywagen visit to the Suffolk/Norfolk coast, possibly so long ago that it was definitely PC – and might even be PB. (Pre Covid. Pre Book. Get with it.)

Back at home, we're endowed with two particular lovely friends, who knowing a thing or two about such stuff, had enthusiastically recommended we visit a delightful town in the vicinity of our travels, about which all I could recall was that it began with the letter 'S'. Thus, on the homeward leg of our earlier journeyings, the CNO (Chief Navigating Officer – keep up) spotted Spalding on our route ahead; I immediately spewed-up vague recognition and in we drove.

A further rewind if you please. During late teenage and early adult years, I suffered from frequent migraine attacks, often presaged by visual distortion, a classic symptom. Thankfully, in later life, the migraines have long since departed but I do occasionally still suffer with the visual issue, thankfully now in isolation of the excruciating headaches and the associated need for twenty-four hours in a darkened room with just a bucket and myriad pills for company.

These days, the visual distortions strike without warning and in the main are now thankfully merely discomforting rather than debilitating. On this particular occasion, such was my excitement at eventually reaching the much lauded and attractive town which we 'simply must visit' that, on approach, my eyesight kaleidoscoped into fragments, whence we were luckily able to park up the Knumptywagen and step out for a remedial breath of fresh air.

Spalding is a mid-sized market town on the River Welland, in the parish of South Holland, Lincolnshire. It appears to boast little in the way of tourist attractions, listing separate Romany and Engine Museums; a bowling alley; Festival Gardens; a Fun Farm and Adventure Land as its highlights. On the day of our visit, it suffered even more by being admired with a fragmentary three-quartered view through two separately functioning optic nerves, while the CNO guided my stumbling personage around a handful of streets before deciding to call it a day and take the wheel to drive her dribbling companion home. Whence we discovered that Spalding was not Stamford.

So here we are! A 'return' visit to Stamford in all its single-visioned, historic, limestoned, architectural and cultural glory. Another Lincolnshire market town, some 20 miles distant from its previous incarnation and also settled on the (more picturesque) banks of the River Welland, which sinuously separates said same settlements. Flowing gently towards its confluence with The Wash, such is the geography of the area that poor old Spalding even gets its river water second-hand.

An almost empty car park absorbed our inconsiderate bulk and we walked the streets agog with wonder. The river meadows; the fine bridges; the bustle of independent and therefore intriguing shops and mullion-windowed hostelries set amidst 600 listed buildings (including five – yes, five - medieval churches, four of which are named after specific Saints while the fifth, All Saints, represents a sort-of ecclesiastical catch-all just in case any unrepresented Angels of The Lord On Earth might take offence).

A newly-awakened Arts Centre, into which high-ceilinged Ballroom we peeped through an open door to marvel at the fastidious internal redecoration underway as we watched; brunch on the pavement at a Scandinoir café, impressive eighteenth and nineteenth townhouses; a brewery; shops displaying art and musical instruments; maskless natives openly greeting each other (and us!) on the narrow flagstone pavements – and so many intriguing passageways and alleys weaving it all together into the delight which had been described to us, so long ago.

So thank you Stamford and apologies to Spalding for my initial confusion. We eventually came, we saw and we have conquered.

Next Stop, The South Coast

Winterborne Came, Dorset, England

We have pivoted. Meaning that we're off again, having barely had the time to evict the tribes of wing-mirrored spiders before they claim squatters' rights.

Pivoted? Well, yes, because this time we pivot our trip around a Covidly-delayed family wedding, to take place at a rather smart venue in the heart of Thomas Hardy's bucolic county of Dorset. And much to do around the pivot point, including the week preceding by the sea in Pevensey Bay followed by the weekend wedding, taking place amidst landscaped grounds and a rather stunning Purbeck-stoned country-house under favourably azure Mediterranean hued skies. After which we're then off to explore the Jurassic Coast via a reunion with another long-lost cousin, so we are – as my Mother would say – being just a little bit busy.

Having sea-sided on the beach where William the Conqueror allegedly made landfall, we travel Dorset-wards and park the Knumptywagen offsite, to then be transferred in our black-tied finery, first to Hardy's Mellstock church and thence to Came House, grandiose in its command of the view over rolling Dorset countryside, made buttery-gold by the recent harvest.

We celebrate the marriage like maniacs, the first big family occasion since Lockdown was invented – and then party into the late summer evening as if the occasion might also be our last. So it is that a slightly bedraggled, bravely smiling group of guests reconvene on the Sunday morning, where we ignominiously park the bug spattered, grimy Knumptywagen on the gravelled forecourt of The Big House, where it attracts the attention of small children and curious adults alike.

The doors are left open for the little flow of visitors to pop in and view the spacious interior; the ingenious storage binnacles; undercounter fridge; 3-ring stove; tiny oven; bijou dinette; over-cab bed and the compact wet-room which combines nifty shower with quaint chemical toilet.

Towards the end of the morning's sociability, as guests begin the take their leave, we find ourselves chatting with the owners of the wedding venue who are – obviously – wellspoken, well-bred and clearly well-old-moneyed. As such they are intrigued by the delightful novelty of the dirty-white wheeled box parked askew on their forecourt – which clearly doesn't sport any of the upmarket badging normally associated with the sleekly-polished limousine marques often to be seen gracing this particular patch of groomed gravel.

"Please – have a look inside" we invite, attempting to mirror the classically upmarket, relaxed confidence of our hosts, as we wander away to wave off others, leaving them both to conduct their own guided tour of the Knumptywagen's interior.

"Lovely" they both pronounce as they rather hurriedly disembark and themselves stride off to attend to other business. It is not until we ourselves make ready to depart that we discover a small, disproportionately malodourous business item has been gifted to us by one of the small, fascinated children who have also been popping in and out, and who had clearly discovered how to use – but sadly not to flush – the toilet.

Onwards.

One Small Step

Llydan Beach, Rhosneigr, Wales

On 20 July 1969, astronaut Neil Armstrong stepped down from Eagle, NASA's fragile, tin-foiled, spider-legged lunar-landing module and placed the human race's very first footprints on the surface of another planet.

Apart from absorbing that semi-interesting historical snippet, observant readers will also note that he was carrying a large backpack, weighing somewhere in the region of 30lbs, which contained his life-support system for the first moonwalk in human history.

Gravity being what it is, he was virtually weightless during his brief sojourn on the moon's dusty surface, whilst in contrast we were enjoying the Isle of Anglesey's earthbound gravitational pull as it anchored us happily in reclining chairs, basking in warm summer sunshine on Llydan Beach.

Having recognised the opportunity presented by a 'surprise' free weekend, we'd liberated the Knumptywagen from storage, dusted it down, remembered to tax it, and trundled off on a spontaneous trip to this small, easily accessible and uncharacteristically sunny island off the north coast of Wales.

Here, through slightly naive landlocked ignorance, we became fascinated by the number of fellow holidaymakers touting large ungainly space-age Neil-Armstrong-sized silvered backpacks along beach paths.

Our piqued curiosity was of course rewarded when nearest neighbours dumped a matching pair of these monolithic packages on the sand nearby, and proceeded to unwrap from within inflatable paddle boards, which came into being, chrysalis-like, amidst some hefty hand-pumping.

These simple craft proliferated along the beach, with feverish pumping (or the occasional high-pitched whine of upmarket battery-operated pumps) providing a soundtrack to accompany the cawing seagulls and general seaside chatter so redolent of our youth.

Once inflated to an alarmingly explosive-looking rigidity, they were then proudly carried (or dragged) to the gently lapping water's edge and launched with varying degrees of aplomb, confidence, skill and tomfoolery by people of varying height, age and body mass.

Those sporting wetsuits generally stepped confidently aboard and – standing tall and proud – paddled themselves serenely towards the distant horizon. Others chose to kneel, some to sit, and some to be pushed seawards by willing partners, one of whom dashed back ashore to embark an over-excited, yapping dog who thence seemed completely at ease crewing the stern of his gently bobbing craft.

Such were their numbers that – as the day progressed- our view out to sea became populated by silhouetted stick-people, as if L. S. Lowry had forsaken Manchester for the day, headed to the seaside and captured the animated scenes in his own painterly style.

And then, as the sun began to set, these proud seafarers came ashore, to release the valves of their pressurised craft, adding yet more alarming space-age sound effects into our afternoon reveries. Gradually, all was packed away; aquanauts donned their oversize backpacks and ambled, in apparent gravity-less slow-motion – back to the busy car park, where presumably they loaded up their own versions of the Eagle and blasted off back to their campsites, B&Bs for rewarding teas, beers and well-deserved dinners, under the benevolent light of a silvery super-moon.

Darkness Descends

Tal-y-Llyn, Gwynedd, Wales

Our Knaus Sport Traveller motorhome has at last been liberated from its winter hibernation; batteries have been charged; interior aired; fridge cleaned; mosses and lichens eased gently from their various toeholds around the exterior trim and a liberal shiny coating of Bobby Dazzler (I kid you not) applied to the bodywork.

And so, we head for Wales – where we open the batting with a perhaps inevitable satnav induced near-disaster, to initiate our Portfolio of Unfortunate Pioneering Experiences. These escapades only seem to befall us amidst the spectacular and easily accessible scenic beauty of the Welsh countryside, and in this instance stems from our innocent use of one of the many online site-location apps upon which we of the Knumptying fraternity draw from time-to-time to find suitable overnight stops when none have been pre-planned.

So it was, that after a successful day's trout-fishing in bright spring sunshine on Gwernan Lake near Dolgellau, we opted to head for a hotel/pub-stop on the shores of Tal-yllyn Lake just seven kilometres away, on the opposite side of Cadair Idris. The clocks having sprung forward, and with the last rays of sunshine illuminating the roadside verges with splashes of cadmium yellow daffodils, we set off with the romanticised notion of parking up for the night at a lakeside tavern – to enjoy welcoming log fires, a pint or two in a thronged and amiable bar and perhaps a warming bowl of home-cooked pub food.

By the time we reached the head of the lake, darkness was more-or-less upon us – and with satnav continuing to gamely guide us, we headed off the main carriageway onto a minor road across which we were soon to encounter a gate, closed against us but not padlocked and assumedly designed only to retain roaming sheep. Through it we therefore passed, continuing along the single lane tarmacked track which hugged the side of the lake. Driven on by our notion of welcoming hospitality, we thought little of the next gates which again were easily opened – although the road surface was beginning to degrade and the width reducing so our wheels were only just continuing to touch tarmac.

Almost imperceptibly (and in direct proportion to the ever-increasing tufts of grass springing up along the centre of the road) our expectations about our destination began to dwindle. Overhanging trees began to scrape the roof and sides of the van and out of the darkness there emerged a large and wholly dilapidated farmhouse. How on earth, we naively asked ourselves, could a hotel out here be practicably serviced via such difficult access – and, if it was indeed to fulfil our expectations, why was there no other traffic sharing our single-tracked and single-minded odyssey?

More gates. Another deserted barn. The lakeside lapping perilously close a couple of feet below our trundling offside wheels. Satnav still upheld a tiny, chequered, flickering flag of hope just half-a-mile further on (and we couldn't have turned round to save our lives anyway) so onward we trundled, now not only stopping to open gates but also to hold the larger tree branches out of our way.

In the far distance, car headlights swept along the main road on the opposite lakeshore, highlighting our creeping sense of isolation as, at walking pace, we 'arrived at our destination': a boarded-up, neglected, stone-walled and wholly inhospitable bungalow which wouldn't have looked out of place in a Scandi-noir murder-mystery.

Perhaps recognising our worried displeasure, satnav then teasingly revealed that our only choice of onward route re-joined the safety of the main road a half-mile further on, so with increasing trepidation fuelled by a glimmer of hope, we crawled on, main-beam headlights carving eerie shapes and throwing shadows into the moss-draped woodland which surrounded us.

At last, there, just beyond the headlamp reach, we discern a final gate fronted by a grass verge, beyond which traffic passed unimpeded on the main lake road. However, between us and salvation lay one more challenge – a fast-flowing river fording the now crumbled track. Unbelieving that we had come so far to encounter this potential impassability, we did the only thing we could have done; clambered out of the van; dragged wellies out of buried storage and waded the ford with tentative steps, backlit from a barely perceptible main beam. Darkened water swirled ankle-deep around our feet which were thankfully finding firm foothold on a stable and solid concrete surface beneath.

OK then. Back in the van; deep breaths; slip the clutch and sail into the water-filled dip; keep the speed up as mountain-chilled Welsh water swirled around our axles and beware of the track cranking tight left at the top of the stone-walled exit ramp.

Ha-ha! Through and out the other side! One gate left. If it's padlocked, we're ramming it, but thankfully it unlatches at our touch and was just about draggable open through the tangling verge grass. Here – illuminated in the headlights – we espy the faded, overgrown and long-forgotten paint of Give Way lines – allowing us to return, slightly scratched, scathed but hugely relieved and triumphant – to reconnect with civilisation as represented by the solid and well-maintained tarmac of the B4405.

Uplifted by a sense of triumph-over-adversity and liberally shaken (not stirred) with great relief, we speedily retraced our route back along the correct side of the lake, only pausing open-mouthed to realise that the hotel we had originally sought was lurking – unlit, unsigned and clearly closed – at the original junction of main road and gated lane down which we had just travelled.

Pulling up here, we placed the telephone call we really should have made before setting off, to awaken a slightly disgruntled hotel landlord who was willing to open his door (in his dressing gown at 9pm?) just long enough to take a £10.00 overnight 'parking' fee from us while suggesting we turn up at nine in the morning when he'd be happy to sell us a great cooked breakfast!

Negotiations concluded, we returned to the van for a nerve-settling and well-deserved nightcap before settling down for the most expensive overnight 'wild camping' we'd ever enjoyed.

Poor Little Fishguard

Fishguard, Pembrokeshire, Wales

Poor little Fishguard. Like a new kid at school, it must have fallen over and scraped both its knees just before we arrived, so was therefore looking a bit scruffy, out-of-sorts and definitely feeling sorry for itself. More pointedly, it was clear its Mummy wasn't going to be picking it up until much later, so it was going to remain surly and miserable for the rest of the day, despite the fact that we'd made a special effort to visit it. Even the Knumptywagen seemed a tad concerned to be left on its own, despite the fact we'd just forked out a minimum of £4.00 protection money for it to stay in the town-centre playground while we wandered the streets in search of breakfast and a spot of enlightenment.

Neither was sadly forthcoming. Maybe our expectations had been set too high when we'd heard about the charming-sounding lower & upper town: the former was just a small and unimpressive quayside (the Rosslare ferry port belonging to a separate part of the town altogether) while the upper town also really couldn't quite decide what it wanted to be, with its fair share of empty retail outlets. A few brave shops imparted a degree of soul but even these seemed a little confused about their purpose so had filled their windows with a peculiar mix of disparate items such as silk scarves, hats, optical instruments and electrical domestic appliances – which combination just confounded us even further.

Even the Tourist Office seemed embarrassed by its own existence, hiding unremarked and unsigned within the cheerful-looking exterior of the flower-bedecked Town Hall. Two gallant ladies lifted their heads tentatively above a high desk in response to our entry and did their best for the town they represented, despite having so little raw material on which to draw. One dear soul – with possibly imagined nervous glances towards her colleague – attempted to furnish us with details about the key tourist attractions in Fishguard. These seemingly consisted of a café down by the lower town quay, where a short estuarial walk could also be taken; a café in the upper town or a home-grown tapestry of an unexplained Final Invasion (which subsequent research determined took place in 1797 and represented the very last foreign invasion of mainland Britain, by a team of crack French infiltrators who fortuitously chose a location three miles west of Fishguard, thus establishing the town in the annals of international history.)

Needless to say we chose to forego a visit to these major attractions, electing instead to seek out a well-hidden Co-op food store (to which we were directed in a lilting Welsh accent by the accolade: "It's not brrillllli-ant, but it's all we've got"). Here we discovered we could have parked the Knumptywagen for free (and spent the £4.00 parking fee on a souvenir optical appliance instead) so to raise ourselves from Fishguard-induced despondency, we embarked on an uplifting bout of grocery replenishment. Late breakfast provisions thus acquired, we liberated the Knumptywagen from an unfriendly corner of the playground and parked up instead overlooking the ferry port, where a recently arrived Rosslare car ferry was disgorging a stream of presumably Irish trucks and cars to provide a spot of visual stimulation and delight with which to accompany our simple in-van breakfast.

Poor little Fishguard. We hope it gets over its grazed knees and perhaps its Mummy might give it fishfingers for tea to cheer it up a little when it gets home. It needs it.

Lobster Saves Pwllheli

Pwllheli, Gwynedd, Wales

Not the sort of headline you'd expect to see every day (unless of course you're a Sun reader), but do please stick around – it'll (hopefully) all make sense in the end.

For better or worse, and perhaps rather cynically, campsites are functionally necessary to our otherwise 'wild camping' ethos. Once in a while, we have to empty-out and fill-up (if you'll forgive the rather indelicate phrasing) but most of the time we prefer to find isolated overnight stops off the beaten track (or at least away from a main road.) In such locations we aim for a good view, a bit of peace and quiet and a minimal sense that we are – in some skewed way – communing with nature.

So it is that today, after three nights of aforementioned wild debauchery, we find ourselves on a farm campsite – rocking and rolling in the teeth of a howling Welsh gale (we couldn't find a weather app that offered any different) – but at least being nurtured and nourished through our bright-orange umbilical power lead. Fresh water has also been piped aboard and the unmentionables have also been disposed of with the assistance of an innocuous sounding 'cassette' and a removable manhole cover.

And already today, we have done Pwllheli. And Abersoch. And Aberdaron. All visited, assessed and enjoyed in different ways, mainly due to the inclement weather which has encouraged us to tour the region in the comparative comfort of the Knumptywagen, alighting only when necessary to either stretch our legs or explore the delights proffered by these three Llyn peninsular settlements.

As if knowing that stormy seas would be more prevalent than calm, Aberdaron was hunkered down in a foetal curl, it's featureless back turned seawards, while the business of the village could be conducted in the comparative shelter of its protected, soft little tummy. Here, gift-shops; inns and pubs; cafés and ice-cream kiosks could provide fulfilment to the gently meandering hordes who'd spilled out of cars parked with due acknowledgment paid to the National Trust, which owns much of this coastline. A stand-out, Austrian-styled, ochre coloured bakery provided both a focal point and an exciting range of sweet and savoury products, of which we availed as if we'd been bereft of freshly-baked-anything for several days, which of course we had. Meanwhile, a stone bridge over the gently flowing River Daron provided a characterful bottleneck for oversized delivery trucks, seemingly bemused by the ebb and flow of indecisive pedestrians all trying to choose between cornets or cake.

Sadly, many of the cafés were Covid-closed, reducing our potential entertainment value considerably so we left Aberdaron behind and drove on to visit windswept Abersoch. On approach, it was clear that this seaside town was a-bustle with roaming herds of pedestrians, all proudly modelling Joules, North Face and Mountain Warehouse on pavement catwalks, bemusement apparent on their faces as the Covidly Closed Café Culture made itself felt here as well. We circumnavigated the town on its nifty little one-way traffic system, failed to find any readily available parking and headed on out again.

Something about Pwllheli had been nagging in my mind, eventually to be realised as a much-publicised holiday camp location, evidence of which was nowhere to be seen. Traffic queued on the main approach road; we flowed slowly with it and eventually washed up in a mundane car park on the outskirts of the town centre. Although rain had abated, the gale force wind tested our door-hinges as we alighted (also modelling Mountain Warehouse, I'll have you know) to visit the beach, from which we immediately beat a hasty retreat with our fashionable mass-market outerwear tearing at its own zipped and Velcro fastenings in the flapping gale.

Narrow pavements were plied by fellow tourists, being accidentally windblown into each other's social distance and there was much ineffective and semi-dangerous stepping into the road to get past. Short rambling queues hovered indecisively outside charity shops, many of these sadly indistinguishable from more bona fide retail outlets. In between these microcosms of human endeavour, other closed shops bravely sported hand-scrawled 'Hope To See You Again Soon' notices in their dulled, cataract-grey windows. Or at least that's what we hoped they said, as most were in Welsh and were probably imparting messages far more inhospitable.

With wind, rain and grey scudding clouds prevailing, we were about to give up and tack back to the Knumptywagen when a sturdy, still-weather-defiant pavement sign caught our attention. A blue painted border framed the enticing word 'seafood' and – to our surprise – the small, compact blue painted and tiled shop was not only open for business but excitedly stocked with all manner of – well - seafood.

Window shelves sported exotic spice mixes enveloped in brown paper; fresh lemons and limes proudly shouted their own exorbitant prices; a basket of cleaned scallop shells (25p each; 5 for a £1) rattled provocatively as you leaned over to disbelievingly examine bottles of Clamato – a definitively New World blend of tomato and clam juice rarely spotted on these shores. Paprika and chorizo quarrelled with each other for attention, and a quietly-spoken bespectacled gentleman, complete with striped fishmonger's apron, held court behind glass fronted counters awash with – erm, well, yeah, like – fresh seafood.

A meaty slab of hake; giant prawns (clearly not harvested from these windswept shores, we didn't care); fresh anchovies slithery with oil; a couple of scallops (whose bright orange roe curled protectively around their mothers, we still didn't care) were all acquired as we salivated our way back onto the windswept pavement. Accompaniments? We must have accompaniments! Fortuitously, immediately next door, a Spar convenience store announced its presence with a delicately typographed 'Deli' sign inscribed on its outer wall. Really?

In we went, fuelled by fish-induced acquisitiveness, and were – quite frankly – astounded by the attractiveness of the interior layout. No sign of fusty rows of own-label baked beans nor plastic-bagged, thin-sliced white bread. Instead, a riot of colour and diversity from a glisteningly fresh vegetable counter; sliced charcuterie and cooked meats; open shelved loose bakery items; wine racked as if we'd stumbled into someone's private cellar; a preponderance of wooden shelves and natural wood claddings; imaginative lighting, décor and layout all immediately transported us to a more exotic and foreign shore than downtown Pwllheli. And then, as almost humble pièce de résistance, we spot the ultimate in Spar convenience-store offerings – a bubbling clearwater tank full of live lobsters, each sporting healthy-looking saturated sapphire blue armaments, on offer at £15 a pop.

We decide momentarily – and with a fleeting degree of sadness – that we have already acquired sufficient piscatorial comestibles from next door and therefore duly reach the tills, sans lobster, but incredulous with awe to have found such an oasis in this otherwise unremarkable town. Independent seafood and live Spar crustaceans? You've just saved Pwllheli.

PART TWO

North to Scotland

An Englishman is travelling through the Highlands
and pauses to drink from a stream.
A passing shepherd calls out
"Dinnae drink frae that, it's all fulla coo piss an
shite."

The Englishman replies in a cut-glass accent
"I'm terribly sorry, my good man, but would you
mind repeating that in the King's English?"

And the shepherd replies
"Och, of course, sir, I was just asking if you'd like
to borrow this tin cup to get a proper drink."

Joke. Probably trad.
If it's yours, please feel free to claim it.

Butcher, Baker, Blairgowrie

Douglas, South Lanarkshire, Scotland

A trip up to the far north of mainland Scotland is planned, to visit places we hadn't managed on our previous trip which was now almost 4 years ago. Our vague objective was to take a few days getting up there, and then let global gravity drag us gently southwards back down the West Coast again, leapfrogging the bits we'd already done and enjoying the bits we'd missed first time round.

Heading north up the M6 and subsequently onwards on the A74(M), we knew we'd need to overnight somewhere. Sensing that Glasgow itself may be a little too overpopulated to provide a true 'wild' camping experience, we arbitrarily selected a random location just off the motorway at Douglas, about which not much was forthcoming from a brief internet search. As it turned out, we were hugely lucky with our choice as Douglas – despite needing a candlestick maker – had everything we could possibly have wished for in a random off-the-beaten-track Scottish village.

A river ran through it; a delightful church sat at its centre; memorials had been raised to famous sons and a battling Cameronian regiment which had formed and subsequently disbanded within its boundaries; an agreeably well-maintained estate containing a large fishing lake (with adjacent parking); a semi-circular and therefore strangely tubular three storey castle ruin standing sentinel over gently undulating estate parkland; ancient trees straggling spreading boughs around massive trunks as if tired from upholding all their limbs; the sun shone; we parked up in glorious isolation alongside the lake; strolled aimlessly to find an empty pub into which we were welcomed by a bored but enthusiastic landlady ('twas she who proudly announced the village boasted a butcher and a baker); two cafes; a petrol station – and all of this within earshot and distant sight of the thrumming A74(M).

An undisturbed and peaceful overnight was followed by a morning's worth of energetic fishing ("There's big pike in there" informed a passing dog-walker, "but they're very canny" – which insight we sadly came to prove) and as our regular sense of disappointment overtook us, we retired to a full Scottish in-van breakfast – enjoying the peculiarly spicy addition of a locally snared haggis.

Onwards around Glasgow and upwards towards Dunkeld, where we'd promised ourselves a re-visit, which didn't disappoint. This charming Tayside townlet was atmospherically busy as we wandered its compact streets; marvelled at the quirkiness of Jeffreys Interiors, set inside a converted church and still playing haunting background music to accompany the delightful weirdness of its stock; acquired ice-creams to celebrate a full day of sunshine, then travelled onwards to Blairgowrie, where our one and only arranged social commitment of the whole trip awaited us.

School friendships seem to either swiftly fizzle out during University Freshers' Week or they endure over years, seemingly never wavering despite long dormant periods, to pick up again without hesitation, deviation or repetition – which is exactly what awaited us in Blairgowrie as we crossed the threshold of a long-term school friend of the Navigator Par Excellence.

Offered substantial quantities of food, drink and unwavering hospitality (including a night in a proper bed) we over-imbibed on all counts – and awoke the following morning to find the Knumptywagen exactly where we'd left it, parked on a nearby side-street (always a relief given the high level of thefts reported through motorhome social networks.)

In drizzling grey rain, we were escorted on a guided tour of Blairgowrie's High Street, where we patronised an intriguing artisan silversmith's shop-cum-workshop and a well-stocked butcher's shop, where several wholly unnecessary purchases had to be made.

An extremely well-stocked Hunting Shooting Fishing shop also drew us in, overseen by an imposing and knowledgeable grey-haired owner, who unwittingly amused us with her response to our enquiry about the availability of live maggots – which we'd been sadly lacking during our earlier fishing at Douglas Water. These, she explained, were not readily available in Blairgowrie as they had to travel by train from England, and unfortunately Blairgowrie lacked the requisite railway station, where said maggots might presumably have alighted and wriggled their way – en masse – along the High Street to her shop, where they would divest themselves of their cumbersome luggage and offer themselves for sale to passing anglers.

Leaving Blairgowrie in weather the locals describe as 'dreich' (for which read 'wet and grey') we headed north to penetrate the Cairngorms, where dreichness soon gave way to snow; road signs warned of ice; alarmingly tall snow-poles marked both sides of the road and every habitation had a sign outside to advertise ski-hire at a cheaper price than the house before. And despite the miserability of the scenery, we did eventually pass through Glen Shee to witness at least 3 skiers actually using the slopes – although, from a distance, none of them appeared to be enjoying it.

Nairn And The Road North

Nairn & Tongue, Highlands, Scotland

Yesterday, we 'did' Nairn where we overnighted on the harbourside and enjoyed a cycle around the slate grey town – which coincided with a war-time bomb undergoing a controlled explosion on the beach – a singularly less-spectacular event than it sounds, apart from the deafening bang and - according to past news reports - a fairly regular occurrence in this neck of the woods.

A brief and strangely enervating Sunday-morning sojourn at a convenient harbourside jet-wash left us £4.00 poorer, but eminently more shiny-looking than when we'd arrived – and that was just the Knumptywagen, (its occupants in need of similar attentions.)

Having left Nairn's local Co-op store bereft of boxed tissues to stem streaming noses (is that possibly just a little too much information?) we trundled north-westwards towards the small township of Lairg, which being Sunday, appeared shut and therefore unable to provide us with a heavily anticipated and sumptuous travellers' Sunday lunch. An in-van repast therefore ensued, overlooking the hydro-electric neck of mini-me Loch Shin, fuelling us for the next leg of the journey, heading along a clearly mapped A-road running due north. The A836 runs directly from Lairg to Tongue and is a remarkable road. For its entire 35-mile length, it's a single-track with passing places. And as if that leaves you slightly incredulous, get this: the road was virtually empty of any other traffic, despite already being within the bounds of the Easter holidays. So numerous were the Passing Places, we lost count of how many there were, each one diligently sporting an individual road-sign to announce its function. It must have cost a fortune to install them all – and we marvelled at the diligence and budgeting strategy of

Highways Scotland, where they might instead have simply installed two instructional signs, one at each end of the 35 miles and saved themselves a wad of cash.

As it was, the frequency of these passing places meant that the seven vehicles we passed throughout the entire 35 miles of the route didn't even need to reduce speed – we just sailed past each other with acknowledging waves as either we – or they – slipped effortlessly to one side and carried on our journeys. And being considerate snail-paced highway wallowers, we also gave way to faster traffic following on behind. Of which there was one (yes, just one) appreciative driver with whom we exchanged acknowledging toots.

Bleak, flat, uninterrupted moorland – cut through by a fast-flowing peat-brown river – rolled to the horizon on both sides. Patches of shattering forestry-work had left swathes of ash-grey stubble across the landscape, looking like iron-filings viewed through a microscope, adding chaotic disarray to the wide-open views. And we just rolled right through it – at times beginning to wonder if we were the last people ever to travel this way.

Tongue marked the end of the day's journeyings; we slipped ourselves discreetly into a corner of a little public car park, stepping out to traverse the estuary and storm Castle Varrich, a single, spirited turret espied standing sentinel on the opposite hillside.

Impressed by the recent installation of a trendy stainless-steel spiral-staircase up the middle of the stone-built tower, we reviewed the drained and muddy-looking estuary stretching towards the distant sea, then walked back feeling we'd now earned a hearty supper, which The Tongue Hotel duly provided, with hospitable welcome and enjoyably impressive food.

Tongue Tied

Tongue, Highlands, Scotland

This afternoon, we reached the north coast of Scotland, that flat-looking bit along the top, which we'd loosely targeted as our 'starting point' for a journey back down all the lovely twiddly bits of the West Coast. We'd already decided to avoid John O'Groats (there's nothing there, advised two travelling nephews who'd been. We little realised that, in our very limited experience, this summed up most of the entire North Coast and not just the JO'G bit.)

The unusually named village of Tongue, nestling unassumedly on the shores of the Kyle of Tongue has therefore become another overnight stop on our journey to date. (You, dear Reader, should also know that every time I type the word Tongue, it makes me smile idiotically – although despite numerous connotations, I've struggled to come up with any greater witticism that the title of this piece, so there you go, I've at least managed to squeeze something in somewhere.)

Following a delightful evening in Tongue, we managed to blag a free water-tank refill from the amusingly-named Tongue Hotel (which stuck-out) on the main road – and set off towards Durness, sadly no longer anticipative of a passenger-ferry crossing and minibus excursion to Cape Wrath, the enigmatically-named north-westerly tip of Great Britain, as (of course) nothing opened until Easter, still two weeks ahead of us.

Our meanderings followed the coastline as much as possible, as we were keen to visit the self-named 'Pete's Beach' in Sutherland, claimed as such by Peter Irvine, author of the excellent 'Scotland The Best 100 Places' – parts of which have informed and directed our route-planning to date. The beach in question is indeed a perfectly proportioned cove of white sand, viewed this morning in perfect conditions, and thus walked to its southern extremity – a fascinatingly striated rock-cliff face in brown & grey, shot through with almost perfectly vertical grooves of a geological format I-know-not-what.

Further west at Durness, a visit to the coastal Smoo Cave also diverted us, where – having previously seen no sign of human life for about 200 miles – we managed to coincide our self-guided walkabout with an arriving coachload of German tourists, all of whom joined us and jostled Germanically for the best position on the rickety timber viewing platform within the cave itself.

Unavoidably joining their throng for a subsequent amble to view the North Atlantic pounding the very top of our country, we did however remain behind long enough to witness two seals besporting themselves in the rolling spume and were secretly smug that – as the Germans had efficiently already re-boarded their coach – we were the seals' only witnesses. Back on the road to find that the only other Durness attraction – a memorial garden bizarrely dedicated to John Lennon (who apparently visited regularly during his childhood) appeared singularly unattractive – and with that we turned ourselves south, in effect properly commencing our West Coast Voyage of Secondary Exploration.

Water Pump Woes And A Windy Attempt To Fish

Scourie, Sutherland, Scotland

Hey ho. The bloody water-pump's packed in. Again. And this time we're on the west coast of Scotland rather than the west coast of France, so the chances of getting it fixed are less than negligible. Several earnest phone calls this morning resulted in the nearest possible solution being back in Inverness, representing over 100 miles of back-tracking across country to the opposite coast, oh – and by the way – they were so busy, their earliest available service appointment was the middle of May (over a month hence) – so a bit like the NHS really, but without all the tedious measurement, form-filling and missed-targets.

An alternative was offered in the guise of a friendly-sounding mobile motorhome technician, this time based in Nairn (where we'd already enjoyed a harbour-side-stay-with-jet-wash two nights previous) but there was little option but to arrange an assignation on that self-same harbourside at 4pm tomorrow afternoon, when David – having checked he had a spare water-pump on his van – would meet us and attempt to remedy our currently arid situation.

"I'll be in a plain white transit van" he said, down a crackly Highland mobile telephone connection. "I'm a bit like one of those private ambulances – I can't advertise on it 'cos I couldn't keep up with all the enquiries." Cunning entrepreneurial plan forming: clone a network of motorhome technicians patrolling the wilds of Scotland and charging an absolute bloody fortune for every call-out. (David, please don't read this before you've fixed us, OK?) Anyway. Accomplished multi-taskers that we are, while all this malarkey is going on, we're also in negotiation with the nearby Scourie Hotel for a day's wild trout fishing on any one of the many lochs severally distributed across what we think we were told was 25,000 acres of prime Highland estate.

The fishing seemed to be wholly managed by an amiable, tweed-clad (English) Hotel proprietor, who was himself juggling our naïve enquiries about boats, lochs and wind direction with the demands of several other tweed-clad (and therefore far more worthy) fishermen milling about the Hotel. More specifically, we were gathered competitively around an absolutely huge, wallpapered map which depicted every loch, contour and track on the estate but also represented – with a sensually curvaceous line of coloured map pins (the border fence with the adjacent estate) where the red-headed pins represented gates set into the general run of blue fence posts.

In schoolmasterly (nay, almost military) tradition, our proprietor wielded a short brass-tipped pointing stick, with which he assigned various lochs to the assembled troops as if doling out missions from which some would never return. And if truth be told, when his brass-tip rounded on us, we ran a metaphorical white flag up our imagined flagpole and surrendered, sadly declining the opportunity since it was (as conceded by the assembled anglers) blowing a freezing-cold easterly hooley; the hireable rowing boats would definitely only go one way down the lochs (and be impossible to row back again); no-one we'd already spoken to had caught anything and it was "a wee bit too early and wee bit too cold fer troot just yet".

We thus returned to our waterless Knumptywagen, ate some breakfast and set off (in the windless warm) on the next leg of the adventure.

An Incident On The Loch Assynt Road

Castle Ardvreck, Sutherland, Scotland

The roads are empty. The sky is cloudless and blue. Arthritic fingers of the occasional sea loch reach through gaps in hills and mountains. The heather-clad moorland stretches to an indescribable infinity. Inland lochs excite the eye, glimpsed dazzling with reflected sunlight like jewels set in mud. Wind-whipped wavelets froth their surface as we sail serenely by, untroubled by traffic or the slight disappointment felt by reneging on a day's fishing for wild brown trout.

Our road runs alongside Loch Assynt and we're headed for Ullapool, when the tumbled ruin of Castle Ardvreck heaves into view, standing still proud on an islet reachable via a sandy beach, so we have to stop. Afternoon sunlight is still powerful overhead in a cloudless sky, and behind us we spot a tumbling sparkling waterfall, which we choose to explore in preference to the slightly more populated castle ruins. The water runs crystal-clear – perhaps whisky-tinged by a hint of peat – but a clean, pebbled streambed lifts the heart and spirits with its delicious crystal flowing clarity.

We stretch our legs onwards beyond the waterfalling stream, rounding a dimple of hill to see an exquisitely positioned whitewashed three-storey house, standing proud but apparently somewhat bemused not to be overlooking the glistening loch. We veer right on a track, espying a stone circle sheepfold in the middle distance, en-route to which we leave the track to stumble upon a macabre shallow pit, full of what appears to be bleached sheep skulls, scattered bones and dislocated, toothed jaws.

We realise on closer toe-of-boot inspection that these skeletal remains are in fact not sheep but the skulls of deer, as it's clear that each has two cleanly sawn stumps where antlers used to be, and in fact a single antler is also found nearby, as if more convincing evidence was required. Slightly unnerved by this discovery, we retrace our steps back to the track, now eyeing the eerie, foreboding house with suspicion that it may have housed people complicit in this skeletal assemblage.

Warm sunlight dispels both the cold wind on our faces and our slight discomfort as we return to the Knumptywagen, peel off now-unnecessary outer layers and join a small gaggle of other tourists to scramble around the base of Castle Ardvreck. From its raised vantage point we can also see the road ahead of us, where – adjacent to what appeared to be a ruined chapel – an unusually large gathering of people could be seen, along with a spattering of hi-vizzed individuals and – as our attention became more focused – the incongruous presence of two ambulances (where on earth had they come from?) parked nose-to-nose at the adjacent roadside.

Too distant to be of anything but passing curiosity, we returned to the van and headed onwards, rounding the next bend to find two cars ahead of us at a standstill, and clearly attendant on a road accident of some sort, the locus of which was behind the ruined chapel, thus obscuring our view.

There was no obvious roadblock although the paramedic activity between the road and lochside clearly involved motorbikes, four of which were visible parked at the side of the road, with an undamaged car between them. As we waited obediently and stationary, the driver of the seemingly involved car walked our line to explain that there'd been a motorcycle casualty and we needed to wait where we were to keep the road clear for the arrival of an air-ambulance.

Over the next hour or so, a sum total of eight other vehicles joined our queue in solemn watchfulness as the air-ambulance did indeed duly arrive, bizarrely electing to land on greensward alongside the loch (and some 500m distant from the assumed epicentre of the accident.) No-one seemed to be in any sort of emergency-induced hurry so we assumed the accident did not involve any immediate danger to life. Eventually, a close-knit posse of people, some hi-vizzed and some in motorcycle leathers, emerged from behind the ruined chapel, carrying between them a stretcher towards the waiting helicopter. After yet more seemingly interminable deliberations, doors were closed and the air-ambulance took gently to the air, languidly heading off in the general direction of what we assumed would be a major trauma hospital, Lord alone knows where.

Ambulances remained; blue lights continued to flash; police had arrived in force and an officer visited the first car in our line, conversed through the window for several minutes then wandered off back towards the scene of the accident. This leading car then conducted a perfect three-point turn and followed obediently by the second car, returned past us in the direction from which we had come.

Slightly bemused by this scenario and lacking any form of other communication or instruction, official or otherwise, we availed of information provided through our open van window by a woolly-hatted and unnervingly over-enthusiastic pedestrian bystander who ghoulishly informed us that there 'may have been a fatality and they're gunna cloose the rood', the veracity of which left us pondering our dilemma.

Officialdom was now swarming around the scene of the accident, and a handful of vehicles from 'the other side' had already been allowed to pass through, so we tentatively (and maybe just a little bit precociously) edged our way forward, passing the epicentre of the accident without let or hindrance from officialdom (and by-the-by glimpsing the tangled wreckage of what we presumed had once been a motorcycle, now half embedded in the turf a good 50 yards from the road-edge, draped with what appeared to be motorcycle outerwear, cut, we presume, from the also-presumed shattered body of the poor unfortunate motorcyclist, who appeared to have simply misjudged – at speed – the bend around which we were now tentatively progressing.)

No-one so much as raised an eyebrow at us as we cleared the melee to round the next bend - only to be abruptly halted by a police car parked at right-angles across both lanes of the road, so as to block our onward direction. A youthful, slightly quizzical officer approached us and with barely disguised rising anger informed us that the road was blocked, didn'tweknow? Well, yes Officer, that's abundantly clear from the position of this Police car – but that's certainly not the case at the other side of the accident and we're very sorry but none of your colleagues saw fit to inform us of such as we passed through their midst not thirty seconds ago. "Aye, well, we hannye had time to get the signs oot yet" came the officious reply, "Ye'll just have to wait here" as he stormed off to erect his long-awaited and cleverly expandable fold-out 'Road Closed' signs.

Thankfully, his female colleague then joined us at our open window, to whom we apologised again in the way of the grovelling English when confronted by persons of authority – in the face of which she smiled semi-indulgently and said "Och, dinna mind him, if ye'll hang on just a moo, I'll move the car and ye can go on your way."

I don't believe I've ever kissed a police officer before and thankfully, her lack of any remedial cosmetic dentistry prevented such an impulsive thought even entering my head. So it was with a suitably deferential and grateful wave, we were duly let pass, much to the consternation and clearly-rising but wholly passive objections of everyone sitting in their cars in the substantially longer queue on the 'official' side of the roadblock.

Lord alone knows what happened to the sorry motorcyclist (or his travelling companions – as we offered silent thanks that the rider hadn't appeared to have been carrying a pillion passenger) and when we subsequently Googled motorcycle accidents in that vicinity for any news of the casualty, there was revealed a slightly sickening catechism of them, so frequent as to be wholly unremarked in local press coverage and therefore demonstrating yet another sound reason why my own mid-life crisis was deferred to the acquisition of a guitar rather than the throbbing two-wheeler I thought my little heart desired.

The Campsite Is Closed

Inverasdale, Highlands, Scotland

We were headed with anticipation to what is becoming a Very Favourite Private Knumptying Spot not far from Poolewe and Inverasdale, the exact location of which is left deliberately vague so we stand a slim chance of finding space for the Knumptywagen next time we visit. Despite the nearby existence of a well-situated official camp-site with all mod-cons, we were slightly flummoxed to find that our own very low-key, help-yourself, leave-your-camping-fee-in-the-honesty-box beachside 'wild' campsite was closed (that's C-L-O-S-E-D) until May 1st (18 days hence) and no amount of wishful thinking was going to miraculously dissolve the chain, padlock and enormous rock which held the gate so cruelly closed against us.

(Sigh!) Visions of a couple of peaceful nights 'camped' on the beach with awning unfurled; loungers out; door-mat on the white sand; barbecue lit under the setting sun; cigars at twilight with Bloody Mary's served prior to magnificent in-van Gourmet dinners – all evaporated like Scotch mist as we swiftly re-evaluated our plans and decided instead to drive to the head of the point, where (slightly incongruously) there existed a monument to the World War II Russian Fleet, which was (in some way I don't fully understand) connected with the Scottish sea-Loch Ewe, which we currently overlooked.

As the afternoon meandered on, we wandered aimlessly about trying frustratedly not to kick rocks larger than would be good for us – and engaging momentarily with a trio of excitable, shiny-bald-headed twitchers, armed with alarmingly huge, camouflaged monoculars, who were seeking any small brown birds we might have seen thereabouts. It is at such times of need that The Trout-Acquiring Pikess Navigator Beyond Equal determined that the small public car park immediately adjacent to OUR beach would now be devoid of lightweight day-visitors (who would have, by now, needed to have headed home for scones) and therefore be wholly available to us where we might establish base-camp, if not actually ON, but at least overlooking OUR beach.

Thus, we made it so. And enjoyed a walk along the tidal edge of pristine sands, marvelling at the gentle waves and thriving rock-pools and pondering the volume of peculiarly huge vehicle tracks etched all over the non-tidal sands and low-level dunes at the rear of the beach*

In fact, having staked a claim to the best view from the empty car park, we even carted the cumbersome sun-loungers; cigars and Bloody Mary's (not on a tray, I couldn't find it) on to the beach itself, where - barely insulated in gloves, puffa-jackets, scarves and woolly bobble-hats - we froze half-to-death enjoying an evening of what-might-have-been, to be followed swiftly by a delightfully warm in-van supper - including a barbecue!

At which point, accidentally and maybe serendipitously, came about our very tenuous and indirect introduction to a gentlemen called Tim. As we cavorted lasciviously, as only Knumptyers can, in the now-empty public car park, a young family arrived in their car to enjoy the evening highlights of an unoccupied beach and, of course, with 3 young children, we got chatting, as you do.

Within but a short while, the two youngest children are examining every nook and cranny of the van (the oldest daughter, probably all of nine years old, clearly felt this level of interest and excitement was decidedly below her) but younger sister and brother wanted to know all about the workings of such a wonderful 'Wendy House On Wheels' that their parents were even exhorted to marvel at our compact washroom and toileting facilities.

While baby brother sat himself in the driving seat and continually sounded the horn (note to Fiat; only let it work when the ignition's on, OK?), daughter number two avidly plotted the interior sleeping layout for it to accommodate all nine of her cousins so they could have a holiday together. Neatly sidestepping her gender-sensitive question of who was the better driver, we engaged in social chit-chat with Mummy and Daddy, to learn that they had been on an excellent glass-bottomed boat trip "with a lovely man, who'd only been doing it for a week and needed guinea-pigs for his tours, which departed from Gairloch (the next loch down) at 10:00, 12:00, 2:00 and 4:00pm daily".

Such unintentional sales-patter couldn't really be resisted, so with the alarming thought of a timed a wakening to make the 10:00 sailing the following morning, we waved our unintentional guests a fond farewell; tidied up and retired to bed, content in the knowledge that we were overlooking (if not actually on) OUR very-most favourite beach on the west coast of Scotland.

**The mystery of such extensive vehicle tracks is solved later in the week. It transpires that OUR beach campsite was closed against us until 1st May because the combined military might of Europe's armed forces have been manoeuvring all over it in tanks, landing craft and many other large, armoured vehicles (while Navy ships and submarines apparently skulked offshore and in the waters of the Loch.) Exercise Joint Warrior has involved "more than 11,600 military personnel from over 17 nations in one of the largest exercises of its kind in Europe" (it says here) and we're just glad it was all concluded before our arrival, as that might have proved an interesting surprise waking up to witness a full-blown invasion – especially while we were without any viable radio or phone coverage!*

Today We Meet Tim

Gairloch Harbour, Ross & Cromarty, Scotland

We visit Gairloch because we're seeking Tim and his glass-bottomed boat. Only problem is, there seem to be two Gairlochs – both based on the linear, Lochside model so prevalent in these parts. And to a certain degree, we've become so overwhelmed by the continuing scenic beauty all around us, we can no longer differentiate between one inland or coastal Lochside village and another.

So we gaily cruise into Gairloch and are mildly bemused by its obvious lack of any boats or harbouresque loch-side clutter, nor any signage offering glass-bottomed boat trips. At the end of the High Street, we therefore effect a perfect Knumpty pirouette and return to the main road, where it dawns on us that what we seek is Gairloch Harbour, a separate entity from Gairloch itself, and this time agreeably cluttered in a start-of-the-season harboury sort-of way.

It's by now five minutes before the advertised Glass-Bottomed Boat departure time as we espy a quaint and newly-painted harbourside shack, here now proudly displaying the appropriate signage, but the door is locked and our only desperate hope is that the boat itself must be in the immediate vicinity (albeit close to casting-off), so the Chief Navigator bales out to sprint across the harbour tarmac – as her co-pilot attempts to park the van.

Success! The boat is located and is indeed about to depart, with a full complement of glass-bottomed passengers, save for two spaces secured by Able Seawoman, Chief Navigator and Dockside Sprinter– whence we are welcomed by our amiable Captain Tim, who shakes us warmly by the hands as we stumble aboard.

In short, the trip was delightful – not so much for any plethora of undersea marvels we witnessed as we peered through glassy portals at seaweed, starfish and the occasional sea-urchin which passed beneath our gaze – but more for the enthusiastic and passionate commentary provided by our expressive host as we puttered about the bay under bright but still chilling sunshine.

Tim really had only been doing these trips for a week – having arrived in Gairloch as a visitor on his own yacht, which he'd sailed up from Ipswich two year's previously – a story in itself. His small crew of avid passengers were indeed his tourist guineapigs as we enjoyed a trip around the bay in Tim's very informative company. Having returned to port, it became awkwardly clear that Tim was taking no fares for these inaugural trips, but such was his infectious bonhomie that there wasn't a passenger among us who didn't press hard cash upon him and wish him well for the coming season as we disembarked.

A Sobering Climb To The Fairy Lochs

Shieldaig, Wester Ross, Scotland

We first heard about it through idle social chit-chat in a pub in Lichfield, some 500 miles south of our current location, but the urge to investigate led us on a backroad from Gairloch to the Shieldaig Loch Hotel, where we found a car park convenient for a hike into the surrounding hills – in search of an unusual World War Two war-grave.

The story is little-known but well-documented online for those who seek it out. It revolves around the tragic crash of a US military aircraft, en-route home at the end of the second World War.

On 13th June 1945 this ill-fated US B-24-H Liberator bomber was returning to the USA from Prestwick airport with 15 airmen on board. This crew of nine was from the 66th Bomber Squadron along with six other 'passengers' – all from Air Transport Command. The route should have taken the aircraft over Stornaway but perhaps due to instrument or navigational failure it was flying over the rugged coastline of Wester Ross where, in heavy cloud, it hit the top of the 981m high mountain Slioch, incurring damage to its bomb-bay doors. It appears that the pilot then attempted an emergency landing in Loch Gairloch but crashed instead into rocky outcrops close to a number of small lochs collectively known as the Fairy Lochs. All aboard died.

The crash-site is now regarded as a war grave with twisted scraps of weather tarnished rivetted aluminium scattered over a stretch of otherwise innocuous-looking heather. A concentration of recognisable engine-cylinders; wheel assembly and propeller blades are also clustered in and around a tiny loch – made all the more chilling and fantastical on the day we found it – by the cloudless blue skies and mirror-calm surface of the loch, out of which wreckage still protruded.

Closer inspection revealed a tiny memorial plaque set into the rocks close by, bearing the names of all those lost. Two small American flags had clearly recently been planted in the heather at its base.

One of the most sobering thoughts of our visit was the respect which had clearly been shown for the site since much of the wreckage has been left untouched here for over 70 years – to provide a telling monument to lives needlessly lost during (and even after) the conflict of a World War.

To lighten our mood after such a fascinating, emotive and humbling visit, we returned to the Knumptywagen; eased off muddy boots and celebrated the fact that we didn't get quite as lost on the way down as we did on the way up.

A Short Cut Across Skye

Sheildaig, Wester Ross, Scotland

Glen of Torridon. Do it. Drive it, cycle it, walk it, run it, whatever your motive force, don't miss it because it's awesome, especially if you're lucky enough to see it in afternoon sunshine as you head for Torridon (which itself sadly proved a bit of an anticlimax.) We didn't stop at the impressive-looking Torridon Hotel or Bar either (as they both looked almost too grand for the likes of us lowly Knumptyers) but instead ploughed on to accidentally discover the highly agreeable lochside village of Shieldaig, basking with its' trouser-legs rolled up like a happy retiree in the evening sunshine.

Here we enjoyed an impromptu and wonderful seafood supper in an amiable and atmospheric bar-restaurant, where they managed to squeeze us in without a booking – and where we subsequently enjoyed lively chat with the locals in the bar – including the bloke who'd just that morning hand-dived the scallops we'd just enjoyed.

On our digestive (for which read sobering) post-dinner stroll in the gloaming along the front, we were further entertained to bump into a well-to-do senior couple wandering toward us, respectively clutching a glass of wine and a full pint of beer. We jokingly challenged them about stealing glasses from pubs, to which they both impishly admitted with juvenile delight. "It's almost our bedtime," they joked "and we're finishing our nightcaps in the Hotel!" We duly exchanged travellers' anecdotes (since their accents singled them out as visitors from well south of the Watford border), during which they beguilingly shared their top travel tip: "Keep a bar in the car-boot, old boy. Put your luggage on the back seat, don't waste good bar space. Only way to travel!" as they boisterously returned to disrupt the peace and quiet of their residents' lounge.

After an undisturbed and recuperative overnight parked discreetly at the side of the road we arose with the seagulls, bought a loaf of bread from Nanny's Coffee Shop and bade goodbye to both the seal in the bay and the (so-far) unobserved sea-eagles reputed to be nesting on the well-forested island just offshore.

Onwards. With an admission to all you NC500 Knumptyers out there who are all keen to know . . . No, we didn't go to Applecross. Sorry to disappoint but we had already decided we needed to save some stuff for the next trip, so we can't report on our white-knuckle, impossibly narrow, heart-stoppingly steep arrival into what seems to have become the launch-location for anyone attempting the North Coast 500 route. Next time, OK?

Instead, we took a short-cut across Skye. In fact, we took a diabolical liberty with the Summer season's spiritual home of nose-to-tail Knumptydom and just dashed – on a wholly traffic-free road – from the bridge at Kyle of Lochalsh down to board the ferry to Mallaig; with only the barest wait-in-a-very-short-line, all in the same afternoon.

So shocking was this admission when made to an inquisitive couple we met at our subsequent (and overly expensive but necessary) campsite stop, that we had to endure a good few seconds' conversational silence as they absorbed the thought of such an heretical action against their most very favourite island in all of Scotland.

"Knumptytravel.com?" enquired the recovering gentleman, observing the discreet promotional branding stickered to the side of the van. "What's that then? Is it on YouTube?" "It's just our blog" we responded. "You can follow our travels online, if you like." "Online?" came the bemused reply. "Oh no, we've only got YouTube – we don't do online." Bless.

Across The Water
Ardgour, Skye, Scotland

We crossed water on two ferries during this trip, each one being exciting yet unremarkable in their own right. Exciting because we don't get out much and unremarkable because nothing awful occurred during either crossing and we were delivered to the opposite shore as anticipated, in a timely, professional and maritime manner.

Our first crossing from Armadale on Skye to Mallaig took place in bright sunshine, with a chill breeze whipping the wavetops – and provided a rare opportunity to examine the tree-scraped roof of the Knumptywagen from our elevated position on the tiny passenger deck. We'd made the crossing as a short-cut route across the southern half of Skye, as an alternative to a longer trip inland via Shiel Bridge, Invergarry and Fort William.

The second ferry crossing was also a short-cut from Ardgour to Corran across the throat of Loch Linhe, which proved far more entertaining as we found ourselves accompanied by a fleet of six or seven souped-up Porsches, a Mercedes SL GVF (GoesVeryFast) and a low slung Ferrari functioning as Wing Commander. All bearing Dutch plates, we'd been soundly overtaken – at alarming speeds on blind summits – by the entire squadron just before we reached the ferry. So unexpected and so fast had been their passing that we became convinced the sleekly diminutive Ferrari might conceivably have 'undertaken' us by simply driving beneath our lumbering bulk. Despite 'Back To The Future'-induced-speeds, as we arrived at the simple roadside ferry-boarding lanes, we found ourselves rather incongruously parked up in line amongst their number, like an austere, pallid and slightly down-at-heel maiden aunt sitting tall and serene in the middle of an unruly kindergarten of boisterous, snot-nosed children.

The all-male entourage of drivers emerged from their walkie-talkied cockpits sporting expensive haircuts, racing jackets and unleaded aftershave, complemented by a smattering of brightly coloured driving shoes. Each dwarfed by the size of their cameras, they snapped away at themselves, their cars and the passing scenery as their drone – launched from the deck of the ferry with casual aplomb – hovered above us and then flew on ahead to record the physical impossibilities implicit in disembarking low-bodied and well-spoilered sports cars from a steeply-angled steel ferry-deck onto a complementarily angled concrete dock.

Oh, how we smiled to ourselves self-indulgently as we manoeuvred our prehistorically slow, lumbering bulk around high-performance cars made inoperable by scrapings of carbon fibre and – waving gaily out of the windows at their hovering drone – we trundled off into a proverbial sunset.

Locking Antlers In Glencoe

Glencoe, Lochaber, Scotland

It was on the glorious road through Glencoe that we continued a rather hazy tradition prevalent amongst motor-homers - a brief, friendly acknowledging wave of camaraderie as we pass one another in opposite directions. On this particular occasion, however, we inadvertently also locked antlers with our opposite number since, as we passed, either one, other or both of us must have drifted too close to the centre line, so in tandem with our cheery greeting, there was a god-awful split-second crash and our exterior driving mirror deteriorated into a glazed mosaic of shattered reflections while the hefty housing flapped limp and broken in the gale-force headwind, hanging like a shattered limb.

Bugger! Lacking anywhere to effectively stop and being momentarily rear-view blinded, it was impossible to see if and how the other driver had reacted - or if it was safe to stop - so we just ploughed on, at least as far as the next available layby, into which we pulled to inspect the damage.

By this stage, our backwards view was already obscured by yet more breath-taking scenery, and we were probably already over a mile apart. With little option but to assume a knock-for-knock neutrality - and barely able to stand upright in the storm-force strength of a chilling easterly wind on this otherwise bright and beautiful spring day, we managed to mummify the broken armature and carapace with swathes of insulating tape. The fragmented mirror was stuck back into its housing so as to retain a degree of rear-view vision, despite this now having the effect of peering through a vibrating kaleidoscope and we resumed the journey.

The Bridge of Orchy Hotel eventually presented itself as a nerve-calming pit-stop, where we decided to treat ourselves to a light lunch. Sadly, given the Hotel's imposing location as the gateway to Glencoe and to some of the most uplifting, awe-inspiring scenery Scotland has to offer, its menu choice was far from uplifting nor inspiring of any awe. The gastronomically challenged offer of Cheese & Tomato Sandwich (note Capitalisation, and allegedly on a choice of bread) languished amongst other unimaginative choices. Yes, OK, served with chips for a tenner, but really? Even the ubiquitous Cock-a-leekie soup, a sighting of haggis or a sniff of locally smoked salmon would have lifted the mood a little. Well done then, Bridge of Orchy Hotel – what a disappointingly unimaginative appetiser to the tastes of the Highlands for any dining tourists headed north.

Wigtown Booktown

Wigtown, Dumfries & Galloway, Scotland

On 11th May 1685, two women in Wigtown, Dumfries & Galloway, were drowned by each being tied to stakes in the estuary of the River Bladnoch and left there while a rushing incoming tide swept their innocent lives away.

This ultimate act of faith and belief, induced by a political King-before-God schism, is now memorialised with both an inscribed plaque and a monumental stone stake set in what is now silted salt marsh, alongside a very fine car park into which – unheedingly – we eased the Knumptywagen at our own slightly less definitive journey's end.

On a lighter note, the Wigtown Book Festival had drawn us forth, encouraged by the durable enthusiasm of friends (along with the promise of a plug-in pitch at their family's farmhouse just outside Scotland's official National Book Town). Boasting, as it does, no less than 15 separate bookshops and an incongruously imposing County Hall posing as a French chateau in the middle of a boulevard-wide High Street, Wigtown thus welcomed us on an agreeably mild autumn afternoon.

In the town, authors skulked secretively amidst an enthusiastic troop of bookish tourists (heavy spectacle frames; untamed hair; long coats and fraitfully upper-class English accents); volunteers; booksellers and a fair smattering of local characters. With our own immediate and busy programme of pre-booked talks, we hastened to sit amongst them in wind-buffeted marquees to enjoy amicable and entertaining chats about recently published books. Having also discovered a delightfully eccentric pop-up bar (in the Victorian first-floor dining room of a magnificently shambolic family home) we staked our claim on Wigtown for the next three days.

Of the talks we attended, our most entertaining was a walking-tour of the town led by local 'Chief' bookseller (and published author) Shaun Bythell, whose family seemingly owned (or laid claim to) at least half the town. This empire included an Airbnb accommodation above one of the bookshops, the tenancy of which entitled the temporary residents to also run the bookshop – an inspirational business model creating sufficient demand to generate a waiting list which allegedly runs to over 3 years.

As a brief aside, one of Shaun's bookshop series 'Seven Kinds of People You Find In Bookshops', is drawn from personal observations of his customers, and includes a passing reference to us Knumpties under the chapter heading "Genus: Senex cum barba (Bearded Pensioner)" thus: "Almost everyone in this genus travels the country in a motor home or caravan like a swarm of geriatric locusts, complaining about everything and never buying anything. The top travelling speed is 45 m.p.h. . . . ensuring that everyone else is late for appointments."

It is also Shaun's passion and commitment to the concept of independent bookshops which causes him to display a shotgun-blasted Kindle, duly plaqued, at the entrance to his shop, alongside a list of exhortations for browsers, the first of which intriguingly states "No whistling".

Meanwhile, our out-of-town, off-grid overnight parking turned out to be in the grounds of an exquisitely located and very beautiful farmhouse – with a sheltered pitch on an almost custom-built walled patio, no less. Here, our bright-orange electrical umbilical cable was laid across a lush (and subsequently Knumptywagen-rutted) meadow into equally characterful outbuildings (incorporating an awe-inspiring woodstore to die for) in this remarkably drone-worthy rural idyll.

We thoroughly enjoyed our visit to Wigtown; we revelled in whisky-fuelled hospitality and the company of good friends; we explored Wigtown and some of its more rural environs; we learnt some stuff; we were entertained and informed by lucid wordsmiths; we ate and drank as if we were on holiday – and we parked throughout our stay for free.

Oh! And yes, we even bought a book.

Food Thoughts From Up North

Ullapool, Ross & Cromarty, Scotland

Travelling in the Knumptywagen with our bijou, on-board kitchenette we more often than not endeavour to feed ourselves 'in-van' – and have enjoyed some restaurant-quality meals prepared from locally-sourced produce on our little inbuilt 3-burner gas stove.

Travelling the West Coast of Scotland, however, literally presents a different kettle of fish in that temptation seemed to lie around every scenic corner. So we tried – on occasions – to patronise the occasional eatery 'en passant' and as the fancy took us.

Now, many people more able than I write extensively about food and although I appreciate good eating as much as anyone else, I'm not sure these humble fingers are able to type about it as eloquently nor descriptively as the true foodies.

So instead – for the record (and just in case you follow in our tyre-tracks one day) – here are the highlights of our dining experiences on this trip.

Blairgowrie: Sadly I can't promote the name of this particular restaurant as – unless our host (a schooldays friend) decides to open a pop-up restaurant – we dined like Royalty in her family home. Here, in anticipation of our visit, she'd taken the day off work and prepared a magnificent roasted side of herb-crusted salmon; a Key Lime pie which just sung its own praises and a selection of cheeses to finish us off. Sadly, it was the accompanying surfeit of fine wines which seemed to do the most damage and we were therefore grateful that this excellent establishment also extended its hospitality to bed and breakfast – thus avoiding a neighbour-awakening stagger up to the only bit of level road in Blairgowrie, where we'd surreptitiously parked the Knumptywagen.

Tongue Hotel, Tongue: A delightful introduction to Scottish seafood which included langoustine, sea-bream and breast of duck. (Yes, I'm aware that the latter isn't currently classified as seafood but it did induce a spot of order-envy across our table.) And yes, I'm also aware that I've struggled to generate anything vaguely amusing from a play on the mouth based epithet of our location. You'll note that nothing has improved in that department since the last attempt – so any witty responses on a postcard please.

The Ceilidh House, Ullapool: What's not to like about a restaurant and bar which includes a bookshop? Especially when the bookshop remains open during restaurant hours and you can simply add your literary purchases to your bill? So in-between sups of a thirst quenching pre-dinner pint, we browsed the shelves and simply handed our book selections to our waitress. Additionally, the campsite in Ullapool was closed (yet again) and the town, understandably, had taken a stand against the random 'wild' motorhome camping which subsequently ensues. Therefore, alongside our bookshop purchases, drinks and food we were able to negotiate our overnight in the restaurant car park, which thankfully entailed no upset to man nor beast. We therefore enjoyed curiously fresh-tasting pickled rollmop herring with horseradish stuffing and an impressive plateful of whole langoustines followed by a bucket of moule et frites as well as a hugely flavoursome venison stew, ripe with herbs and a perfect accompaniment to a glass of fine red, the provenance of which I neither know nor care.

The Seafood Shack, Ullapool: Oh my! These are the sort of places we came to Scotland to find. This small daytime eatery didn't exist on our last visit to Ullapool and – since it occupied a slot on the same road as the Ceilidh House – we walked past it on the afternoon of our arrival just in time to catch sight of its blackboarded menu before it closed for the day. And that's where the delightful commitment-free nature of Knumptydom scores highest for us – with no onward bookings to honour and time-commitments to absolutely nothing and no-one, we vowed to hang around in Ullapool until The Seafood Shack threw open it's wooden gates at 12 noon the following day. What a treat! Our late brunch therefore comprised two servings of Smoked Haddock Hash – a delightful mix of the eponymous fish, nestling in crispy kale undergrowth laced with crispy potatoes, a dill-infused crème-fraiche dressing and topped off with a poached egg. All of this self-served al fresco at giant recycled cable-reel wooden tables – which came under heavy demand as more and more customers arrived. And for those readers who recall the Kevin Costner film, 'Field of Dreams' – The Seafood Shack fulfilled that film's classic ethos: If you build it, they will come.

Shieldaig Bar & Coastal Kitchen: A bustling locals' bar with a seafood restaurant on the mezzanine level above, who again squeezed us in without a booking and treated us to an atmospheric and very fresh seafood supper. Hand-dived local scallops were served atop slices of black-pudding; the freshest, meatiest, whitest halibut ever served in Christendom followed, accompanied by a spring-onioned mash, mange-tout and samphire, all of which wasn't quite enough to discourage a shared sticky-toffee pudding to follow – redolent with dates and setoff beautifully by a quenelle of vanilla ice-cream on the side. It was here too, with drinks in the bar afterwards that we met the diver who provided the scallops.

Sunnyside Croft Campsite, Arisaig: Mentioned here not for its clinical and pristine cleanliness; its slight environmental obsessiveness and it's locked-down shower-block where you annoyingly needed to depress a button every 12 seconds to keep a flow of water cascading over you, nor the eye-watering fee of £38.00 for an overnight stay (that's with electric plug-in – but we did need a water-and waste service, so decided to swallow it anyway) – oh no, none of those things! Instead, it provided the location for a memorable in-van seafood extravaganza, with sea-fresh moule and scallops (acquired earlier in our journeyings from a delightfully well-stocked and family-run seafood shack just over the bridge on Skye) accompanied by broccoli and pasta-shells, within which individual mussels nestled, each happily glued into place by the unctuousness of a cream-with-white-wine sauce.

Loch Leven Seafood Café, North Ballachulish: A respite opportunity since the recommended Kishorn Seafood Restaurant was – guess what? Yes, closed as we sailed past it earlier in the day. We were instead received at Loch Leven ("We're open 7 days a week") – with rather a breathless panic due to our status as unbooked walk-ins, but a table was found for us. Despite feeling rather pressured by a rushed and rushing waitress (rather incongruously speaking broad Estuarial English) we managed to get ourselves outside of home-baked bread with an olive oil dip; sizable portions of moule and clams; roast baby potatoes and a side of greens in a cream sauce all washed down with a couple of decent-sized glasses of Muscadet. And the following morning, passing by again after a roadside overnight at The Narrows on Loch Leven itself (ironically directly opposite a delightful-looking campsite which would have been a 20-mile round trip to reach) we availed of a bag of crab-claws from the Café's associated seafood shop.

Then there was our disappointingly mundane lunchtime stop at the Bridge of Orchy Hotel to be finally followed by a return visit to a welcoming and accommodating venue at Luss on Loch Lomond, where they were very happy for us to overnight in their car park in exchange for a few Scottish pounds spent in their restaurant.

The Loch Lomond Arms Hotel: A cosy nook in this bustling Hotel Bar Restaurant provided time for reflection on our journey so far, fuelled by the provision of a shared starter of Black Pudding & Haggis Scotch Egg followed in good order by rack of lamb with mash and peas; a bavette steak with frites served with an uplifting and flavoursome chimichurri sauce alongside mushrooms and an exquisitely grilled tomato on the side. A shared dessert of rhubarb crumble presented in deconstructed mode; with strips and croutons of rhubarb, crumbled Scottish shortbread and thick Crowdie cream flecked with ginger. Malt-whisky nightcaps were enjoyed in the van, with the blinds drawn and our LED lighting sapping as little power as possible from the Knumptywagen's heavily punished leisure battery, and before we knew it, the new day had dawned whence we set off south again, on the penultimate day of our Scottish journeyings.

Going Home, Going Home

Kinlochleven, Lochaber, Scotland

Many years ago we had the thrill of moving house to discover that our new next-door neighbours were a duo of accomplished professional musicians. The Early Birds specialised in original children's music – which provided a touching and much-loved soundtrack for our own daughters' childhoods. One particularly memorable and moving track revolved around a child's view of things seen 'from the window of my Daddy's car', where the chorus still chimes in our heads every time we turn for home in the Knumptywagen: "Going home, going home, there is nothing quite like going home".

And so, with that emotive music reverberating in our memories, we headed onwards in light flowing traffic through Glencoe south towards Loch Lomond and hence onwards on the last leg of our fortnight's trip. Stands of tall Scots Pines punctuated the horizon, with low sunlight strobing through their ruler-straight bare trunks turning them into giant green-tufted bar-codes, as we slipped into individual silent reverie about the highlights of our trip into the wild west of Scotland . . .

Pete's Beach isn't apparently called that, but I suppose it helps to protect its true identity as one of Scotland's Bestest Westest Coast beaches, which it certainly appeared to be on the day we found it, despite a rare overcast sky; a perfectly proportioned golden-sanded cove with a clear sea breaking gently – it was truly picturesque, highly photogenic and surprisingly unpopulated. Layered rocks scattered the perimeter while a rust-coloured cliff closed off its southern edge. We enjoyed leaving our footprints in the wet sand, almost as if leaving a signature to claim the beach for Knumptydom, as well as for Pete! (See 'Scotland The Best 100 Places' by Peter Irvine, published by Collins)

Nairn. Mentioned again here because we did visit twice – the second time to replace our failed water-pump, reported elsewhere and involving a 200-mile round trip – good job we had no other plans. And Nairn's got a wonderful statue on the harbour, of a woman with kippers. And a wonderful beach. Not the one that fronts the town; the one on the other side of its eponymous River. Slightly hidden behind a large and sociably mixed campsite, it goes on for miles of gently curving sand backed by gentle dunes and a golf-course. We set off to walk along it but within a mile or so of trudging through soft white sand, felt a bit like John Mills and Sylvia Sims so turned back for an Ice Cold In The Knumpty Van instead. Nairn also boasts a two-vehicle jet-wash; agreeable public toilets; posh-looking restaurants; a handful of thriving pubs; a high street (with shops!); cafés and a well-stocked supermarket – all complementing its attractive harbour which doubles as a drag-racing strip for the local youths' souped-up Corsas, Adams and Fiestas, all sporting wide-mouthed and therefore very loud exhausts.

Pubs & Football. There are two pubs we vaguely patronised during our trip which don't get a mention elsewhere – which were both coincidentally related to the Chief Navigator's unquenchable passion for televised football. The Argyle Arms in Ullapool was very quiet in the late afternoon when we enquired whether or not they'd be showing the Liverpool vs Chelsea match later that evening. 'Well, och, yes, I'm sure we could sort that oot fer ye' responds our amiable host. 'Give me a minute' as he disappears into the darkened hinterland of the Hotel's back corridors. 'Would this do yeh?' he enquired minutes later, leading us into a small, separate and completely unoccupied bar, clearly mid-refurbishment. 'I'll make sure the TV's on when you get here – just help yourself!'

Which we did. In fact, due to a prior gastronomic appointment up the road at the Ceilidh House, we didn't actually reach the Argyle Arms until half-time – but true to his word, our private TV room had been tidied up and remained our own exclusive domain for the remainder of the match, in exchange for just a meagre couple of pints (we couldn't fit anything more in!) And as we emerged – bleary-eyed back into the main bar – it was to be greeted by more than several surprised turning heads, all of whom were fully immersed in an intense Quiz Night, through whose midst we skulked with muttered 'good nights' out onto the street and back to the exclusive domain of the Knumptywagen.

The Tailrace Inn at Kinlochleven also provided welcome respite, if only in the form of yet more bloody football, this time in a comfortable locals' bar where some of those were amused and entertained by us arriving 'hotfoot' from a couple of hours in a howling, finger-numbing gale force wind. Prior to our arrival, we'd been attempting to fish the 'narrows' of Loch Leven where our only catch had been a small and mysteriously rust-coloured fish, a photograph of which was passed around the bar in order to confirm its identity as a small codling. "I've used bigger fish as bait" was the most amusing riposte we received as we warmed our hands around two very cold pints of Guinness.

Strange, incongruous architecture dominated this village: a huge, utilitarian brick-built edifice housed the World's Biggest Indoor Ice Climbing Walls while another large, unidentified and therefore mysteriously sinister-looking building sat above the village, like a backdrop to 'Where Eagles Dare'. Below this, nestled a cluster of houses all uniformed in a bold cream and red colour scheme, reminiscent of raspberry-ripple ice cream. And for anyone amongst our dedicated readership who gives a tinker's cuss: Liverpool 2 – Porto 0 and Liverpool 2 – Chelsea 0.

Hurrah and "Up the lucky Reds" (as my father used to shout.)

Douglas. We can't quite get over our stroke of luck in finding Douglas. Not that he was lost, he was just waiting for us to turn up. A little like Nairn, it was another place we visited twice – but this time voluntarily – as it provided such a beguilingly delightful beginning and end to our round trip. A river runs through it; there's a string of fishable lakes set in gently rolling estate parkland; a ruined castle; historic monuments and church. The village has all the amenities you might need in the form of pub; cafés; petrol station; butcher's and baker's – along with easy parking and – as we discovered while overnighting 'wild' alongside a birdwatcher's dream lake – warm and friendly dog-walkers. Thank you, Douglas, we will return.

LSM&UC. When we become too old and decrepit to clamber into the Knumpty cockpit anymore (let alone mount the ladder to our corduroy-lined over-cab bed), we've decided we needn't give it all up – we'll just become LSM&UC – from which we'll earn a handsome retirement living. LSM&UC? Easy! Limited Space Maximisation & Usage Consultants.

Like many a motorhomer of our acquaintance, we do like to pack it all in – so come rain; shine; up-hill or down-dale; fishing, cycling or hiking opportunity; outfits for dining out or dining in; relaxing lounge- or beach-wear; a sudden need of cable-ties, corned beef, waterproofs, Post-it notes, wellies, folding chairs, windbreak, outside lighting, walking boots, gaffer tape, tin foil or a screwdriver – we need to know we have it all to hand. Hence every cubby-hole, cupboard, under-seat or overhead storage locker; external bike-rack or the (rather confusingly named) 'garage' is always packed (very carefully) to maximum capacity and weight-loading. Thus, we combine our inherent OCD traits with Tetris-induced packing skills and – as yet – have found ourselves lacking nothing that we might conceivably need.

But when it comes to the home leg, it all goes completely to pot. Standards plummet as we celebrate the fact that we no longer need to be scrupulously tidy with all our goods and chattels. In short, everything we use on our last night just gets stuffed wherever it will go – in a sort of glorious celebration of rank packing irresponsibility. Everything that isn't already tied down just gets piled into the shower-cubicle/toilet: fishing rods, wellies, coats – even a mercy dash last-minute courier consignment of silver punchbowl and LCD TV – just gets bunged anywhere, rendering the habitation area of the van virtually uninhabitable, as we now loudly rattle our way back down the M6, singing loudly to cover the unpacked cacophony.

PART THREE

Covid 19 Pandemic – Lockdown

"From this evening, I must give the British people a very simple instruction. You must stay at home. You should not be meeting friends. If your friends ask you to meet, you should say No".

Boris Johnson, UK Prime Minister
March 2020

Join Us On Our Journey

Lichfield, Staffordshire, England
(COVID-19 Lockdown)

Whoa! Hold on – now don't get all jittery. Despite suggestions to the contrary, we are not, repeat NOT, out and about in the Knumptywagen. Far from it. In fact, like so many of our fellow Brits (let alone the motor-homing fraternity) we are locked-down, staying home, saying "no", protecting the NHS and hopefully – albeit indirectly – saving lives.

Yet let me please introduce you, gentle reader, to the Forth Bridge. Especially as those of you well-versed in the field of span-engineering will recognise that this is just one of three more-or-less adjacent and magnificent crossings of the Firth of Forth, which threads its way to its confluence with the North Sea just above Edinburgh, Scotland.

The more didactic amongst you may also recognise that the Knumptywagen would have experienced a degree of great difficulty crossing the Forth on this particular structure, since it carries the main London to Aberdeen railway lines, as opposed to any road traffic.

Opened in 1890, the structure is built from 53,000 tonnes of steel held together with six-and-a-half million rivets. It's 2,467 metres long (that's over a mile-and-a-half in old money) and its painted surface area is approximately 230,000 square metres. And therein lies its biggest claim to fame – as a metaphor for a task which proves to be never-ending.

Hence, its relevance seems apt as we conclude our unknowingly epic locked-down activity of painting the hall and landing of our Victorian-era house. Now, as a brief aside, I've deliberately used the descriptor 'Victorian' here, so you'll be left in no doubt as to the extent of our self-determined 'journey'. With three floors, two landings and two-and-a-bit flights of stairs, our task was frickin' huge at the outset, but what-the-hell, we figured, we had plenty of time and not a lot else to do with all this Covid-imposed spare time.

In uncharacteristic anticipation of lock-down, colour charts had earlier been acquired from our local decorating supplier; swatches stuck on our two-tone walls; samplers purchased (at extortionate cost for such piddling pots) and painted patches applied in various locations to ascertain the effects of what little natural daylight permeates our semi-detached, single-sided domicile.

What no-one told us as we made our final decisions was that the dark-blue 'Ink Well' colour selected for the lower half of the walls would be so disproportionately packed with pigment that it would be thick and sticky to apply and – perversely – would also need an average of three coats to achieve a uniform finish. Thankfully, the floridly named 'Gardenia' (a 21st century euphemism for 'magnolia') needed only two coats – so between us, it's only taken two weeks to complete our journey. And that's without any of the miles of white gloss woodwork for which, thankfully, we had the foresight to procure the services of a professional decorator, who will now – no doubt – be unable to commence Phase 2 until we're all released from the grip of this confounded virus.

Since our task seemed never-ending, your esteemed and humble author turned (briefly and uncharacteristically) to the statistical dark side to measure and calculate that our painterly efforts amounted to a disappointing and slightly less-than 0.001 percent of the efforts involved in the continual repainting of the Forth Bridge.

And as if this was insufficient disappointment, our final ignominy came with the installation of three new wall-lights – candle-like sconces which dictated the use of trendy, bronze-glazed LED filament bulbs (which were admittedly described as 'very warm white'). Sadly therefore, as dusk falls, our beautifully redecorated labour of love is lit with such a powerful, orange glow that it actually appears to be on fire and – despite all our efforts – the house now feels as if it's burning down around us.

Two Wheels Good, Four Wheels Bad

Lichfield, Staffordshire, England
(COVID-19 Lockdown)

Two wheels good, four wheels bad. Yeah, I know – it's a misquote from George Orwell's 'Animal Farm' – from which you may infer that some relevance to our current Locked-Down status in this Sceptred Isle will emerge as this tale unfolds. As citizens of such, we're exhorted to take our daily exercise without using our vehicles, so I guess that strapping a couple of surfboards to the Knumptywagen and heading for Cornwall isn't quite what HMG has in mind. But if we can't use four wheels, can we use two?

Well, her Worshipful Chief Navigating Troutess thinks so. And has a cunning plan to combine localised exercise with exploration of our environs by boldly leading a two-wheeled expedition along the wide and leafy-green towpaths of not one, but two canals both local to our home-base in leafy South Staffordshire.

Just a tad over four miles from home, Fradley Junction sits at the conjunction of the Trent & Mersey and Coventry Canals, which between them share 131 navigable miles and a total of 89 locks. Normally a popular, bustling canal-side hub boasting characterful public house (colloquially known as the Mucky Duck); narrow boat hire; camp site; café; picnic area and nature reserve – it was Uncannily Covid-19 Quiet and, truth be told, all the more appealing because of it.

We both own bicycles. Giant bicycles, in fact and – for the hard-of-hearing – that's their brand, not their size, just in case you've envisaged us precariously mounted on huge penny-farthings. Acquired separately and independently of each other, the coincidence of the brand and their almost-matching silver-grey paintwork is about where the similarity ends, since one is a standard 'hybrid' pedal cycle – while the Navigating Troutess's just happens to have an engine.

Can you hear the cries of protestation at that last throwaway comment? No, I know it's not a real engine in the strictest sense of the word, but it is electric and it does assist when the pedalling gets tough. And mine doesn't. So I have to exert myself beyond the call of duty while the Navigator Par Excellence whirrs serenely alongside, issuing gently motivational encouragements towards my progressively reddening face.

Since I therefore consider my own two wheels to be bad, I am lucky enough to be compensated with due consideration (as befits my age and station) when routes are planned. As most canals thankfully don't flow uphill, towpaths are a fairly safe, level and easy-going option upon which we can take our Corona-induced daily exercise.

And, as previously advised, Fradley Junction provided a perfectly isolated and delightful location at which to stop and feast on our pork-pie-and-banana picnic, romantically cossetted in a rear-mounted wicker basket – before saddling up for a semi-enjoyable and almost-entirely self-motivated ride home.

Pressing The Big Red Button

Lichfield, Staffordshire, England
(COVID-19 Lockdown)

Living as we do in central England, we're not very far from the middle section of the M6 Toll. In fact, within six miles of home, we have a choice of two junctions via which we can either access or leave the UK's only toll motorway.

However, at £11.80 for a one-way ticket, we find it prohibitively expensive to travel one half or the other of its smoothly tarmacked length in the Knumptywagen, opting instead to use a particularly tedious (but far cheaper) stretch of the A5 to go north, or a dual carriageway stretch of the A38 when headed south.

Which saddens me deeply, since I was the person who actually opened the M6 Toll.

Do you want to read that again? Your esteemed yet humble author actually opened the M6 Toll.

Not quite single-handedly, I admit, but as near as dammit when the moment arrived – at 10:10 hrs on the 9th December – a cold and slightly misty Tuesday morning back in 2003 (when it would have cost a mere fiver for our motorhome or a van.)

At the time, I was a working member of a local event-management company and we'd already been involved with our client, the private company which owned, built and would operate the new road on a 50-year lease.

Thus, sometime in early November we were briefed on the requirements for the opening and its attendees – comprising national and local press; Minister for Transport Alistair Darling; Police; Road Haulage chiefs; Health & Safety Inspectors; VIPs; company staff and management; estimated total about 120 people. Actual date to be advised (on 24 hours' notice), all sworn-to-secrecy and all highly confidential.

Oh, and yes, can you sort out a gathering place and a viewing/ filming/photography platform for the nation's media at Weeford, please, adjacent to the southbound Toll Plaza. And almost by the way, can you also come up with a clever way to open the UK's very first toll motorway, pretty-please?

Well. As you'll know if you've travelled it, rites of passage are granted by barriered tollbooths where, in exchange for a fee paid by either cash or card, the barrier is raised and the vehicle proceeds. So there wasn't really much to play with except the moving barriers themselves. With a total of 10 booths spanning the width of the carriageway, it seemed to make most sense that we arranged each barrier to be raised in sequence across the entire width of the road. Simple.

Given that Alistair Darling would need to feature prominently, we built him a plinth with a shiny steel pillar topped by a Big Red Button, which he would push with aplomb to signify the official opening of the road. This would be the cue for the operative in Toll Booth One to raise their barrier, whereupon the immediate neighbour would raise theirs, thence onwards. Barriers would thus be raised in a sequential salute to the arriving horde of traffic which the Police would hold back with a rolling roadblock, out-of-sight towards the new road's confluence with the 'old' M6.

Since no-one trusts a politician to do what they're supposed to do (along with some technical issues which I won't bore you with) it was deemed expedient that The Rt. Hon. Alistair Darling's Big Red Button would work most efficiently if it was wired-up to absolutely nothing. Instead, to commence the barrier-raising sequence, we would use a proven, nifty little hand-held wireless radio-cue transmitter which our client (let's call him Mr B) would press simultaneously with Mr D's pressing of the BRB. After extensive testing, this would be the method for a clear, electronic signal to be sent to the first booth, thus setting the barrier sequence into motion.

So it was that, on the actual chilly misty-morninged day, I attentively positioned myself alongside client Mr B on our own little plinth with our own, carefully plotted uninterruptible line-of-sight to the BRB. But as The Rt. Hon. Mr D began his spiel, Mr B – experiencing a sudden onset of abject nervousness at the magnitude of his task – bottled-out and fumblingly passed me both the transmitter and ultimate responsibility.

And so, as Mr D did indeed pronounce the M6 Toll open and pressed his BRB, it was actually me who discreetly pressed the transmitter-button, setting in motion the planned and timely opening of the M6 Toll. A slowly rolling truck and car convey, ably escorted by a perfectly timed phalanx of Police cars, thus processed through the barriers to sully the virgin tarmac of the UK's first and only toll-motorway, and we all went home to get warm.

If only I'd had the foresight to ask for a free lifetime pass.

RSPB Big Garden Fishwatch

Lichfield, Staffordshire, England
(COVID-19 Lockdown)

Enjoy an hour with nature and . . . see the drama unfold on your doorstep.

So read the enticing blurb for the RSPB's annual Birdwatch survey, conducted over one weekend in January, and presumably involving many more bored locked-down twitchers than ever before.

Enchanting images of small songbirds populated the colourful website and – thus enthused – we set aside an hour to contribute our checklist to the national tally.

With the demise of our aged cat last summer, we were keen to re-establish a garden into which small songbirds could again venture without feline fear. Thus, a variety of birdfeeders were slung amidst the branches of our straggling apple tree and although this arrangement hasn't yet induced a feathered feeding frenzy, we were optimistic for our hour's observation from our 'hide' behind the kitchen window.

Our garden also features a raised pond, built when our children were small to allow access without danger of falling in. As such, it's hosted many a fairground goldfish, most of which survived their traumatised provenance and grew to a decent size. Some even produced offspring – such that – in its heyday – we were able to count over 20 fish. (A definitive tally proved incalculable as the damn things insisted on swimming around during critical headcounts.)

The problem was, we weren't the only ones keeping a tally. To our concern, an RSPB approved heron had also identified the opportunity of a feeding frenzy and became a regular visitor, often strutting proudly around our garden like an officious equerry at a Royal garden party. Continual shooing; Heath-

Robinson-style net-deployment and eventually a surface floating anti-heron grid all proved ineffectual, to the point where 'More Than A Score' was gradually whittled to a confidently countable 'Seven.'

And then, as if in celebration of the protection afforded to it by the RSPB, one morning we discovered that the Seven had been herroned down to Zero, which possibly explains why we conducted our Birdwatch session fully equipped with all the usual requisites: binoculars; checklist; pads and pens – along with a nagging desire for an air-rifle.

Here Comes The Corona Man!

Lichfield, Staffordshire, England
(COVID-19 Lockdown)

A childhood memory now, made pertinent by the discomforting grip of the current global pandemic. Although my recall is fragmentary – and your immediate reaction, dear reader, may be one of incredulity at the imminent unfolding of a supposed fantasy – The Corona Man did indeed exist.

In my minimal and clumsy research for this piece, I came across varying definitions of the word 'corona'. The most prevalent of these related to auras around the moon, although in the context of this particular rambling, I much preferred the allusion to a 'crown' since that better implies a regality or superiority to the range of overly sweetened, flavoured carbonated bottled waters ('fizzy pop' as it was known in my childhood years.) So yes, all hail The Corona Man, with his yellow lorry and door-step effervescence.

If memory serves me right, this was no small, tin-pot, localised venture either. Large, open-sided lorries carried crate after crate of Corona: a nationalised fizzy pop in myriad colours, each of which vaguely represented its purported flavour. Vibrantly radiant red and fluorescent green denoted Cherry and Limeade respectively; Ginger Beer sported a curious semi-opaque beige cloudiness; lemonade was transparently clear (and therefore too dull to be a flavour of desire) whereas Cream Soda – whilst also disappointingly clear – enjoyed the exotic mystique of a surprisingly torpid creaminess and was therefore all-the-more desirable to my uneducated palate.

My currently 95 year-old Mother, whom I have recently quizzed about the subject, seems also to recall that Dandelion & Burdock was another family favourite – a darker, treacle coloured concoction which neither myself nor two younger brothers could be convinced was derived from plant-based ingredients, especially as none such items could possibly have formed a key element of either our diet or refreshment regime, as far as I can now remember. Every week, whilst there was little anticipation of his arrival, once the yellow lorry rolled to a halt outside our house, excitement would escalate to fever-pitch in the scant seconds it would take us to tear across our small suburban lawn; leap the low border wall like a troupe of thirsty gazelles and peer excitedly into the rows of crates, each arrayed facing outwards at a slight angle so as to present an easy method of selecting and removing the choicest of our selections.

As I now look back on that heady childhood era, this door-step delivery seemed to be but one of many which kept us supplied with provisions. Alongside the more obvious
Milkman, I also seem to recall a Coalman (we had a shed dedicated to the bulk storage of 'coke' for our aging central-heating boiler). I also seem to remember erratic deliveries of boxed groceries from the Co-Op Lady, whom I once surprised at our backdoor by wishing her a polite 'Happy New Year' one morning in what was probably mid-February.

To cap it all, every other Saturday, a man called Brian would arrive on our doorstep clutching a bucket and sundry other paraphernalia in order to wash my Dad's car. (I mean, how Nigel Slater is that?) At some point during my blatant observations of his working practices, I know I also asked him if he'd wash my bike – presenting myself, I'm now sure, as a completely snooty and precocious arse of a child – which I probably was.

And whilst it couldn't be classed as a door-step delivery, I also recall we would acquire fresh wet-fish from an avuncular and white-coated fishmonger named Edgar, whose overlarge and ruddy ears were fascinatingly elephantine, flapping in time to accompany his fishmongery monologues as he joshed semi-suggestively with his queue of adulating suburban housewives.

Then, to conclude these Covid-induced reminiscings, there was Uncle Matt – a tweedy gentleman possibly sporting a tightly-clipped, greying military moustache – who ran the local sweetshop. Here, when the mood took us, we could also indulge (nay, rejoice!) in the height of adult sophistication. Clustered in an excited gaggle around an ancient, wheezing freezer, we could choose between two iced lollies – Lager & Lime or Cherry Brandy – each as garishly over-coloured as our favourite pop. These pocket-money trophies clearly implied ingredients which involved the mysterious and as-yet forbidden alcohol, upon which we would therefore regularly pretend to get – as overheard during our parents' infrequent suburban dinner parties – just a little bit squiffy.

I Want To Go To Tenby!

Lichfield, Staffordshire, England
(COVID-19 Lockdown)

I'm alarmed to realise that I'm in urgent need of an engineer to fix my Nostalgia Valve. Mine is clearly faulty, as it is currently leaking heavily into these various ramblings (for which please read 'literary masterpiece') in an almost uninterruptible stream.

Possible causes of this technical failure could be the recent swell of VE Day reminisces, but I reckon the valve itself has been under pressure since lock-down, when bimbling around in the Knumptywagen and recording many of our travelling experiences became a dangerous, anti-social and unauthorised activity.

So, exhorted by a dear friend and mentor, I've felt it incumbent upon me to continue to push an erratic supply of vaguely travel-oriented blatherings onto paper. Thus Tenby. In Pembrokeshire, South Wales. Many of you will be familiar with this charming and delightful Pembrokeshire seaside town. Granted it's not the most hospitable location for a Knumptywagen as most of the recognised campsites are just a little too far out-of-town. Instead, we have been wont to follow our touring ethos of 'wild' camping (as discreetly as possible, you understand) and to only stay in suitable locations for an overnight or two where circumstances allow. Thus, on our visits to Tenby, we have tucked ourselves unobtrusively into the huge coach-and-car park hidden in a quarry-like setting from where a short scramble gets you onto The Croft above and overlooking the uplifting expanse of Tenby's fine North Beach.

But it is not to these visits that I wish to allude. Instead, with the Nostalgia Valve yet to undergo repair, I shall let its pressured stream bear us back to childhood holidays on those golden sands. I had assumed that we must have enjoyed many family holidays here, although Mother believes we only took two summers – one in the Castle Hotel (we think) and one in a quaint terraced house located right on the Harbour Beach, which might have been called Fisherman's Cottage, but now can't be traced in my limited, impatient and inept research.

Whatever. It was in this house we enjoyed a summer of fun: crabbing; rock-pooling; wandering the magical streets and Castle Mound (adorned with real cannons, I'll have you know); picnicking on the beach and playing a boardgame called Flounders, amongst other holiday delights. These included a mackerel-fishing trip with a skipper whose name, I still recall, was Jimmy - a weathered, traveller-like-figure with pony-tail and pirate's ear-ring, both of which fascinated me in equal measure to the writhing, silvery-blue mackerel we liberated with abandon from their rightful domain in glittering Cardigan Bay.

Another memorable holiday delight was our daily visit to a small, shed-like kiosk nestled cosily against the upper-harbour wall. From amidst an impressive array of buckets, spades, fishing nets and beach-balls, a lady here would sell us pocket-money lollipops from a jar – exotic in their flattened, disc-like shape, their caramel colour and a now-long-forgotten flavour.

It was to here, much to my overwhelming amazement and excitement, that one of my Mother's numerous brothers, Uncle Jack – visiting us for the day – escorted me to facilitate the purchase of an aspirational gift, the likes of which I had never believed I could possibly ever own. As balsa-wood gliders go, this surely was the pinnacle: a feat of engineering which included a large rubber band; an oversize red plastic propeller and even a wiry bit of undercarriage with working wheels, ostensibly to facilitate a runway take off, under its own motive force.

The simple but awe-inspiring components were duly unpackaged and assembled on the harbour-side, where we sat, my Uncle and I, our legs dangling as if A.A. Milne might have had a hand in it. The small fragile flying machine took shape in front of my eyes – both still agape at my good fortune – until the craft was pronounced in a ready state. A finger-winding test of the propeller caused the stretched elastic band beneath the fuselage to twist once, then twice then knot itself into a taut, straining skein of bulging, latent power.

Onto the firm, flat sand surrounding the harbour, where our maiden flight was self-aborted when its rapidly unwinding propellant exhausted itself as the undercarriage slewed sideways into the frictional sand. An aerial hand-launch, therefore, was deemed our next sortie, proving slightly more complex than expected, as Pilot Uncle Jack had to hold both the fuselage in conjunction with the propeller, to prevent it unwinding before launch.

Whoooo hooo! There it goes! And so it did. With a gentle thrust the little craft – its spinning propeller all but invisible to the naked eye – gamely climbed above head height, pitched and yawed a little, climbed gloriously higher – and then flew straight into the unforgiving harbour wall, where it broke into pieces and fell to an ignominious crash-landing on the sand. A sudden unbelieving silence ensued. We ran to the crash-site and forlornly collected up the broken parts. Even now, I can still recall the combined sense of both sheer elation and abject disappointment – each experienced in almost the same breath.

And yet, in the face of this abject disappointment, like a Magician wielding both top hat and rabbit, Uncle Jack had a further avuncular treat to impart. With a gleam in his eye and not a word spoken, he diligently replaced the shattered pieces into the paper-sleeve wrapper, drawn with a conspiratorial smile from his pocket. 'Come with me' he said, and while I wiped a tear from my eye, we returned to the lady in her kiosk where – disbelievingly – I was exposed to my first experience of adult duplicity. Here, with head held high, Uncle Jack unashamedly proclaimed that the aeroplane we purchased less than an hour ago was 'like this when we got it' and tipped the shattered pieces onto the counter.

Transfixed with awe, I recall very little of the ensuing negotiations, except my dazed and incredulous state as I walked back onto the shining sand, clutching a brand-new replacement balsa-wood plane – in the company of an Uncle who was now – in my eyes - both a Hero and a Petty Criminal.

Two Way Traffic

Lichfield, Staffordshire, England
(COVID-19 Lockdown)

Stay at Home became Stay Alert – and travel as far as you like to take your daily exercise.

Given the slightly ambiguous nature of HMG's recently updated Covid-19 advice, we (assumedly akin to thousands of fellow citizens) – have taken it into our own newly- empowered hands to interpret these directions – and used them to justify retrieving the Knumptywagen from storage.

Avid readers now familiar with our tales (you know who you are, thank-you-very-much-indeed) will be aware that our motorhome has enjoyed an overwintering sojourn away from home. At the end of last year's season, we were able to secure a slot in a rural farm-based storage facility where it has been parked up, forlorn and not-quite forgotten for the past six months.

But – as the sun has begun to shine a little, both meteorologically and metaphorically – we've felt a growing need to retrieve and revive the old girl – just in case we can put her to her intended use again, sometime anytime soon.

So, early one sunny evening just this week, we kitted ourselves out with a set of heavy-duty jump-leads and set off (in a recently acquired open-roofed car) for a refreshingly novel, post lock-down drive into the Staffordshire countryside.

The journey is an agreeable one of about 30 minutes on good old-fashioned A and B roads, taking in well-hedged, sweeping arable countryside as well as a reservoir. The sun shone and traffic was light, so our spirits were already lifted by the time we arrived.

To conform with Government guidelines and to justify our journey, we thence took our daily exercise with a brief perambulation of the Knumptywagen's perimeter and were pleased with the outcome, as we'd both half-expected a far-sorrier state than that in which we found her. Bodywork was still fairly white (or at least less green and grimy than anticipated); nothing seemed to have fallen off; the interior was dry, and she was still standing foursquare and upright on tyres which all seemed to have remained at least semi-inflated.

A first attempt to start her up confirmed our foresight in bringing the jump-leads as the battery was well and truly flat. However, on opening the bonnet of our new 'donor' car, our enthusiasm was confounded as we discovered the exposed car-battery boasted only one terminal. One terminal? How can that be? I have two jump leads in my hands here and in all our admittedly limited knowledge of things automotive, both your esteemed author and the Last Capable Map Reading Navigating Troutess On The Planet were aware that you need two terminals to which to connect jump-leads.

The car battery, our passive and indifferent foe, sat supine and half-concealed beneath an immoveable bulkhead, providing no chance of slipping in even a probing finger, let alone a bulky crocodile clip. A strange and complicated set of braided wires also snaked up from the black depths to grasp a series of bolted terminals atop, this all covered with a red plastic guard which looked like the Devil's claw, so we took that as a warning and decided not to attach anything to this lethal-looking arrangement either.

Can you therefore picture the furrowed brows; the quizzical facial expressions and the Stan-Laurelesque scratching of heads as we stared disbelievingly into the engine bay of our passive Peugeot? One terminal? Two jump-leads? How can that be?

The car handbook was bloody useless. On a slightly dog-eared page 134, it imperiously assumed that the only circumstance in which you would ever need to access the car battery at all was to connect it to a 'slave' battery in order to start the damn car. Nowhere did it even acknowledge or consider our forlorn and powerless Knumptywagen, now standing passive, impotent yet still anticipative before us.

Phones out, Google consulted. YouTube awash with over-confident Americans each taking three minutes to promote their 'channel'. An enthusiastic bearded gentleman provided explicit and hugely complicated electrical instructions to camera seemingly from his driving seat while hurtling along a busy motorway and – the final straw (I kid you not) – a bare seven second piece where some idiot-git who remained out-of-shot (thereby avoiding receipt of a torrent of live verbal abuse), simply lifted the bonnet and pointed to the battery location within the Peugeot 308CC engine compartment. End-of. Dick.

A glimmer of understanding was at least provided by an online forum, which suggested attaching the black jump-lead to a bare-metal car-part – but then neglected to define to what the other end might be attached. We thus tried a variety of tentative combinations – vaguely sensitive to the risk of electrocution; sparks of arc-welding magnitude or a Knumptywagen-consuming fire – all of which failed to provide the necessary spark.

And thus, with little else in the way of an inspirational solution, we availed further of HMG's Covid guidelines and drove all the way home again; swapped ourselves and the jump leads into a second car (by way of further exercise) and set off for a repeat trip into the hinterland, content in the knowledge that we did, at the very least, know that this car had two terminals on an accessible battery.

A Cautionary Tale

Lichfield, Staffordshire, England
(post COVID-19)

We've had a couple of little day trips out in the Knumptywagen recently, in an attempt to benefit from the slightly more relaxed Lockdown Rules governing the movements of the British people, which alarmingly seem to include us, for goodness' sake. Both trips have also involved a spot of fishing as a means-to-an-end and both have been enjoyable, uplifting, rewarding yet challenging in their own right.

Given that the poor Knumptywagen has lain idle for several more weeks than originally intended, it has seemed slightly strange to re-familiarise ourselves with the rigmaroles implicit in setting off on a journey, not the least of which was navigating ourselves out of our narrow back-lane, now made even narrower by an overgrowth of hedging, which caressed (a softer verb than scratched, I find) our unwashed sides as we lumbered out of captivity and onto the highway.

And it's here, as we bowled jauntily along the country's still dangerously pot-holed A-roads, that a fleeting scene from a Woody Allen film came to my mind. I can only assume that – after a long, Covid-enforced layoff and in my role as Driver-In-Chief – my reacquaintance with the wallowing size of the van brought the scene to mind, since vehicles travelling in the opposite direction all seemed to pass with more perilous closeness than I ever recall.

What if they were to cross the line? What if the oncoming driver cut the corner, or overtook on a blind bend, or simply drove head-on into us to relieve some deep-seated psychosis built up over the past weeks of Lockdown?

Oh, Woody Allen – save me from this unwarranted anxiousness! I became convinced that if

I could just find the clip, it would purge me of these strange unwanted visions and sense of foreboding. As I recalled, the scene conformed to Mr Allen's normal level of amusingly dry and visual wit and I'm pleased to report that I eventually tracked it down to his 1977 opus, 'Annie Hall', all of which demonstrates, in one fell swoop, how much spare time we STILL have on our hands during these languid and disturbing times.

Well, dear reader, you'll be enlightened to learn that within forty-seven minutes of the opening credits (and in a scene lasting all of 14 seconds) Woody's character, along with cookie-girlfriend Annie (more than ably played by Diane Keaton, who else?) visit her family in the country for the first time. Here, after an awkwardly amusing 'first-date' meal, Annie's brother Duane (played by a youthful-looking Christopher Walken), privately confides in Woody that he harbours a suicidal desire, when driving at night, to turn his wheel into the path of an oncoming vehicle – and thence goes on to vividly extol the gore and carnage which would thus ensue.

With perfect comic timing, cut then to Woody & Annie being driven back to the airport. By Duane. At night. In the rain. As the camera pans across all three of their faces, sat side-by-side on the front bench seat, and comes to rest on Woody, we see his traumatised expression as he glances nervously across at Duane at the wheel, who is, of course, staring into oncoming headlights through the swishing wipers.

So, having fulfilled my slightly obsessive investigations, I'm now feeling purged, fulfilled, re-balanced and safe enough again to assume a seat behind the wheel and travel out in the wallowing Knumptywagen – where we might just acquire a handful more tales of derring-do to impart in due course.

And the fishing trips? Well, they're a different story.

When The Wind Blows

Lichfield, Staffordshire, England
(post COVID-19)

Avid readers (that's all three of you) will be aware that the previous tale hinted about a fishy story – and who am I to deprive such a faithful, committed and ever-eager readership?

As anyone who has yet ventured far from home to take their exercise will now realise, public facilities (for which read 'conveniences') are understandably closed while Covid-19 continues its unabated dominion over worldwide human activity. So it is with some small, satisfied smugness that we can take our own toilet (and other self-contained mobile facilities, of course) with us when we either exercise or fish, both of which are now authorised by HMG for personal and socially-distanced indulgence.

The Navigating Chief Map-Reading Troutess had previously turned her hand to a spot of research and discovered a trout fishery not far from home – of which we were surprised not to have had any prior knowledge. Patshull Park appeared to comprise Hotel, Golf-Course and Trout Fishery all in one, a holy trinity of delights just over an hour's drive away from home. Adding the twenty minutes it also takes us to navigate out of our little back-lane, we thus arrived mid-morning at a delightful fishing lodge set in the grounds of a Covidly-closed Hotel, alongside an open and functioning golf-course at the head of an allegedly Capability-Brown enhanced lake approximating – we were told – a whopping great 75 acres.

Large amounts pf paraphernalia were thus enthusiastically unloaded from the Knumptywagen into a punt-like fishing boat, pre-hired for our exclusive use, such paraphernalia including our electric outboard motor along with various layers of weatherproof clothing and fishing tackle aplenty. Off we set, toodling (that's marine terminology, OK?) amongst other fisherpeople who themselves were toodling in their own boats, all of us seeking that elusive spot where fish might be gathered beneath the increasingly rippling surface of this vast lake.

And therein lies the necessary jeopardy without which this wouldn't be a tale to tell. As we gently pootled, (another one tossed in there for free, OK?) the wind was gathering pace and our comparatively high-sided craft – abetted by two well-wrapped bulky bodies each offering unintentional sail-like resistance – was blown at cartoon-like speed across open water into the weedy tail of the lake – as far away from the shelter of the Lodge as it was possible to get.

Our genteel electric outboard sadly proved no match for what turned out to be a 35mph headwind but at least the experienced foresight of the Warden had furnished us with a pair of oars (and a spare battery, God-bless'im). Logic therefore suggested that we take to the oars, set the motor to Warp Factor Eight and head back to port.

Not a bit of it. At full motive power and straining at both oars as if pursued by Vikings intent on rape and pillage, we made absolutely no headway whatsoever. Waves were now slapping against the prow; grunted expletives blew from our mouths like chaff and with as much effort as we could muster between us, we were blown ignominiously sideways into a lakeside reed bed, where we came to grateful rest. And here we remained for the time it took for our laboured breathing to normalise and for a tangled bale of waterweed to be unwound from the propeller.

Other anglers could be espied dotted across a wind-lashed distance, each happily anchored and hunkered down in their favourite spots, clearly still managing to catch fish. Here we were – effectively marooned, fishless and without anything to sustain ourselves, since our picnic lunch remained safe from harm in the Knumptywagen fridge, where we had forgotten it in the bustling excitement of our maiden voyage.

After half-an-hour or so, the gusting wind took on a more contemplative demeanour, at which point we bent to our oars again; squeezed a couple more watts of power into the outboard from the thoughtfully provided spare battery and forged our way, ripple by ripple, out of the reeds and back into the body of the lake.

It became clear from later inspection of a large aerial photo hanging in the Lodge that we had cruised unknowingly into a narrow venturi where well-wooded lakeshores converged to funnel the already powerful wind into the maelstrom which cast us away for the afternoon. Thankfully, the day was not a complete write-off as – moored within safe striking distance of the Lodge and in the lee of a low dam wall – we were both able to chalk up a catch each before heading back to the shelter of the Knumptywagen – and a very late, very welcome lunch.

On The Road Again

Carreg Ddu, Gwynedd, Wales
(post COVID-19)

As a precursor to a little trip away in the Knumptywagen, we had a strangely dysfunctional day prior to departure. Our local locksmith came out to fit a replacement cylinder lock to the van's habitation door – a task that should have taken no more than an hour – but then, may the Good Lord bless him and his clever little set of secret-agent tools – he decided to also have a quick look at our faulty under-seat electronic safe (yes, you heard me right) and spent the next three hours sorting that out, sprawled across the floor of the Knumptywagen, working tirelessly in both an awkward space and the uncharacteristic heat of a summer's day. This magnanimous act of personal ambition (he refused to charge us any more than his original quote) did however delay us from loading the van with all that was necessary for our planned trip northwards, to undertake what we'd already decided to christen The Lakeland Loop.

Then, news broke that the ill-defined geopolitical region known as Greater Manchester was to be locked-down in celebration of Covid-19 with immediate effect, preventing us from stopping off to visit daughters in Chorlton and therefore catalysing a reappraisal of our route north. Since baby grandson in Chester was thankfully not embraced by the revised lockdown area, we learnt that he could (with the agreement of his parents) find time to make himself available for legitimate smooching.

Post-smooching, we would then also be perfectly placed to reach Wales – more specifically the Llyn peninsular, an area we'd been keen to explore since memories of childhood holidays emerged from an unrelated review of family photo albums some time previously.

So. Round off the day with a quick visit to the vets with the aging family pet of some 15 years, to return home sadly, but not surprisingly, cat-less, RIP Millie. A sundowner shopping expedition then ensued, to acquire provisions for both a socially-isolating, aged Mother and ourselves; ignorantly load the van with the sort of lightweight summer clothing dictated by that particular day but not sadly and subsequently demanded by Welsh weather – and we're ready to roll!

Caernarfon was a very agreeable surprise, viewed as it was on a gloriously sunny Sunday, from a secret Knumpty location on the opposite side of the River Seiont. Imposing castle walls, turrets and battlements were almost completely besieged by families all madly crabbing from the harbour walls, so our gentle perambulation became an entertaining natural history lesson, provided by legions of Scouse seven-year-olds all keen to show off their hauls of gullible crustaceans haphazardly stacked and gently stewing in clear plastic buckets.

Following an enjoyably scenic hike along an edge of the Menai Strait, we were disappointed that Covid-19 guidance provided a perfect excuse for the tired, littered and shoddy surroundings of the nearest waterside pub. Here, staff Indifference and Ineptitude vied for pole position as we tried to secure a couple of pints of beer. Disappointed with our libations and as the evening cooled and summer foreclosed on its lease, we decided to dine in-van and thence enjoyed a peaceful overnight.

"If you don't like the look of the weather on your phone app, get another app" seemed fitting advice for the following day, as another dose of sunshine, tempered by a fresh seaside breeze, surprised and delighted us as we made landfall at Morfa Nefyn, midway along the Llyn peninsula's north-west coast. A cliff-top inn offered free motorhome parking in exchange for food consumed in the restaurant, and with locked-down Wales celebrating their first day of indoor-dining, we booked ourselves a table for two.

Prior to which we enjoyed a fantastically sunny hike along the coastal path, most of which skirted the well-manicured fairways of the local golf course. This enabled us to enjoy at first hand spectacular scenery out to sea and witness the wooden ineptitude of cryogenically defrosted lady golfers attempting to hit golf balls in some form of competition which the All Knowing Navigating Chief Troutess Golfing Handicap of 19 Soothsayer pronounced to be a Texas Scramble, which it clearly was.

The Ty Coch Inn sits in a prime location on and overlooking a golden curve of sheltered sand on a tiny skin tag of geography named Carreg Ddu. On this delightfully sunny afternoon, its outdoor bar ("We're closed if it's raining", said the signs) enjoyed a well-managed queue of socially-distanced punters, trailing onto the beach amidst the bustle of the British middleclasses. Family groups were all taking the sea, sun and sand without a care in the world and demonstrating not one hoot for the demands of racial diversity which currently so troubles the rest of the world. (It's really no surprise that this area is colloquially known as Sutton-Coldfield-By-The-Sea)

Chatting families stood knee deep in gently lapping water; pleasure boats pootled in the bay; enthusiastic youths cooled rising sap by charging en masse into the miniscule waves and we sat in the glorious sunshine with pints of beer and pub-sandwiches, simply lapping up the ozone-charged cross-shore breeze and the atmosphere of a lock-down-released August day on the beach.

"Just download the app and you can check-in with us; view the menu; order food and drinks and even pay your bill" breezed our cheery waitress by way of welcome to our evening booking back at the overnight pub. Little did they seem to realise on this celebratory first day of Welsh 'indoor dining' that their entire socially-distanced, track-and-trace, device-based ordering strategy was wholly reliant on a wi-fi signal which self-evidently did not exist in this particular establishment. Since it's claimed that even Kazakhstan enjoys better internet coverage than most of Wales, why would you pin your entire Opening Day Covid-19 Restaurant Recovery Plan on a flawed high-tech solution that completely bypassed the historically well-proven, low-tech keystone of the hospitality sector – good old-fashioned human interaction – conducted at a socially responsible 2m distance?

Which it wasn't, of course, as slightly confused yet still inanely smiling staff lost all sense of the new normal and simply leant on our table while beers and food were ordered by mouth and delivered by hand. As such, we enjoyed mediocre food and paid in full ("What do you mean, there's a half-price Government-backed initiative?") yet still enjoyed free overnight parking with unrivalled and magnificent views across the beach at Morfa Nefyn.

On balance? Result.

PART FOUR

Flavours Of France

"How can you govern a country which has
246 varieties of cheese?"

Charles de Gaulle
President of France
1959 – 1969

The End Of August: We Set Off For France

Plouvien, Brittany, France

Travel broadens the mind - and while I don't mean to be detrimental to the motorway network of Great Britain, I don't believe the author of that quote was talking about the M5 here. We did however enjoy a smooth and surprisingly free-flowing trip down it yesterday, failing dismally to broaden our minds with a newspaper crossword while covering a surprising 225 miles to reach Plymouth docks in good order with a brief and minor diversion for a social visit in Bristol en route.

Sufficient wi-fi? Well, yes, typing this in a lounge area of 'Armorique' – a Brittany Ferry – as we cross a thankfully only-slightly-swelling English Channel towards Roscoff, I'm worried that if I switch apps mid-channel, so-to-speak, I'll be left staring at the whirring-wheel-of-weak-wi-fi for as long again as I've been waiting for this page to load.

All is well with our journey so far. An overnight stop in the dockside queue of other early-arriving motorhomes was disturbed far too early by the Port's designated 'knocker-upper' who awoke us from our slumbers at dawn. Ample time to brew a cuppa and then join the same queue to roll into the bowels of Armorique (apply the handbrake and engage first gear, please sir) and then retire – having first consumed Full English (served up with a French accent) — to a surprisingly spacious sea-view cabin to sleep off our disturbed slumbers.

Roscoff greeted us with bright sunshine and we were quickly processed into a convoy of anxious motorhomers, feeling our way, en masse out of the port and onto French roads – our first outing onto the continent of Europe.

Satnav, in the inimitable style of most modern technology, insisted on providing us solely with guidance through Finland so, ably assisted by an ace navigator who thankfully comes from the last generation of map-reading humans, we progressed through the edges of Finistere towards our selected first destination for the night – a France Passion location at Plouviens, which had also piqued our interest being located on a trout-farm.

We reached our destination, a picturesque but unremarkable rural family home set in a wooded and rivered valley to find it was indeed a trout-farm – as we discovered on a brief exploratory walk-about. Free-flowing waters of the river fed into cricket-pitch sized concrete tanks – in which huge and well-camouflaged trout languidly swam. We met our host, a few attempts at each other's language established the commonality of failed conversation, and we retired to the Knumptywagen for yet another brew and to ponder what we might do next, having settled too far from the town of Plouvien to make a cycle trip or walk there worthwhile.

At The Sign Of The Flashing Green Cross

Camaret-sur-mer, Brittany, France

Joie de vivre! The French certainly seem able to demonstrate the joy of life far better than us Brits. They also celebrate Pharmacies to a surprising extent, as each village or town we've travelled through so far seems to always have at least two, advertising their presence with overlarge green neon crosses flashing excitedly outside their premises.

And this morning, when we stopped in Plabennec for our first boulangerie visit of the trip, we were amused by an outward demonstration of French joie de vivre, mounted proudly on the wall of such a Pharmacy.

While we Brits are busy bolting publicly accessible defibrillators to the outside walls of our retail and office premises in a seemingly desperate advertisement of our current national state of health, the French, God bless 'em, are mounting Durex condom dispensers on theirs. I kid you not. There, proudly mounted on the wall of a busy Pharmacy, was a 24/7 put-your-money-in the-slot emergency condom dispensing machine. And not a defibrillator in sight!

So. The sun is shining, almost too brightly to see the screen as I type – sitting in the Knumptywagen, which is perched in a small car-park overlooking the blustery harbour and sea-front of Camaret-sur-mer, a cheerfully agreeable resort on the tip of the Presqu'Ile De Crozon peninsula, to which we have wended our way, after departing our trout-farm stopover of the night previous.

For the record, the evening prior, we enjoyed a 90-minute forest walk – accompanied by un grand chien belonging to the fish-farmer, and which appeared to be half-dog and half-bear as it hurtled around our feet and splashed noisily in the river along the banks of which we walked. Alarmingly, it then disappeared completely before our half-way point, to greet us cheerfully on our return to the Knumptywagen, a cool 11,000 paces up on our earlier tally. This thankfully justified an all-you-could-eat Ready Steady Cook in-Knumptywagen dining experience – enjoyed while relentless rain splashed noisily on our roof for most of the evening.

Morning thankfully provided a clear blue sky as we trundled off-site in search of the much-anticipated "aires" – free-to-use service points specifically for motorhomers – and for which we had a map dedicated to their locations throughout France. Well, despite the map and some more excellent navigation from The Last Capable Map Reader To Walk The Earth, could we find the damn things, which should have been locatable in municipal carparks? Non. Until we reached the small and intriguingly named riverside village of Hopital Camfrout, (an historic place of healing beside a sinuous stream, apparently) where we pulled up and wandered around on foot, almost giving up hope of locating the indicated Aire, when there it was – a small stainless steel monolith, sprouting taps, holes and gullies, into which we were delightedly able to empty waste-waters, refill and refresh and generally dance around like excited schoolchildren who'd just been given an extra day's holiday for performing well at Speech Day.

Suitably refreshed and replenished, onwards we trundled, on surprisingly quiet roads and across amazing bridges as we reached the west coast for which we'd been aiming since we'd made landfall at Roscoff.

Now chronologically out of kilter, the story finds itself back at Camaret-Sur-Mer, where – after much driving about (including a gentle and rather surprising trundle through the middle of a funfair being set-up on the quayside) we parked up above –

and overlooking – the town. Continuing bright sunshine coaxed us out for a walkabout, although a stiff sea breeze kept us moving – out along the harbour wall and past the most amazingly large boats – all timber hulled and all abandoned very neatly together in an orderly row, rotting gently for the benefit of numerous photographers (including us), all striving to achieve the most artistic angles and pictorial compositions. The quayside Fisherman's church sat squat alongside a solidly Napoleonic-looking, four- square moated fortification and provided yet more photographic opportunities.

As evening arrived, we ventured into the town again, where the funfair was just getting its legs out, and while stallholders braved the continuing sea-breezes, we found the quaintest of quayside restaurants, the imaginatively named Restaurant Del Mare where, in broken Franglais, we managed to order dinner.

Emerging now into true darkness, we might have found the funfair in full swing had there been anybody else but us to patronise it. The lights were flashing; the sound-systems were pumping; the smell of frying doughnuts mixed headily with that of freshly-stranded barbe-a-papa and whilst being the sole inhabitants might have been a bit of an exaggeration, we did feel slightly sorry for the generally glum faces of the stallholders as a trickle of potential punters mostly promenaded in an orderly line down the middle of the street, avoiding as best they could any temptation to part with their money.

There were, however, two points of note on each of the two Hook-a-Duck stalls: they were both offering real live goldfish in plastic bags as prizes, a sight unseen since it was deemed politically incorrect (and probably downright cruel) to offer such livestock as motivation in the UK. And for those less fortunate clients who may only have hooked enough points to warrant a prize off the back-wall, these prizes were very clearly arranged into the best demonstration of gender-stereotyping since the advent of public toilets. One side of the stall was festooned with childrens' novelties in every conceivable shade of pink, while the other half of the stall proudly displayed a range of camouflaged military-derived toys you could ever hope to shake a stick at.

Serendipity And The Water Pump

Quimper, Brittany, France

Today has been A Very Good Day. A Very Good Day indeed.

Why? Because it began with the disappointing and very complete failure of our faithful and unremarkable servant, the Knumptywagen's water-pump. This device lurks unseen within our onboard fresh-water tank, and its role is to provide a supply of water, on demand, through two taps; an ingenious little loo-flush and – on rare occasions - our onboard shower. (Posh, eh?)

Its silent demise at this early stage of our 3-week tour was therefore a bit of a disappointment and conjured up rather dry and unpalatable thoughts of the rest of our journey, unless we could get it fixed.

Enter our magnanimous and welcome friend, Serendipity. She arrived as she always does, unannounced and shyly introduced us to page 69 of this year's 'France Passion' guidebook which featured an advertisement for a nationwide network of motorhome dealerships, primarily spread across eastern France, with just three dots on the tiny map denoting rays of hope on our western seaboard.

Well. As if she hadn't already done enough for us with this small gesture, Serendipity decided she'd put in a full-time shift on this sunny Saturday, and in doing so, turned what might have become a complete Bad News Potential Time-Consuming Disaster Day into Trala-la-la Dance Amongst the Daisies.

And just to contrast our extreme good fortune (because, if we're honest with ourselves, nobody really likes a full-blown good news story, do they?) what follows juxtaposes and contrasts (a) what actually occurred with (b) what would normally have happened, OK?

1a: 'France Passion' guidebook advertisement.

1b: No book, no advertisement, or at the very least, no advertisement noticed.
2a: Three of the highlighted outlets from a possible twelve were on our side of France.
2b: None of them were anywhere near us.
3a: One of the three was in Quimper, through which we were headed anyway.
3b: The nearest was bloody miles out of our way.
4a: We found it! (No thanks to our Satnav, which still thinks we're in Finland.) We arrived at 10:30 to find it was open until 12 noon.
4b: Our service department is closed on a Saturday.
5a: The Navigator Without Equal had pre-programmed Google Translate with the problem, translating it into French on her phone, thus to present this information to an amused and impressed dealer on arrival.
5b: We're English. We don't speak foreign languages and were therefore unable to communicate.
6a: The dealer spoke English.
6b: Gallic shrugs.
7a: A mechanic was available immediately and diligently got stuck in – to a tight and very awkwardly accessed water-tank to examine the problem.
7b: Our service department is closed on a Saturday.
8a: Within 10 minutes, he'd located and stripped out the inaccessible pump.
8b: Worried shaking of heads; conspiratorial muttering; sucking of teeth and sharp intakes of breath. "Who sold you this then?"
9a: The dealer had a suitable replacement pump to hand, seemingly amongst a box of random spare parts.

9b: The part will need to be ordered. It's Saturday. Therefore, part unlikely to arrive before Monday, call it Tuesday just to be on the safe side.
10a: The mechanic fitted the new-found pump immediately – with efficiency, knowledge, care and diligence.
10b. Our service department is closed on a Saturday.
11a: The dealer totted up a simple bill for the parts, charged nothing for the labour; the whole episode was completed within 60 minutes of our arrival and cost us just €63.00 euros in total.
11b: We were presented with an extortionate and inflated bill, charging a premium for our unannounced arrival; the problem we presented and the inconsiderate timing of our visit.
12a: We were simply waved off with a smiling "merci" and no heart-wrenching pleas to like them on Facebook.
12b: We left with a bad taste, feeling we'd been taken advantage of and with strong demands to be rated on Facebook.

There. That's why today has been A Very Good Day. And sadly, dear reader, it doesn't end there, as our unfolding story hasn't yet got anywhere near our overnight stop at the shellfish farm. Can you stand the suspense if that waits until the next chapter? Think you're going to have to!

Apres Le Deluge

Concarneau, Brittany, France

Today it has rained. And then it has rained some more. In fact, il a plu beaucoup. It wasn't unexpected however, as the Navigator Par Excellence is also The Weather Girl in her spare time, so we were appraised of the situation even as we sat out yesterday evening on the deck of our shellfish farm, where the lowering sun was to witness our consumption of molluscs, crustaceans and ubiquitous frites.

However, we mustn't let this continuing excitement run ahead of us, and yesterday's exploits were promised today, as we did get rather carried away over a water-pump. So, you're naturally and curiously asking at this point, what happened during the rest of our day? Well, I'm very glad you've asked – because, like it or not, you're about to learn more. And it involves a trip down what would normally be classed as Memory Lane, since we returned to visit Concarneau, a largish town on the west coast, where approximately 26-ish years previously, we had holidayed with several small and therefore demanding offspring. Admittedly, we were accompanied by relatives who were themselves also parents of similarly youngish offspring, so what should have been a holiday of mutual support just turned into a fortnight of five a.m. starts and mutual abject exhaustion. And it rained then too. For a fortnight. So much so, in fact, that the clasps on our cheap suitcases, stored under beds around our rented maison, all turned rusty – a tale which has entered and remained firmly embedded in family folklore.

So, Memory Lane having been extensively redeveloped into Exhaustion Highway, our arrival yesterday into Concarneau triggered absolutely no recall of that previous visit whatsoever. It was however, a very pleasant experience, as our motorhome gave us privileges denied to lesser beings, in that we could access dedicated parking at an Aire, on the site of the now-disused Gare, a mere step or two into the centre-ville.

What amazed us was our collective numbers. There were motorhomes bloody everywhere. Mostly bigger, grander and more modern than ours but we delighted in the fact that one of the few remaining spaces available happened to be right next to exactly the same make and model as ours, bearing German plates and (wouldn't you know it) occupants who spoke perfect English. We congratulated each other on our impeccable taste in 'camping car' as the French rather quaintly call them; fed the parking machine a paltry sum and strolled in warm sunshine down a bunting-dressed High Street to a delightfully cosmopolitan port, with a choice of pavement bistros, restaurants and creperies.

Our earlier water-pump activities had left us sans breakfast, so our first task was to indulge in two large savoury galettes (Breton buckwheat pancakes) stuffed full of every conceivable breakfast item we could think of, sitting in the sunshine at tables outside one of numerous eateries overlooking the mediaeval walled Old Town, which neither of us again could recall from our previous visit.

Suitably fortified (geddit?), we entered the Old Town and were taken aback by a pedestrian Main Street positively buzzing with tourists, lined on both sides by low-ceilinged but cavernous shops, selling all manner of upmarket souvenirs; trendy art, jolly-matelot stripy sweaters and various intriguing sweetmeats. In addition, English was suddenly heard to be the prevalent language. Not, I hasten to add, from the good burghers of Old Town Concarneau, keen to extend entente cordial or to boost their sales, but by the predominance of drained-looking English parents pushing buggies, roaming the cobbled alleyways and explaining patiently in that teeth-gritting way of the angrily suppressed English middle classes just why Jocasta and Henry couldn't have yet another bag of marshmallows and James, please stop poking Sophie with your pirate sword or I'll take it off you. Ah, happy days.

A walk around the old town walls extended itself accidentally into a continuance along a promenade-of-sorts, and with her now pedestrianised map-reading skills still well to the fore, The Chief Navigator reported that our gentle Fit-bit measured stroll of over 10,000 paces led us back to the Knumptywagen, almost unidentifiable amidst the assembled Concourse d'Elegance of The Knumptydom of European Nations.

Onwards. Turning to our France Passion Guidebook of interesting places where we could stopover for free (ostensibly in exchange for our purchasing goods or services from our hosts) we sped as best we could towards a shell-fish farm, purporting to offer a range of farmed oysters, clams and other shellfish plus crustaceans such as crab and lobster.

As expected, the facility was on the coastal water's edge at the end of a pine-lined lane and – perhaps inevitably – was more industrial than picturesque but we claimed the last slot amongst five other motorhomes; introduced ourselves (as instructed by the guidelines) to a fairly indifferent host and set about peering into all the gurgling tanks full of passive oysters and humongous lobsters. A decision about our evening dining plans quickly turned positive when we found a tabled-deck overlooking a sheltered tidal bay, and a menu which provided a vast array of seafood. With classic French salesmanship, a table in the completely empty restaurant could be made available to us at 7pm and no later, so – excited by the prospect of hot in-Knumptywagen showers, we spent the next frenzied 15 minutes readying ourselves to dine out.

We enjoyed our simple meals of moule mariniere and crevettes-something-or-other (which Google managed to translate, intriguingly, as "shrimp pupils") but my-oh-my, we were rather outshone by the couple on the next table who seemed to have ordered the entire Atlantic Ocean. This amazing menu item appeared to offer the entire edible content of the second largest ocean on the planet, served up on one huge platter, with two full-sized shell-on crabs as its centre-piece, surrounded by ring after beautifully arranged ring of oysters, clams, mussels, langoustine, prawns and shrimps, the latter of which simply clung over the edge of the dish as if to the gunwales of a sinking ship. We couldn't even begin to guess what it must have cost, but they did have the biggest, smartest, longest, flashiest motorhome on the pitch.

Gonflage And The Baguette Machine

Château-Gontier, Mayenne, France

When we acquired our motorhome three years ago, it became clear from the documentation that it had spent most of its time on the Channel Island of Jersey. How it came into our possession through a dealership on the outskirts of Birmingham remains a mystery, but it had been well-maintained and – unlike many of the options we'd already viewed – sported tastefully understated upholstery thankfully sourced from the stylish but apparently extremely limited Migraine-Avoidance Range.

It did, however, have a particularly noisy, rattling cab – which over time we became used to, even though it rendered the radio virtually useless, even with the volume control wound up to Threshold of Pain level.

As with a lot of other motorhomes, ours spends most of the winter months going nowhere – remaining foursquare and static on a patch of hard-standing at the rear of our house. Having replaced the worn front tyres during the summer last year, this January we replaced the worn rear tyres – and the effect has been transformational. As we immediately experienced setting off for March 2018's maiden voyage, peace and quiet reigned supreme; the rattling had reduced significantly; we could converse at a comfortable level and even the subdued and reverent tones of Radio 4 presenters burbled at an audible level for the first time in our journeyings.

Moral of the story? Well, presumably (and yes, as advised in the motorhome press, but ignored by those of us who thought we knew better) leaving a 3.5 tonne vehicle resting on its tyres for any length of time (either on Jersey and/or the outskirts of Birmingham) is going to misshape them imperceptibly – to the point that their insignificant lumpiness was obviously contributing to a significant amount of cab noise, which we'd just assumed was normal for a motorhome.

Yes, it's an expensive remedy if your tyres haven't actually worn out, but even visual inspection hadn't identified that our tyres had even become misshapen, so we didn't attribute our excessive cab-noise to this issue.

Come the autumn, then, we've decided it'll be well worth the inconvenient effort of jacking the van up to take the weight off the tyres, which will hopefully preserve their innate and beautiful roundness which, in turn, will permit future in-cab social conversations – and Radio 4 – whilst journeying.

And OK, just for you insatiable fans of Knumptydom, here's an added bit of tyre related malarkey, resulting from our trip through France, when we struggled to find anywhere to pump up our well-journeyed tyres. Who'd have guessed that we should have been looking out for 'gonflage' when we had instead been erroneously seeking 'pompe du pneus'?

As it was, we eventually found an unmanned roadside service area, primarily featuring several DIY car-washing bays, alongside which was a simple coin-slot air-compressor unit where we were able to check and gonflage our tyres. What fascinated us most, however, in this completely automated environment, was a free-standing, outdoor, baguette-dispensing machine. Shall I say that again? A baguette-dispensing machine. In exchange for yet more coinage, we could have helped ourselves to a baguette (freshly baked, judging by the aroma) and delivered through a Perspex slot in much the same way as you might grab a can of Coke or a bag of crisps from the machine at your local swimming pool.

This passive machine, standing sentinel amidst gonflage and arid car-wash bays, provided us with much intrigue for the onward leg of our journey, as we speculated on how often it would have needed to be replenished, and how fresh the contents would remain, standing in the sunshine (or more accurately, the rain) all day long.

Finally, what made this particular conversation even more fulfilling as we hurtled further southwards in search of better weather? It was our ability to hear and be heard at autoroute speeds, at last made possible by our lovely round, and now properly inflated, tyres.

Concerning A Visit To Vannes And Some Attempted Refreshment

Vannes, Brittany, France

What does it take to make a cup of coffee? And that's not a trick question. Really, what does it take? Even doing it 'properly', it's not – I hope you'll agree – the world's most complex task. And if you do it for a living, professional-like, it should be even less complicated, yes? Well. Stand by for an uncharacteristic rant. Because this morning, in the picturesque and historic city of Vannes, in an otherwise bustling and very agreeable covered market, it took three-point-five people all of fifteen minutes to serve up a cappuccino and a hot chocolate.

Three-point-five people? Well, yes. Three of them seemed to be dedicated to the task full time while the point-five was clearly designated to visit me every so often at the counter, look quizzically at the receipt I was clutching (which was slowly turning into papier-mâché in my increasingly desperate and sweaty grasp); smile knowingly and then wander off again.

Two of the three seemed to be the proprietors of the coffee-stall, the third – judging by their shared taste in outlandish eyewear – possibly a daughter. And therein lay the difficulty. The Holy Trinity of Attempted-Coffee-Dispensation were clearly far too busy trying to look fashionably stylish with their oversized, horn-rimmed, dual-coloured spectacles and their 'Je suis Francais, vous connaissez?' attitude that their primary raison d'etre had clearly long since been lost to a sad triumph of style over content.

As such, they all clattered about behind their counter, clouds of steam and froth flew about the place, clientele (are you liking the lingo creeping in here?) gathering exponentially while they continually crashed into each other rushing from the till to the coffee-machine (ooh, pardon!) and back again, sloshing milk and coffee-grounds around the place with gusto, but sadly not quite managing to MAKE ANY BLOODY COFFEE!!!

Eventually, an outcome emerged and we were able to triumphantly enjoy our petite dejeuner, as solid rain continued to pour down outside. (You were wondering why the hot chocolate, weren't you?) We were a bit damp and needed comforting – with oven-warm pastries bought from an adjoining stall which was far less fashionable and therefore infinitely more efficient. And ha-ha, look at us, we're eating them at the coffee-stall's tables and they're too 'busy' to do anything about it. Result!

Vannes was, as the guidebooks advised, well worth a visit, and we enjoyed the rest of our brief pedestrianised tour of the old town as well as the classic 'painting-by-numbers' treelined streets. The cathedral was mid-Sunday mass as we stepped inside and it was gratifying to see a healthy congregation giving their all to an unidentifiable hymn, while the pervading smell of incense transported us both back to earlier and more youthful times.

The cathedral was also the first place we'd witnessed to act as refuge to a straggle of homeless individuals, one of whom was sporting a very hipster beard and smoking a cigar in between swigs from his can of extra-strength lager as he squatted aimlessly in the main doorway. Vannes was clearly a good place to be homeless.

The rain persisted as we stumbled by chance outside of the impressively solid mediaeval and well-preserved city walls into a beautifully planted and lawned linear park which led us back towards the yacht-cluttered port and the welcoming and dry interior of the Knumptywagen, where The Navigator Without Equal soon had us back on the road again, heading south as – assumedly – that's where the sun was shining.

A Bit About The Landscape

Camaret-sur-mer, Brittany, France

What about the landscape, I hear you cry. Tell us more about the landscape through which you must surely be driving all those kilometres? We need more detail. We want to picture it in our mind's eye, through your eloquent and well-observed metaphors and similes. Paint a picture for us so that we may feel part of your trip, your journey, your odyssey.

OK. It's mostly green.

For the most part, we've kept off the autoroutes and used good-quality and well signposted secondary routes, through rural areas, all of which have had a neatness and tidiness that you don't seem to see in the UK. Farms, many of them arable, don't have the same amount of abandoned clutter, outmoded equipment and rusting, tumble-down barns. There's plenty of cattle in the well-ordered fields but no sheep spotted yet (although a boucherie in Vannes market had the most fantastic array of lamb, including double-sided Barnsley chops, although I suspect they weren't called that in this particular arrondissement).

We've also been staying at 'France Passion' sites – a very simple, word-of-mouth marketed national network of rural facilities which offer free overnight parking specifically for motorhomes. We're therefore mostly off the beaten-track and although many of the sites wouldn't be described as picturesque, they are 'real' and provide an unembellished insight into rural France (which, so far, has indeed proved mostly green.) When we arrived last night after-hours at a site which included a Farm Shop, we were able to negotiate with our Host to open said shop and allow us to procure sausage; lettuce; cider; a bottle of very fine Muscadet (currently lubricating the author as he types); a bulb of garlic; butter (just patted into a vague shape and wrapped in greaseproof paper); tomatoes; potatoes and a jar of local apple sauce, most of which became a very palatable in-Knumptywagen supper as the quietening dusk fell around us.

In terms of the greater landscape of the North-western French coastal region, we did witness one striking feature as we left Camaret-Sur-Mer, to drive across country with an early morning mist solidifying in the heather-swathed valleys. A precipitous bank of heather and ferns at the side of the road was floodlit by the low-angled light of morning sunshine, illuminating a carefully curated gallery of spiders' webs – literally hundreds of them, each the size of a dinner-plate – arrayed in close proximity across a hundred metres of foliage, with every carefully woven silken strand exquisitely and delicately highlighted by myriad droplets of morning dew, mirroring the sun and providing the most breath-taking natural artwork.

The only other observation to offer is that the landscape is Impressionistic, reflecting the vivid juxtaposition of colours (OK, mainly differing shades of green) which dominated many of the semi-abstract Impressionist paintings we all know, admire and love – but can't attribute to specific artists through a frustrating lack of in-depth knowledge of the subject. Suffice it to say that the landscape and its artistic representations feel somehow cyclical in that they continually inspire, inform and interpret each other. Does that make any sense?

Must be bedtime.

Pornic And A Religious Experience

Pornic, Loire-Atlantique, France

I've never been to Heathrow's Terminal 4. I'm told it's vast and a triumph of modern architecture stroke engineering. I have however, been to the small regional French town of Pornic's local supermarket and I tell you what – it would give any one of Heathrow's international terminals a run for their money any day.

The slightly unfortunately named Pornic (which spell-check continually informs me should be spelt 'Pernicious') doesn't appear in any of our tourist guides which could be why we found it such an unassumingly pleasant small harbourside town. Built around a coastal inlet, and featuring (as most small, unassuming French towns do in these parts) a whacking great chateau-style castle and similarly imposing yet unremarkable stone-built church, Pornic was laced through with ambling alleyways and narrow lanes hemmed by blue-shuttered terraced primary domiciles.

The quayside presented a view of deep and unctuous-looking mud-banks, in which a variety of small boats were randomly studded. The significant height of the harbour walls over which we leaned served notice that the tide was currently out, although it was clear that once it returned, the scene – sans mud – would prove far more picture-postcard.

Pavement cafes and bars dotted the quayside and a modern tourist office drew us in to enquire, in our usual hesitant and halting French, about fishing prospects inland, at which point (of course) the already smiling assistant segued into English to explain the local map.

It seemed a strange feature of Pornic that it could be both eminently coastal yet also immediately rural, as to the rear of the tourist office a canal began to wend its way inland. With our backs turned to the harbour, the view was – yet again – of green and verdant countryside. Returning tout suite to the Knumptywagen, we travelled along a prescribed route along the identified canal, to find a small off-road area where we parked up (as it turned out, for the night - although this wasn't due to a surfeit of landed fish).

During the human race's tenure of the planet, it's become a learned response that some form of bait goes a long way towards aiding the fishing process, especially when your method of choice is rod and line. In our case, we sadly had no real bait of any type, save half a baguette. This didn't really help our cause, as no matter how diligently we squeezed bits of the damn stuff onto our hooks, it rarely displayed sufficient tenacity to stay on during the casting process, let alone once in contact with the water.

So it was that, for the second time that day, Ernie came to our rescue. We've no idea where the nickname came from, or how we assigned it to the French supermarket chain of E. Leclerc, other than the initial 'E' had to stand for something, so Ernie it became. And it was Ernie who'd seen fit to build the vast, airport-sized supermarket just on the outskirts of meek little Pornic.

Hence our return visit, because on our earlier grocery shop, having strolled the aisles of plenty, we'd spotted a section dedicated to fishing tackle. (It was alongside the teaspoon aisle, to which we'd headed previously - because we needed some teaspoons – and to which precise location we were miraculously guided, as if by divine intervention, within this vast and awe-inspiring retail cathedral.)

Plenty of rods, reels, nets and general paraphernalia and then there, just above comfortable reach, were hung some enticing but eye-wateringly expensive artificial baits. Ironically, we had to lean on a lower unit to reach these piscatorial jewels and only then realised that the lower unit was, in fact, a small refrigerator in which was stored every conceivable colour of live maggot and the rather more traditionally coloured earthworm, all securely packaged in little bait-sized pots, at about an eighth of the cost of the artificial versions. Result!

A quick hike to the tills via the sweetcorn aisle – (did it really have an aisle dedicated to sweetcorn, or am I just making that up?) and Ernie, God Bless the Patron Saint of Supermarche Francais, had supplied us with a quasi-religious experience, as well as the presumed unique opportunity to be the only shoppers in Christendom ever to have graced a moving supermarket till-belt with worms, maggots and sweetcorn as the sole constituents of a grocery shop.

Of Sunflowers And Soldiers, Chicanes And Shutters

Various Unidentified Villages, Gironde, France

As we amble gently south, we're slowly getting the hang of the various regions of the French Atlantic coast. In some respects, our Satnav's inescapable infatuation with Finland has encouraged our increased use of good, old-school paper maps and these, combined with the unrivalled skills of The Navigator Par Excellence, have meant a far greater sense of place as we've been able to recognise when we're crossing from one distinctly mapped region into another.

So, when we made landfall in Roscoff, we found ourselves in one of the many featured locations of the Shipping Forecast, Finistere – from where we continued into the Loire Atlantique & Vendee, thence into Charente-Maritime and then (currently) the Gironde.

It was the transition between Charente-Maritime and the Gironde which seemed most distinctive, in that suddenly, the arable fields around us were almost completely filled with sunflowers. Their purpose we could only guess at – seeds or oil derived therefrom – but they were clearly (and sadly, from a visual point of view) past their best. In fact, they were formed up in forlorn battalions, uniformed in tattered brown and faded yellow, all facing in the same direction, each and every one of them shamefacedly drooping their heads as if in defeat, and all seemingly marching in retreat across the landscape.

In contrast – and marshalling these defeated ranks – fields of ripe maize marched alongside, their golden bayonets poking aloft in close formation, each one standing tall alongside their soldierly comrades as they proudly marched the vanquished armies of sunflowers towards their final fate.

Meanwhile, in the seemingly deserted villages through which we passed, three things proved of note. Firstly, most of them genuinely did seem deserted. Honey coloured stone villas, terraces, cottages, houses – call them what you will – all seemed as if the holocaust had arrived just ahead of us and wiped all evidence of human habitation off the streets. Yes, the occasional car passed us by – the occupants staring rather more than they should have done, presumably at the unfamiliar-looking number plate on the Knumptywagen, but probably more likely in horror since our driver, as they perceived it, seemed to have her head down, buried in a large, unfolded paper map.

Secondly, the French could clearly teach the rest of Europe a lesson or two about traffic-calming. In obvious fear of any of the non-existent pedestrians being mown down by passing vehicles, each village is preceded by a suspension-challenging speedbump, which continues to shake the entire contents of the Knumptywagen, no matter how slowly we edge ourselves over them. (More to the point, despite best efforts, they have completely wrecked – of all things – our cutlery drawer, which will need serious refurbishment back in Blighty). Once the speedbump (always topped with a superfluous painted pedestrian crossing) has been negotiated, we enter a series of delightful, high-kerbed chicanes (reminiscent of those fairground rides which thrilled us as kids when we were let loose in small, motorised cars which steered themselves around a circuit, regardless of our childlike, committed and enthusiastic turning of a completely disconnected steering-wheel). These chicanes are planted with flowering shrubs, herbs, and other flora – all of which brush both sides of your vehicle and deliver an overpowering psychological constraint to your speed as you – quite literally – admire the daisies as you pass through.

And finally, since your average speed is now slower than the apocryphal horse-and-cart-through-central-London's-rush-hour (and your vehicle, is in effect, being kept on the carriageway simply because it's clattering off the containing kerbs), you have time to marvel at the shuttering which covers each and every window you're passing. I'm not kidding. Whoever won the Window-Shutter-Manufacturing-and-Installation-Contract-for-All-OfFrance must surely now own Monte Carlo. We've never seen so many window shutters. Open, closed, weather-beaten, faded, newly painted, nearly all of them very beautiful in their own right – every single house has about eight hundred of the things. They're everywhere. What a coup. You can just hear the sales patter now: Look, you hang 'em on every single window and they keep the heat in and the heat out. You don't need curtains, and they make your home look, well, sort of French, n'est'ce'pas?

John Deere Invades Dijon

Dijon, Burgundy, France

The Channel Tunnel was a virginal penetration for our Knumptywagen and very smoothly it went too, especially as we'd misunderstood the duration of the underground journey by incorporating the hours' time difference between the UK and France, so our expected 'crossing' of one hour and 35 minutes took just 35 minutes, which made us feel vaguely disappointed by our endearing stupidity.

Out we popped onto what my parents always referred to as 'The Continent' and found the nearest autoroute on which to hurtle south, headed for Reims as first stop, courtesy of nearby Jonchery-sur-Vesle where we had found a welcoming and authentic French bistro for beer and food prior to a romantic overnight in an Ernie Leclerc supermarket carpark nearby.

Onwards then down more autoroutes (paying the tolls to speed our journey) where Dijon became our next stop. Yes, famous of course for its mustard but also, we'd read somewhere, for gingerbread because the city straddled historic European spice routes. We were headed for a basic (i.e. cheap) motorhome stopover or 'aire' but arrived too late in the day and found it already rammed full. As luck would have it, this aire was immediately adjacent to a proper, riverside campsite and as we joined a two-motorhome queue at the barrier, a guy emerged from the office to tell the driver of the van immediately behind us that the site was now full. Our skin-of-the-teeth-last-available pitch was perfectly acceptable and the site was an interesting mix of tenting motorcyclists (they do love revving their engines for no apparent reason, don't they?) as well as mixed nationality Knumptywagens and caravans.

Dijon itself was but a short cycle ride alongside a picturesque river and we enjoyed a pedalled cruise around gently thronged pedestrianised streets, eventually finding a classic covered market, closed, but ringed by bustling pavement restaurants and café bars.

It seemed as if the circus had also arrived in town at the same time, as a parade of agricultural vehicles led by two very new, very shiny and very large green and yellow John Deere tractors clogged up the perimeter streets. Their massive tyres dwarfed slightly anxious diners as they rolled close by – to be followed by manure-splattered pick-up trucks containing an array of bleating and mooing farmyard animals, staring impassively as they witnessed parts of their cousins being consumed before their very eyes (avec frites, naturellement.) The entire market area ground to a healthy-smelling halt as horse- and cattle-boxes were unhitched and manoeuvred into display positions in any available space. Caricatures of French farmers with ash-extended, white-tipped fag-ends bimbled about, gesticulating and shouting at one another while their drifting smoke covered up the more bucolic aromas.

By this time, we'd managed to secure ourselves ring-side seats at a pavement café bar (almost as dangerous as at a proper circus) while an entertaining and mixed collection of Motorists of The World – who'd become unwittingly interspersed within the whole vehicle-based farmyard parade – themselves became stationary exhibits of frustration, resignation or amusement as we watched them sitting in their open-topped Fiats, Ford Mustangs or Porsches, slowly marinating in their own Gallic annoyance and the smell of manure.

Eventually, the farmyard circus managed to disband itself into an area alongside the market where they immediately used a pre-established giant barbecue to start cooking wholesale samples of the meats which were clearly still represented by the live calves, cows, goats and horses (blinking benignly as yet more cooking smoke drifted into their twitching nostrils) and which were now tethered passively alongside the cooking area like some bizarre form of petting zoo.

Having now completed our own repast and enjoyed the chaotic and delightfully free entertainment, we saddled up and retraced our route back to the campsite in the lowering late evening light (sadly still without spotting any evidence of either mustard or gingerbread outlets.) Here, we enjoyed an in-Knumptywagen nightcap, put ourselves to bed and were eventually lulled to sleep by the sound of large-capacity motorcycle engines being overrevved needlessly into the small hours.

The Grapes Of Paulliac

Paulliac, Gironde, France

I do sometimes wish I was a wine buff.

The problem is, for 'buff' read 'snob', and I'd hate to think I was snobbish about anything. (Well, apart from inappropriate behaviour in public; expressing one's opinions too loudly; loud bassy music emanating from cars whose drivers really should know better and – let me see – oh yes, people who know a lot about wine and can therefore combine the words liquorice, blackcurrant, legs, apricot, lingering, tobacco, nose and vanilla in one sentence without ever being challenged or considered a bit odd.)

But if I had been a wine buff, the French countryside through which we've been travelling would have had far greater meaning – because it is undoubtedly wine-country. Our travel-guidebooks had all provided lightweight insight into what we should expect when we entered the regions around Bordeaux. Vines, mostly. Acres of them. Sorry. Hectares. Delightful rolling fields full of vivid, lively green rows, all combed neatly across the landscape at a surprisingly uniform height and bearing – at this September harvest time of year – cluster upon dangling cluster of luscious, shiny black grapes.

Their volume and accessibility – growing mostly in unfenced fields alongside major highways – are clearly a temptation to passing motorists, as we witnessed at a brief pull-in stop to consult our roadmap. By pure chance, it seems we were in the vicinity of the Rothschilds' estates – whose famous labels of Mouton-Rothschild and Chateau-Lafitte are bywords for high-end wines, so we can only assume their grapes are also highly prized as we witnessed an amusing act of highway robbery.

A small Peugeot hatchback with French numberplates pulled into the layby just ahead of us, driven by an aging Madame – with a similarly aged female passenger, both of whom were sporting oversize sunglasses hinged beneath giant and heavily bouffanted fin-du-siecle hairdos. These, perhaps inevitably, were offset by twinsets and pearls, although the passenger's were disguised beneath a trendy silver-grey padded gilet. As the car came to a stop, the passenger slipped nimbly out, casually entered a row of unfenced vines and emerged, smiling conspiratorially at us with a large bunch of grapes now comically and theatrically semi-hidden beneath her overwear. With a flamboyant gesture appropriate to her age and apparent station (as a grape-buff, perhaps?) she slipped back into the Peugeot which then graciously fishtailed its way back onto the carriageway and away into the sunset.

We could just imagine the two Madames cackling like naughty schoolchildren at their audacity as they sped off and then – after a moment's or two amused contemplation – decided what-the-hell; got out and did exactly the same (but minus the fishtailing departure, obvs!)

Lessons Learnt

Epernay, Marne, France

Although the title of this piece could sound as if some disaster may have befallen us, I'm pleased and delighted to impart that no such thing has occurred. In fact, having sensibly acquired a motor-home-specific Satnav (in the form of the thoroughly recommendable Garmin Camper 770 with extra SD card so we can take ALL of Europe with us) this piece has been declared a UNESCO World Heritage Jeopardy-Free Zone, so if it's a swashbuckling tale of adventure you've tuned in for, you'd be better off switching channels now, OK?

The lessons learnt are simply those observations we've made as our trusty Knumptywagen has so far rattled us a healthy 977 miles across Europe to a pit-stop in Bergamo, Italy.

Lesson 1: On the roads abroad, there are many motorcyclists. If one overtakes you, there are more. Always a minimum of two, and more often than not a whole shoal of them, weaving past you and then exercising a slightly unnerving stretching-their-legs-exercise (which we're assuming may be some sort of secret sign, shared and known only amongst themselves, possibly to mean: "You stupid Brits and your stupid Brexit and that stupid Oaf of a so-called Prime Minister who started it all and why don't you just all eff-off out of it and leave us to our own foreign-ness, eh?")

Lesson 2: If a motorcyclist is travelling solo, it's odds-on that he's on a moped and may therefore be safely overtaken. Optional "eff-off" hand signals may be used (in retribution for his fellow-motorcyclists' Brexit foot-waggling) but bear in mind that the size of your motorhome may well have obscured his view of your hand-signals anyway, rendering them a complete waste of time, effort and nationalistic bravado.

Lesson 3: When motorcyclists have gathered en-masse for a rest-stop and removed their helmets, they are ALL hairy blokes who are ALL older than you.

Lesson 4: Or, exceptionally, when some other motorcyclists remove their helmets at rest-stops, they are women. These are ALL always younger than you.

Lesson 5: Where have all the Brits gone? (Well, strictly speaking, not actually a lesson, but last year touring the West Coast of France, we were bloody everywhere.) Now, there are very few of our fellow Brits on the road at this time of year. In any form of vehicle whatsoever.

In fact, in terms of numberplates spotted and waved madly at, we're still in single figures. (Good job then, that we weren't playing Number-plate Cricket – or any other travelling road game designed to keep us distracted on long journeys. No matter how old we are.)

Lesson 5: If you visit a Champagne house in Epernay at 11-o-clock in the morning and indulge in a tasting, even though it was the budget single-glass option and not the full five, you WILL accidentally buy an entire case, then remember you've parked the Knumptywagen on the opposite side of town and will have to carry the heavy box all the way back to it.

Lesson 6: The one-way traffic system in Epernay prevents you bringing the Knumptywagen to the Champagne house and your shoulders will therefore subsequently ache for 24-48 hours as a salutary reminder to curb your impulsive nature, even though it was classed as discretionary holiday expenditure at the time.

Lesson 7: You can get away with overnight 'wild' camping almost anywhere, as long as you're discreet about your intentions until everyone else has left the carpark you've barged your oversized bulk into. Only then should you put your levelling ramps out. Leave no litter, empty no wastewater and draw all your blinds before you put your flash new LED interior lights on. And don't forget to close the black-out blinds behind your drawn net curtains, otherwise those local residents peering suspiciously at you after nightfall are going to think they're watching a home-grown and silent version of the opening credits from 1995's James Bond film, 'Goldeneye' as you prepare for bed.

Lesson 8: As you progress higher and higher into the Alps, your ears 'pop' from the difference in pressure. Swallow hard to clear it and do not – under any circumstances – release the built-up pressure in your toilet-cassette until you're back at sea-level again. Disastrous consequences will befall you if you do not heed this cautionary advice.

Lesson 9: Italians on campsites enjoy standing around in groups and speaking very loudly to each other. I tell you, you won't find this sort of antisocial behaviour in Keswick, oh no.

Lesson 10: Future chapters – when nothing particularly exciting has happened to us – may well utilise this thinly-disguised and allegedly knowledge-imparting device as a recurring theme, for which – under UNESCO guidelines – the author makes no apologies.

We Visit Hyperbole, Alliteration And Lamarche-Sur-Saône

Lamarche-Sur-Saône, Côte d'Or, France

Our journey onwards from Chamonix was rife with hyperbole. Breath-taking, awe-inspiring, spectacular and amazing scenery unfolded around every hairpin bend. Of which there were many. On a steep and winding descent into what became the Vallée du Rhône, a roadside layby provided a breath-taking, awe-inspiring, spectacular and very vertiginous view (ooh, a spot of alliteration there, just for good measure) downwards into a valley below us.

A clearly identifiable dual-carriageway ran arrow-straight along the length of the wide u-shaped valley in the distance below us, looking like a huge and therefore spectacularly amazing airport. To the right, another more natural-looking V-shaped valley headed off into misty sunshine, green and forested and in stark contrast to its highly developed neighbour.

Our route down was so steep and the views so awesome, it felt as if we were coming into land as we dropped by alarming degrees on a low-geared mountain-hugging road. Before we'd fully recovered from the hyperbole, we were on the flat and headed along Runway E62 following the Rhône towards Lake Geneva.

We sneaked through Switzerland, slightly speed sensitive (OK, I'll stop it now) because we hadn't purchased a 'vignette' – a windscreen sticker which basically denotes that you've paid the requisite fee to travel on the autoroutes. At something in the region of 36 euros per year it might have been good value had we decided to declare ourselves Brexit-neutral and take up residency. However, our plan was to cross back into France at Creux within an hour and this purchase didn't seem to be particularly good value. It was with a disproportionate sense of impish excitement, therefore, that we made it across the border unchallenged by Swiss Guards and headed onwards to our next pre-selected overnight stop, mentally stashing the saved fee in our ideological Good Excuse For Dining-Out fund.

Auxonne was just off the A39 about 35 kilometres south east of Dijon, and the nearby 'aire' we'd found was reported to be a quiet, riverside location. We found it delightfully so, in fact, and undaunted by the several motorhomes already on site we swiftly deployed awning and chairs in strong afternoon heat under yet another clear blue sky. The River Saône flowed past our door; serene, green, wide and gentle. A lone fisherman wading from the end of the simple slipway – and a couple of fishing boats which came ashore – excited us at first, but it really was very hot and there was no sign of any catch, so we relaxed in the shade and let the world float gently by. The view was made more picturesque by a moored cruiser (sporting a Swedish ensign, of all things) which became the subject of a spot of online research to realise that this classic boat was indeed registered in Sweden – and was also a full year older than yours truly!

As is usual for rural France, the small village of Lamarche-Sur-Saône was buzzing. A closed bar; a closed hairdressers; a closed butchers; a closed bakery; a main road so devoid of traffic that we thought it too might be closed all contributed to the irony of this paragraph's opening sentence. Devoid of any sign of human habitation (apart from an exhausted-looking bloke pushing a pram – with whom we exchanged slightly startled 'bonsoirs') we gave up on the idea of a cooling Kronenbourg or Pelforth at a characterful pavement café and returned instead to enjoy a gentle Turneresque sunset while we drank our own beer. And perhaps more pointedly, were forced into saving our 36-euro Swiss fee for another day while we instead enjoyed a delightful under-awning dinner in the gloaming.

Bright and early the following morning, we discovered the bakers, butchers, the road and even the bloody bar to be open. There was no sign of the bloke with the pram (sleeping maybe?) and so it was we replenished our victuals and set off again onwards, ever onwards.

Mustardless To Montreux

Montreux, Riviera-Pays-d'Enhaut, Switzerland

Impressively loud birdsong awoke us from our slumbers at Dijon's riverside campsite (long before the motorcyclists did) and following an uber-gastro in-Knumptywagen breakfast of fresh apricots stewed with a soupçon of Cointreau (being the only vaguely viable cooking liquid we could find) stirred into thick French yoghurt, we were soon on the road out of Dijon, disappointedly still with no sign of mustard or gingerbread outlets.

Today, we would keep off the autoroutes and as a result, enjoyed a truly delightful drive through classic French countryside, under clear blue skies and a smiling sun on virtually empty roads, some of which ran ruler-straight for miles amidst rapidly greening arable fields specked with tall, cylindrical grain-stores and large, single-storey agricultural buildings.

Given our lumbering bulk, our general speed was comparable with that attainable on the autoroutes, although this was reduced to 50kph through each village, this variable proving a pleasing distraction from the thrumming long-distance thrash of previous day's journeyings.

Poplar-lined stretches of road loomed suddenly ahead of us in the diminishing distance, welcome shade was cast as we ran between their breeze-shuffled leaves – from which we'd emerge again onto open highway, with no discernible reason why these spectacular runs of trees started and finished as and where they did. In some locations, these towering Poplars were instead replaced by runs of the classic painting-by-numbers Plane trees, sporting dappled bark and which became green-leaved arches enclosing the whole road, as if we were driving through the naves of verdant, sunlight-dappled cathedrals.

It being Sunday, when even fewer of France's gallant citizens than normal emerge onto their village pavements, we were surprised to come across a roadside boulangerie, open for business and happy to sell us a fresh, warm and crunchy-feeling lunchtime picnic baguette, to be complemented (to our even greater surprise) by further comestibles acquired from an also-open and welcoming Boucherie Charcuterie in the same village.

Our onward inertia carried us towards the Swiss border, made evident by both the gradual change in incline and subtle changes to the domestic architecture, as more and more wood began to appear as the core construction material – eaves particularly beginning to overhang the buildings they protected by what was quickly becoming alpine dimensions.

As such, the road began to climb into the foothills of the Alps, indigenous wooden chalets becoming the norm, as were sleepy-looking caramel-brown cows gazing comically over stone walls to show off almost-imagined story-book bells affixed to wide collars around their necks.

With little demarcation, we crossed out of France and into Switzerland, now intent on reaching our planned overnight destination of Montreux on the shores of Lake Geneva, where a little bit of distant family history was hopefully to be revisited.

Chateau Chillon And The Hotel Splendid

Montreux, Riviera-Pays-d'Enhaut, Switzerland

Prior to our departure from the UK, friends more widely travelled than us had hinted that we may find Switzerland expensive, so we'd previously determined that we'd dine in-van whilst within that country's precincts.

It turned out to be a good plan because as we made preparations to cycle into Montreux that evening from our Swiss suburb, a thunderstorm put paid to that ambition and we did indeed dine in-van that night.

The following morning dawned damp, clearing and fair, so we unracked the cycles and set off along a lakeside path designated for the purpose. A delightful ride – with early-morning views across Lake Geneva towards cloud-shrouded mountains – saw us reaching Chateau Chillon, a magnificent and clearly historic building edging the lake, and therefore providing easy pickings for the photographic enthusiasts who were already beginning to murmurate around its base.

Our intended but uncertain destination was a Hotel in Montreux itself which had provided Seafield Convent School Choir with accommodation 40 years prior for their (elsewhere reported) appearance at the Montreux Festival. Would it still exist after all the intervening years? Would The Musical Navigator recall its location? And would we find it on our short cycle ride? Yes, yes and yes. The Hotel Splendid had indeed survived and we found it located in a surprisingly impressive spot on Montreux's main drag. Upgrades seem to have included a very swish, illuminated interior sign proclaiming its name – which seemed a little extravagant since this only therefore advertised its existence to resident guests, who presumably already knew which Hotel they were staying in? But hey, it provided the chance for yet more wry and hopefully vaguely humorous observational cynicism from your author.

Objective achieved, we sought out a bakery but could only find a convenience store, which – as per earlier warnings – inconvenienced us by charging over eight quid for two pastries, a baguette and a couple of peaches, although we still felt this to be justified on the basis that was the only monetary benefit the Swiss were going to squeeze out of us – and we had just stayed the night for free.

So, back to the van, reloaded and set off on yet more upwardly exhilarating alpine roads towards our next key objective – the Grand St Bernard Tunnel – to take us out of Switzerland and on into Italy. This indeed it did, in a spectacular feat of mountain engineering. Following a sunny pitstop for brunch in a roadside alpine meadow, we approached the tunnel through a lengthy run of still-empty road, enclosed within a tunnel-like concrete overhang, pillared and open to the continuing mountain views on one side – presumably to protect the approaches from snow and maybe falling rocks?

The Grand St. Bernard Tunnel (it says here) was opened on 19 March 1964 as the first road tunnel through the European Alps. It's an impressive 5,798 metres long; is absolutely ruler-straight for almost all of that length (and why wouldn't it be, if you're going to all the trouble of blasting your way through virgin rock underneath one of the planet's major mountain ranges?) and it has two lanes, thankfully one in each direction. Our access point on the Swiss side stands at 1,918m above sea level and on emergence into Italy, we were at a similarly impressive 1,875m.

We emerged into daylight under a similarly lengthy run of protective open-sided tunnel on the Italian side, where we commenced another spectacular, hair-raising and hairpin-bending descent onwards towards our next planned destination.

Crumpled somewhere into one of the numerous and cavernous Knumptywagen door pockets will be the tunnel toll receipt, which – if I could be bothered to go and find it – would remind me what we paid for the privilege of driving through (virtually on our own as there continued to be very little traffic) but put it this way: it was surprisingly less than we'd anticipated so, a bit like our experience of Switzerland in general, we felt as though – on the whole – we'd got a good, old fashioned bargain from our brief and rewarding stay.

Don't Stop Me Now

Montreux, Riviera-Pays-d'Enhaut, Switzerland

An unintentional musical theme joins our story briefly here, as we reach the Swiss lakeside town of Montreux. Bear with.

Our approach had brought us over challenging alpine roads, most of them driven by The Navigator Par Excellence, who had accidentally volunteered to do a spot of driving just before a fortuitous bend in the road revealed that it rapidly became tortuously steep, twisted, narrow and frighteningly unfenced for most of the uphill route.

A tumbling, sparkling river had gouged its own chasm of Knumpty-swallowing proportions to our immediate right and accompanied us almost to the summit of the range overlooking Lake Geneva and its floodplains, which we viewed at a brief stopover when the forest momentarily cleared and we were able to revert to our more traditional travelling roles.

Down we went, around yet more hairpin bends, continually buzzed by shoals of foot-waggling motorcyclists who were clearly enjoying the full width of the spectacular, unpopulated road, with only a slowly wallowing Knumptywagen to impede their maniacal, knee-scraping progress.

So, into Nyon we rolled, heading left towards Lausanne along the lakeshore as best we could, eventually being persuaded by insistent signposting onto a higher and less scenic road. From here, we eventually reached Montreux itself and headed optimistically for a 3Knumptywagen aire located lakeside within the town itself. Sadly, our optimism was misplaced as no such location existed, resulting in some fairly hairy manoeuvring to extricate ourselves from a teemingly busy cul-de-sac. Our sheepish English grins fell on stony ground with askance glances from the good burghers of Switzerland who clearly felt we should forthwith and immediately remove our enormous, bug-spattered and inappropriate four wheeled British bulk from their genteel and very tidy Swiss lakeside promenade.

Onward then, we knew not where, until the suburb of Villenueve provided us with respite in the form of a public carpark adjacent to an open-air swimming pool adjacent to the lake. The day was ending and swim-suited families were clearly gathering themselves to return home, so the initially busy car park quickly and fortuitously emptied to leave us the pick of the spaces. With no sign of any overnight parking restrictions, we settled into a tree shaded corner overlooking the now deserted swimming pool, Lake Geneva and a semi-distant historic-looking lakeside building which turned out to be Chateau Chillon.

So. To the musical connections. Unbeknown to us and only discovered when we subsequently cycled back into Montreux itself, there's a great big and very realistic statue of Freddie Mercury in typical stage-pose situated on the lakeside promenade. It's there because, apparently, up until his untimely departure, he had made Montreux his home. But his global fame pales into insignificance when compared to our real reason for visiting the town synonymous with its own annual International Music Festival.

For it was here that, over 40 years ago, the Navigating Rune Reader Par Excellence gave voice to her own musical contribution as a member of her convent school choir – which, with an average age of just 11 years old – performed several modish and popular choral numbers in front of an international and highly critical judging panel and (assumedly) an audience. Although at her own admission, few accurate memories now remain, the performance was (and remains) encapsulated for all time into a small, thin and now scratchy sounding 7-inch disc of black vinyl. From this (or at least its now converted digital version) there emerges a delightfully innocent aural representation of Seafield Convent School's unique performance at the Montreux Festival – under the steel-ruled guidance of a Sister André, who would rehearse her musical scholars by using the steel rule against the back of their legs should they so much as falter with the delivery of any musical note. Did they win anything? Not that any surviving evidence suggests, but memories are revived and relived every Christmas in our household when this unique memento is replayed incessantly to anyone naïve enough not to have heard it all before.

Beckoned By Biarritz

Biarritz & Saint-Jean-de-Luz, Pyrénées-Atlantiques, France

It had to be done. Biarritz lay ahead of us, stamped into a niche on France's south-western coast by an epoch now best defined by tiers of jaded glamour.

Its reputation as an elegant and desirable seaside destination became established in the mid 19th century, when Napoléon III and his exotically Spanish wife Eugénie elected to take their leisure here, imbuing the resort with strong enough credentials to remain a well favoured, sophisticated destination well into the 21st century. So in we trolled.

Right into the bustling, belle époque and cosmopolitan heart of this grand old dame of French coastal resorts. And round we went, swirled within a miniaturised version of Parisian rush-hour traffic with wide boulevards encouraging a typically Gallic disdain for any concept of lane discipline. Round we went, unable to find anything resembling roadside safe harbour, grinning and waving maniacally at the hooted remonstrations against our weaving, half-blind bulk until - following several similarly fraught circuits - Biarritz simply spat us out onto its other side.

During the dawning realisation that Biarritz was clearly not for the likes of us, The Chief Navigating Officer Sans Equal had managed to locate an alleged Campsite Aire on the southern outskirts of this disgruntled town, to which we then wended, this time through incongruous suburbs. Here, we found a patch of waste-ground fortified around its perimeter with ragged high wire fencing and an equally incongruous candy-striped barrier, closed against us. As we paused here with our sun-warmed bonnet reluctantly sniffing the late afternoon air, it became apparent that we were now staring into a semi-permanent travellers' enclave, and the more we stared, the greater number of ragged, tousle-haired children gathered beyond the barrier to stare back at us.

Hmm. Waving hesitantly, we retreated into another increasingly competent U-turn and headed back onto the open road, southbound, towards we knew not where.

The dot which represented Saint-Jean-de-Luz on our delightfully archaic printed roadmap was large enough to straddle the Spanish border, so as we arrived at Camping la Bord de Mer, hastily researched en route, we were only sure it was still in France from its name. Dusk and rain had begun to fall; the site was cliff-top but well-sheltered and had a space or two for a couple of Biarritz rejects.

We booked in. And hang the expense – if we stay for two nights, we get the day in between to languish on the beach and swim in the sea, right?

Wrong.

Having humped ourselves and our bathing kit down the cliff path the following morning, under a clearing sky, a brisk Atlantic breeze and a warming sun, we made camp for a day on the beach. As did a team of semi-hunky Lifeguards, who then wandered the shoreline, blowing whistles at anyone rash enough to have entered the water and multilingually requesting that they vacate the sea as conditions were très dangereux pour nager.

Over time, the beach became more populated with anticipative bathers, all held at bay by the patrolling lifeguards, who were collectively determined that none shall pass to enjoy the rolling Atlantic surf. So on the beach we all sat, staring wistfully out to sea like rapidly wizening mariners squinting towards the beckoning horizon.

At lunchtime, we interpreted a lifeguard's whistle as signifying half-time and - leaving our worldly goods in a tidy (and therefore unpilferable) pile - we wandered into the town in search of diversion, revelry and lunch.

Which we fulfilled in the form of snack-bar sandwiches enjoyed aboard a "Dotto" train – one of those blue-and-white, road-going diesel tractors done up to look like a bag of Tate & Lyle sugar crossbred with a Mississippi paddle steamer and towing several passenger carriages in similar guise. From here, we cruised the unassuming palm-fringed streets of Saint Jean-de-Luz, waving regally at bemused pedestrians, before returning to the beach and rejoining what had now become a class-action vigil against the Lifeguards.

As the heat of the afternoon began to wane, so did we - sunbathing languidly with little else to do – until the pattern of patrolling was seen to lessen when the Lifeguards gathered at the water's edge as if for a post-match debrief. The crowded beach lifted their collective heads and sniffed the air of change.

And as the whistling Lifeguards at last took their leave and headed for home at the end of their shift, we howled with primeval joy and raced as one to the sea's edge, plunging headlong into the same breaking waves from which we'd been protected all day. As far as I know, not one us drowned.

Turnaround Tapas

San Sebastiàn, Basque Country, Spain

And this Tourist Guide booklet, in English, is just one euro, gracias. This smiling conclusion to our second engagement of the day with a native of San Sebastián ended well, we felt. The smiling tourist officer had explained the city's layout with the aid of one of those big, tear-off-a-big-jotter-pad of street-maps – on which she'd biro'd salient points of interest (upside-down of course – they're always upside-down) and then in conclusion offered us a glossy little booklet, from which I've been able to elicit some interesting facts about the city we had chosen as the turn-for-home destination of our trip.

I say 'second engagement of the day' because our first was the best introduction to a city that a visitor could expect: it rained heavily. And as a result of this unexpected turn of events (The Part Time Weather Girl had designated that afternoon to be one of bright sunshine), we found ourselves hurriedly taking shelter in La Perla, a chic bar/restaurant, embedded in San Sebastián's elegant Promenade and apparently part of a Thalassotherapy Sports seawater treatment centre which – and I quote – 'was one of the most important spas in the world in its day.'

Our slightly damp and disarrayed arrival was greeted by a smiling and welcoming barman with a knowing, expansive gesture over an array of tapas which left us staring boggle eyed, as if we'd just penetrated the innermost hallows of Tutankhamen's tomb. As it turned out, this array of delicacies was a shallow representation of what we were to discover later, but at the time, it represented shelter from the rain as well as an impromptu lunch, as a small selection of delicacies was washed down with a couple of welcome beers, with the Knumptywagen now staying well and truly put until the next morning.

And while we discovered the culinary delights of tapas, the rain eased off and the sun did indeed emerge as predicted, with almost enough warmth to steam the pavements dry as we sauntered from our baptism back onto the Promenade.

We continued our saunter towards the old town area, while technology was quietly shadowing our every step, in the form of a little electronic device worn by The Navigator, which would later report that we had completed over 22,000 paces during our visit. This accounted for over two days' worth at normal expectation so as we walked we were mentally gearing ourselves up for a blow-out dinner of Beano-esque proportions later that day.

As it was, we just kept walking. The lure of the wild Atlantic led us through the port area, past the Aquarium and out around Mount Urgull, a rocky outcrop which served as part breakwater and shelter to the port area, topped by an imposing stone statue of Christ-Not-Quite-The-Redeemer, but a passable impersonation, nonetheless.

This 'New Promenade' allowed us a bird's-eye view of the Atlantic waves breaking over rocks below us, foaming with such a viscous and vivid whiteness that it looked as if vast cauldrons of uncooked meringue were being churned beneath our feet. This unplanned walkabout provided us with views of Lurriola – the third beach in San Sebastián's triumvirate of surfing, overlooked across a haphazard dumping of massive, motorhome-sized cuboid chunks of breakwater slate, then led us gently back into the Old Town again.

Here we enjoyed a stroll through a narrow and engaging network of street-bars, cafes, restaurants and shops, just busy enough to impart a true holiday atmosphere without being overwhelming. An old-world, brightly lit and fantastically stocked tobacconist on a corner drew us in with its cabinets of cigars and undisguised array of cigarettes, appearing positively defiant in its full-frontal and unashamed exposure of the leaf-that-shall-no-longer-be-named.

The more bars we passed, the more their epic displays of tapas became a form of food pornography, until one in particular – Taberna Aralar – caught our eye, with chandeliers of smoked ham joints providing a perfect foil to the abstract visual chaos of every conceivable bite-sized foodstuff in every conceivable colour of an abstract artist's palette. Old, tobacco stained wood lined the bar, the floor and the walls; the clientele was bustling, colourful and noisy and we decided – without a word passing between us – this should be our dining destination later in the evening.

Searching For Sites In San Sebastiàn

San Sebastiàn, Basque Country, Spain

There exists a very helpful website for those of us with a need to know, called searchforsites.co.uk and this provides user-uploaded details and reviews on campsite locations throughout Europe. This had sadly reported a spectacular lack of anywhere in or near San Sebastián where Knumptyers may find safe harbour, save for a single location – an Aire (an area dedicated to parking one's Knumptywagen and which normally provides the essential water-and-waste facilities we deem so important to ongoing life in a cramped-space-on-wheels) located within the city about a mile inland from the sea.

The online reviews of this particular site were not exactly glowing. Often full, busy, cramped, out-of-town – but when needs must, you give it a try anyway. La Chef Du Mapping et Le Weather (Part-Time) had deemed it appropriate to arrive at said Aire at a point in time in which the previous night's occupants would be departing, and as such, we rolled up at about 11:30 a.m., to find about half of the 50 spaces unoccupied. Planting ourselves firmly in one corner and deploying our levelling ramps (a sure sign of overnight-intentions if ever there was one) we were pleasantly surprised that the site was much better than we'd anticipated. It was tucked into a quiet and unused corner of the University campus and surrounded by mature greenery.

Each parking-space had mown grass growing through clearly defined hard-standing, so the appearance was pleasing enough – and certainly a little more hospitable than some of the supermarket car parks we've snuck onto in our time. Yes, the spaces were close to each other – there would be no luxuriating in recliners under an awning here, but hey, we were in San Sebastián, levelled up, safe and secure, and ready to hit the town.

Our arrival here had been preceded by a depressingly dull, rainy and very slow journey from St. Jean De Luz, across a completely unremarked border crossing between France & Spain where not one jot of signage denoted the edge of one country and the beginning of another. In fact, having thought we might have needed to wave our passports at someone, the transition seemed solely to be marked by a subtle change in the brand of car-showroom which proliferated along this section of the route, from Citroen to Seat. But hey, that's Schengen for you.

So. Here we are and off we set, enticed by high expectations and a clearing sky, we set off on foot towards the sea, a walk of about 30 minutes amongst fresh-faced students swirling through the University campus, looking variously studious, anxious, hip, trendy or down-at-heel but all, without exception, alarmingly young.

Our return to the Knumptywagen at about 4pm – having negotiated and used the local bus service (with the help of advice from the local Tourist Office) – was far quicker, less taxing on our legs and just as sociable. And yes, the reviews were true – the site was now packed full – looking more like a mobile-home showroom than a campsite, as 49 sleek, shiny, bright white mobile homes crowded around our one little Knaus. A smattering of UK number plates was in evidence, including our immediate neighbours – a young family with two boisterous young boys ("Tom! I won't tell you again, put your Crocs on when you get out of the van, and take 'em off again when you come back in! Gnaaagh!")

A brief rest-up, siesta-style and then - dressed for the evening - off we set again, back into town, our new-found confidence making mincemeat of the bus-stop locations and associated numbering and ticketing systems; direction of travel; even knowing where to ding the bell for the stop at which we needed to get off - all led us into an evening of tapas indulgence we thoroughly enjoyed.

The Pogles of St. Émilion

St. Émilion, Gironde, France

Readers of my generation will likely recall with childhood nostalgia the work of Oliver Postgate (1925-2008) whose naively innovative animated children's TV programmes included Noggin The Nog; Clangers; Pogle's Wood and Bagpuss (with whom – despite his undoubted popularity – I never really got on.) As far as I can recall, the Pogles were an aged and ageless couple of shuffling diminutive forest-dwelling folk, where – being totally dedicated to each other – they simply ambled about looking after the flora and fauna therein.

I mention this by way of introduction simply because yesterday evening, we attended a 'degustation' of local wine at a vineyard run by Monsieur et Madame Pogle themselves.

Arriving alongside several other motorhomers during the late afternoon, we were all invited – nay, commanded – by M. Pogle himself, to attend said tasting at 'six heure aujord'hui', emphasising this appointment time by much tapping on the back of a bony wrist which presumably should have borne a watch, but didn't.

So it was, at the appointed hour, a motley assemblage of Knumpties Of The World convened in M. Pogle's homely kitchen, to be welcomed by himself (accompanied by his wizened, diminutive and bustling wife) to both their home and to their wines. We awkwardly – and with the greatly enhanced politeness attributable to a mix of people who find it difficult to communicate – settled around the kitchen table where M. Pogle took his place at the head, perched on a slightly elevated stool. Meanwhile, Mme. Pogle, God bless her, bustled in and out with huge, black, knotted knuckles of vine wood, which she fed into a gentle fire burning in the grate of their 'open plan' lounge. This was incongruously decorated with a very 80's and therefore very faded full-size Habitat photo-wall graphic of a sunny woodland glade – which I guess enhanced the sense of being in Pogle's Wood even further.

With a triumphant and slightly impish smile to her husband, Mme. Pogle approved his commencement of the 'degustation' and we surrendered ourselves to an animated but incomprehensible description of each of four bottles of red wine, which were sloshed out with alacrity into all our sampling glasses, the gentlemen's measures being notably grander than the ladies'.

Our immediate neighbours at the table turned out to be Welsh so, having indirectly insulted them by whispering how crap the English were at learning other languages, we established a sort of mutual interpretation service, each couple exchanging with the other whatever we thought M. Pogle might be expounding on.

During these desultory exchanges, we were able to establish that M. Pogle was a heritage octogenarian of some 88 years; his crystal-eyed, fire-fuelling wife a couple of years his junior, and that they'd been married (and making wine) for over 60 years.

As the session progressed, we all became (perhaps inevitably, given the measures now being poured) far more voluble. Fractured Franglais began to be exchanged across the table and there was much uproarious laughter, at what we sadly had no idea but joined in nonetheless, in the forlorn hope that it wasn't directed at us. At one point, our host began flailing his arms about and making drinking gestures, which we decided was how he kept himself fit, as these exertions were accompanied with a very interpretable 'trois bouteilles par jour' and a glint in at least one of his rheumy eyes.

Yes, of course, we all signed up to buy some wine, one couple quietening the room as they asked, in the style of Oliver Twist, to taste some more then promptly ordered three cases of the stuff, while we Brits looked at the floor and muttered that we might manage a bottle or two.

Job done, we staggered with our genuine Chateau-bottled Saint Émilion booty back to the Knumptywagen, now fired up and fuelled with sufficient bravado to attempt a pre-planned fifteen-minute cycle ride into the nearby town of Saint Emilion itself.

Off we set but on approach we became aware that many more cars than might be normal were parked and cluttering the grass verges some way out of town. Our curiosity was consolidated when our access was impeded by a temporary roadblock (including cycles) guarded by good-natured Security operatives, who smiled benignly as we locked up our bikes and wandered down a cobbled street into Wineville itself.

Saint Émilion was (and hopefully still is) a truly beautiful – and quintessential – French village, its major difference with many of the others we'd passed through being that it appeared to be well populated by humans wandering around its cobbled streets. And what cobbles! The Health & Safety brigade would have enjoyed concreting over them all to provide a stable and accessible surface, but we managed to hobble gamely into the heart of a bustling small, aged and homely town. The honey-grey church tower had just been illuminated from within as dusk was falling and we stumbled by accident into its bowels to view the arched monolithic cavern beneath the church tower, carved out of solid limestone in the 12th Century.

Looking out from a vantage point at the base of the tower, a delightful public (and well restauranted) square lay beneath us, so it was towards this location which we then clambered down a precipitous cobbled alleyway stumbling around unpretentious narrow lanes to explore the rest of this amazing UNESCO World Heritage site.

Homage to the grape and to wine abounded, and when we eventually found ourselves a restaurant table a deux under the spreading plane trees, we each enjoyed a verre du vin to accompany our one and only dinner en plain aire – under a thankfully clear and darkening sky.

Our visit had accidentally coincided with an annual cultural celebration - the Journee du Patrimoine, a country-wide celebration of French heritage where over 17,000 historic monuments open their doors for free. As such, the town was buzzing with activity including a march of the wine-tasters dressed in ceremonial robes - and apparently to conclude with a splendide firework display.

It was, however, getting slightly chillier than comfort allowed as we finished dinner, so we decided to return to our bikes and thence to the warmth of the Knumptywagen, in the hope that we might get a glimpse of the later fireworks from afar.

In that we'd been able to eat outside for the first time in our trip so far, our timing could only have been bettered had we taken the decision to set off ten minutes earlier. As we cycled back towards 'home', it began to rain. And as we cycled, it became heavier. And then it absolutely sheeted down. So much so that it became virtually impossible to see through the rain, especially as we had our heads down as we stood on our pedals and hurtled into the blackening night. Drenched on arrival, the bikes were simply dumped alongside the Knumptywagen, and we drip-dried ourselves before ending our Saint Émilion evening with a reviving glass of cognac.

And then the fireworks started. Mon Dieu! If only our line of sight from the sheltered interior of the Knumptywagen townwards hadn't been blocked by an enormous pear tree, we would surely have enjoyed a spectacle of the festival, as the display went on for a full – I kid you not – 40-minutes, non-stop. Drifting noise, smoke, pelting rain and the assumedly dampened 'oohs' and 'ahs' of a distant crowd reached us from a distance, all clearly emanating from a massive pyrotechnic spectacle, the likes of which we didn't get to see at all.

French Cuisine, Michelin Stars And The In-Van Dining Experience

St. Émilion, Gironde, France

Even alien beings, who may have lived their entire lives in a galaxy far distant from our own fair and lovely planet, would know that France is renowned for its cuisine.

It's a fact. And if I had any to hand (facts, that is) I could expand on that point and reference how many restaurants there are per capita in France compared to – say, well, Germany, Finland or Great Britain.

Then I could go on to explore the proliferation of great culinary French chefs, but apart from recalling the names of Albert & Michel Roux; that one who lives in Oxfordshire (can't remember – maybe he IS a Roux?) and that hairy bloke on the telly who smokes a lot, pretends to be French and does a TV ad for Knorr stock cubes (I ask you), I'm afraid I'm currently a bit thin on verifiable truths here.

Then of course, there's Michelin, with its coveted star-ratings for top restaurants around the world. Which leads me briefly to proffer the fact that many people in the know seem to suggest that the gastronomy of northern Spain far outclasses anything the French might offer, although most of that is down to nothing more than personal taste and opinion, of which there currently seems to be an overwhelming banquet.

But all of this set me to thinking about the exceptional calibre of our own In-Knumptywagen Dining Experiences as we've travelled the length of France's west coast. It would have been amusing to have travelled this great distance on the aforementioned brand of French tyre too, as we could then claim to have dined out courtesy of Michelin throughout our trip.

However, having inspected all four wheels of our remarkable vehicle, and recalling that two front tyres were replaced just prior to our departure from the UK, then I'm sad to report that we're now half-Michelin and half-Uniroyal, so what follows is a selection of our Melange Du Pneus 3-Star Dining Menus, prepared in-Knumptywagen almost exclusively by The Queen of The Road Map and Sometimes The Weather, when she wasn't engaged in either of those two other commitments.

Tuna salad, ham salad, various combinations of light, freshly prepared lunches, always based around sliced fresh tomato; varied and exciting salad leaves dressed with a house-speciality honey & mustard dressing we named 'Yellow Tail' after the empty half wine bottle in which it is stored; hard-boiled eggs with mayonnaise; coleslaw, cous-cous and whatever else caught our eye in the markets. And bread, of course - although in France especially, that's almost a separate topic in its own right.

Baked chunky (unidentified) white fish served on a bed of spinach with hard-boiled egg and cheese sauce, new potatoes and broccoli. (We asked for 'Popeye' in the greengrocers as neither of us could remember that spinach was 'epinard'. It worked.)

Seared pan-fried duck breast, served with a fresh tomato and red pepper ragu followed by a cheeseboard selection.

Pan-fried duck breast (we bought two of them in a market and they were huge, so we shared one between us, twice, if you see what I mean?), sliced onto a bed of apple-sauce, served with new potatoes and optional side-salad.

Saucisson (well, sausages really but they were infinitely more continental than insipid pink Richmonds) served on a bed of apple sauce (yeah, you're on it – too big a jar for one serving), sweetcorn and new potatoes.

Fresh gambas cooked and served shell-on with a house speciality cocktail sauce.

Peppered veal casserole (it got cold in the evenings, OK?) served with plain boiled rice and caramelised carrots.

Tuna, shallots & peas with lemon juice in a white-wine creme-fraiche sauce, served with petis pois and pasta.

Pork cutlets with sweet chilli and tomato paprika sauce and new potatoes.

Chicken in a white-wine sauce (unusually, not the M&S tinned variety) with broccoli and rice.

And tonight's specialite de la maison? A les resets cassoulet avec saussicon, pomme du terre et l'ognion all sautéed en les haricot cuit du Heinz en sauce tomate.

In almost all cases, our Knumptywagen meals are served with a local wine, generally procured from the location in which we were staying and rounded off with a square of dark chocolate and maybe even a local brandy.

Cheeses were also acquired, but their strong French aromas filled the Knumptywagen every time we opened our tiny fridge, so they tended not to be included on the Menu Du Jour. Merci beaucoup, Messieurdame, servis tu compris, bon soir et bonne vacance.

Hamfist And The Fishing Shacks

Blaye, Gironde, France

When we first met Hamfist, we were still on our outbound journey south and had just crossed the wide and muddy Gironde by river ferry from Blaye, about which more another day, perhaps.

From our France Passion guidebook, we'd identified an overnight stop at a vineyard on the Medoc side just north of Paulliac (which we were prevented from visiting by the final knockings of a marathon race taking place there with the narrow roads down to the river simply clogged with cars and dazed-looking runners wrapped in silver blankets.)

In most instances, we'd simply arrived at the designated FP location, been briefly greeted by whoever we could find, and pointed in the general direction of where we were to park the Knumptywagen. On this occasion, we were greeted by a gentleman of late middle age with a decent height and girth on him – looking a little like a Gallic version of Jeremy Clarkson with a weather-leathered face. As we shook hands and grunted unintelligibly at each other, we noticed he had the most enormous hands. Roughened and ruddy from agricultural toil and (presumably) viniculture, our poor unwitting host immediately became known to us as Hamfist (which rather amusingly translates as 'Jambonpoing' in the vernacular.) Anyway, he waved us towards a field alongside his ordered rows of vines, almost within stone-throwing distance of the river, where we parked up and immediately set out to walk the estate and stretch our journeyed legs.

Along the edge of the mighty, muddy Gironde we'd already noticed a repetition of fishing shacks, like small sheds built on stilts to stand proud of the tidal river waters. Each shack was approached by a length of stilted walkway above the reeded margins which allowed passage from land. These walkways were fenced along their length and protected at their landward ends by stout timber doors, padlocked and bearing variously painted legends, all of which basically translated into 'Private – Keep Out'. Many of the shacks looked forlorn and derelict, although we did espy one in the far distance on which could clearly be seen human silhouettes against the late afternoon sky.

The most fascinating element of these shacks – and the feature which imparted an almost Vietnamese look and feel to the river's edge – were the fishing nets themselves. These huge nets – one per shack and each about 4 metres square, were simply stretched flat on a square lightweight framework, hung centrally and dangled horizontally from a hefty pole which angled out from the hut, above the water. As we watched from afar, we could clearly see the net being lowered, raised, and fussed over by the occupants of the shack in our line of sight.

Intrepid explorers as we are, we managed after several short-cuts (which turned into mud-impeded dead-ends) to reach the hallowed, gated entrance to the occupied shack, and surprised an elderly bearded Monsieur by both our emergence from the rushes and our inquisitive tourist-like presence.

Surprisingly perhaps, instead of turning his shotgun on us, he muttered something in French and accompanied this with a beckoning motion, opening his gate and in effect ushering us with smiling nods along the rickety gangway to his hut.

And so, the mystery was solved. Our speculation, based on evidence seen at the market we'd visited in Blaye, was that the nets were used for catching shrimps – of which there were obviously plenty on offer on the market stalls. However, Madame, who – perhaps typically – was operating the net and generally running the show, soon dispelled this theory by uncovering a large bucket full of hefty-looking mullet.

For the uninitiated, the mullet is a large, silver-grey scaled sea-fish, with a characteristic wide mouth at its blunt front end, and twin pectoral fins each set at an almost forward-facing angle. Such is their appearance that the mullet tends to look like an underperforming and therefore slightly disappointed flying fish. They are also devilishly difficult to catch with rod and line, hence this primitive but clearly effective method of scooping them from not much more than a two-foot depth of swirlingly opaque brackish river water.

We were not induced into the pivoted raising and lowering mechanism of the net – this was hidden away in the windowless interior of the hut, although the pole itself did emerge to the rear and was counterbalanced with a large, bell-shaped weight. It was clear that this feature aided the frequent net-dipping, and subsequently held the net in an accessible position to allow the catch to be scooped out with a separate long-handled net wielded with efficient and practised ease by Madame Mullet herself.

And so we took our leave, thanking our hosts for their brief and welcomed insight. Hastening through a night of drumming, tumultuous rain to the following morning, we sought out Hamfist to procure some of his estate-bottled Medoc to add to our growing collection. Within minutes of making our request (in our best fractured French) Hamfist demonstrated an uncanny fulfilment of the epithet we'd foist upon him, as he was the most ham-fisted vintner we'd yet encountered.

First, he couldn't find the keys to his cellar; then he couldn't find a couple of the bottles we'd requested, despite there being hundreds of them laid out in front of us. Then he had to affix foil bottle caps, which of course had to have green 'export' stickers applied to the tops – which we discovered on an adjacent table as he bimbled into the darkened vaults of racked oak barrels in search of them.

While he roamed ineptly to and fro we noticed his tasting table, set out for some future event, no doubt, with labelled boxes of Ikea's cheaper wine glasses rather dispelling any magic we may have felt from being in the presence of such an array of oak casks, fine wines and fruity-looking labels.

Even at the point of payment, the provision of some trifling amount of change seemed beyond his capabilities and he disappeared again, this time into the similarly darkened depths of his own kitchen, where he patted his pockets and rummaged interminably (despite our protestations and suggestions that the change was 'pas de problem') and eventually emerged triumphant, clutching two tiny coins in one of his huge ham-fisted hands.

We Cross The Muddy Gironde

Blaye, Gironde, France

The riverside town of Blaye had been mentioned several times in our guidebooks as being one of the 'lesser-known' wine-producing towns of the Bordeaux region and in the hope of sniffing out some lush wine bargains, it was therefore to Blaye that we made our waye.

Arriving mid-morning and without having breakfasted, we were excited to find a local market in full swing in the centre of this unassuming town. What the Guidebooks seem not to have mentioned (although this was probably reader-oversight) was that the town was dominated by a huge and imposing mediaeval citadel, which provided a backdrop to the market and - well - to pretty much everything else as well.

Finding space in a carpark on the river's edge, we immediately sallied forth in search of comestibles, to discover that the extensive and colourful market arrays of fresh fruit, vegetables, charcuterie, cheese, meats, shellfish, underwear and kitchen aids didn't quite fulfil the brief, so we repaired to a roadside cafe-bar, fortuitously deciding to take seats inside to escape threatening rain. Fortified by the only item available on the menu - ironically, a platter of charcuterie and cheese - as we tucked in, the rain arrived and abated and we set out to storm the bastion of Blaye.

The UNICEF World Heritage moated citadel was vast and remarkably well preserved. We marvelled at the towering stone-built walls and were surprised to find that within their protection a couple of small pavement restaurants were thriving, as was the tourist office. Built to provide the city of Bordeaux – lying some 30 miles upriver – with protection from marauding river-borne enemies, the Citadel had been remodelled in the seventeenth century by a gentleman named Vauban, whose reputation as a military architect and engineer was clearly of great national pride.

One aspect of the Citadel which owed nothing to its historical importance - and which certainly wasn't mentioned in any of the informative multiple-language graphic panels which were dotted about – was that, at the time of our visit - it was besieged by a phalanx of motorhomes. 'Camping car' spaces had been designated around the perimeter moat (signs for which we'd complete overlooked on our arrival) so the juxtaposition of massed ranks of 21st century leisure vehicles with 12th century stone walls provided a sharp and thought provoking contrast.

Having exhausted ourselves with our bastion-storming and market-wandering activities, we repaired to the Knumptywagen and were just settling to a relaxing cuvette de thé, when our attention was drawn to a short queue of vehicles quietly growing on a small service road in front of us and which – on further intrigued inspection – turned out to be lining up for a ferry. Further inspection identified a viable 21 euros one-way fare across the Gironde River and a departure time of less than 15 minutes. With little in the way of further consideration and still with tea in our cups, we impulsively joined the queue, tucking ourselves happily in behind a beautifully burbling, open-topped, personally plated British Bentley in classic racing green.

A good-natured, slightly haphazard loading of vehicles and passengers ensued, with an upper deck allowing us a unique opportunity to examine the rarely seen roof of the Knumptywagen and decide it really would need a damn good wash when we got home.

The Gironde is a mighty river. About a mile across, it swirled forcefully around us, the colour and consistency of milky, boiling coffee as our vessel skated sideways across the tidal flow. Passing fortified islands and docking expertly on t'other side at Lamarque, we were swiftly disgorged onto the Medoc, a peninsular of wine-country which we might eventually have reached by road, but only via a significant detour. Our Bentley burbled off powerfully into the chateau-speckled countryside ahead of us, as we mere mortals washed up the teacups and wallowed gently onwards in its wake.

Binic. Très Agréable

Binic, Côtes-d'Amor, France

With a view to positioning ourselves within easy striking distance of the ferry port of Roscoff in preparation for our return home, The Navigator Par Excellence had guided us away from the wind- (and sadly mostly rain-) swept French Atlantic coast to kiss the edges of La Manche, where the wind dropped, the inhospitable waves abated and we found ourselves in the lowkey and therefore very agreeable harbour-town of Binic.

Binic featured little in any of the tourist guidebooks we consulted during our trip, save for a tiny dot on a map placed by companionable and better prepared motorhomers than us, who had provided an extensive (and very beautifully catalogued) list of suggested locations which led us here.

Gratifyingly, we were clearly expected, as the now familiar "Knumptyers This Way" signage appeared on our approach to the town. A visit to the Tourist Office confirmed the availability of an 'Aire' just a little way inland from the attractive harbour, to which we wended our way, to find ourselves both pleased and disheartened in equal measure in that there was space for us amongst well-ordered double-semicircles of other Knumptywagens, all parked up with just a noggin of breathing-space between each one.

We dutifully followed suit and parked up, unhitching the bikes and immediately setting out on a cycle-based exploration of the town. Centred around an attractive inner harbour which was almost as well-populated with abandoned yachts as the Aire was with motorhomes, we enjoyed the relaxed and welcoming atmosphere of the open-fronted cafes, bars and restaurants. A little further beyond the Harbourmaster's funky-looking postmodernist architect-designed offices, an outer harbour played host to an array of motorboats, all at that time mired in mud, but all facing the gap in the harbour wall in excited anticipation of a returning, liberating tide.

There was an end-of-season emptiness to the promenade – which terminated in a combined gap-and-tunnel through natural cliffs allowing access to a small, contained sandy beach beyond. This picturesque arrangement imparted a sense that we'd reached a continental version of Tenby, with a bit less overt commercialism and a complete dearth of Scouse or Brummy accents.

The sun shone. And we were warmed. In fact, it became so uncharacteristically warm that the Restaurant waitress who greeted our enquiry about a table for two for their hoarding-advertised lobster lunch became quite concerned that we wanted to sit outside at one of her pavement tables, in full sun. Until, of course, she realised from our accents that we were not only English but also Scouse and Brummy – and left us to roast while we tucked unashamedly into delicious lobster and frites.

Meanwhile, a couple of maverick motorhomers had parked up on the harbour front, giving us license to join them, which we did, moving the Knumptywagen stealthily (and with some small degree of guilt) from the crowded Aire to find ourselves a level kerbside spot with an unimpeded view of the outer harbour.

This was protected from the ravaging sea by an impressive stone-built breakwater wall which extended its protective arm out to a small lighthouse on its point. It was clear from the gathering of anglers already awaiting the incoming tide that this was an optimistic place to cast a set of mackerel-feathers so, replete and with lobster-reddening skin, we then quickly made our way to join the throng, having tackled up a couple of our own trusty fishing rods.

We'd already noticed that the beaches surrounding the harbour were unusually flat and extensive in their width, which confirmed our speculation that the tide would return swiftly. This it indeed did, rising at a surprising pace up the harbour walls and allowing us all – with unrehearsed synchronicity – to hurl leaded lines and flailing feathers into its swirling thrust. With these endeavours, a few of us landed small, but nonetheless rewarding mackerel, which we then took back and pan-fried like sardines for supper, with lemon and buttery juices mopped up with nubs of baguette.

We were so enamoured with the accessible charms of Binic that we stayed parked up on the harbour front for two nights, enjoying walks around the town and the harbour as well as a brief and thoroughly British attempt to sit on the beach (this adventure cut short by a disappointing and lengthy withdrawal of sunshine.) A further cycle-ride led us to the intensive exploration of a harbour-side and impossibly over-stocked Chandlery shop (with which I was so excited that I'd be happy to have my ashes sprinkled within); the best Boulangerie Patisserie of the whole trip and finally, a surprise street-market which sprang up overnight – hosting an amazing selection of stalls including a horse-butcher; goats'-cheese specialist; greengrocery featuring multi-coloured carrots and spiky-walled pyramids of artichokes and finally a spectacular stall dedicated solely to onions of every conceivable shape, size and pungency.

Roscoff eventually exerted its influence and we reluctantly set off for the ferry, via yet another airport-terminal-sized Leclerc hypermarket to fill the Knumptywagen's remaining nooks and crannies with souvenirs, gifts and well, yes, since you ask, some wine. In good time, we joined a queue of other homebound motorhomes – feverishly cleaning the interior of the Knumptywagen while-we-waited (much to the obvious amusement of the couple parked up behind us) before rattling and rolling onboard for the journey across La Manche back to dear old Blighty.

Man Cannot Live By Bread Alone

Binic, Côtes-d'Amor, France

We've enjoyed visiting the various boulangeries we've come across during our travels. More often than not, they've provided the only sign of life in otherwise comatose villages, open all hours and always staffed by a ruddy-faced, portly Madame. Possibly, there's also a farine-dusted husband lurking in a backroom, who is drawn out by the intrigue of our English debate about which shape of baguette we should choose on that particular visit.

And when the Boulangerie is also a Patisserie, well, Heaven can wait. Even in the smallest, most de-populated settlements, the range of patisserie on offer is simply astounding, with glass-fronted displays layered with choux delights; individual tartes topped with every conceivable form of jelly-glazed fruit; layered mille feuilles so deep that anyone choosing to consume such a delight would need a snake-like unhingable jaw to facilitate safe passage; beignets of such lightness and fluffiness, filled with apple, apricot, caramel or jam that it's impossible to believe they translate simply as 'doughnuts'; small quiches whose tiny, handwritten labels boast of such exotic content as shrimp, crab, tomato, goat's cheese, aubergine, peppers, caramelised onion or indeed any combination of the above; cascades of gleaming white meringues stacked to represent a chalk cliff fall; honey coloured light and spongy madeleines each shaped like a tiny toy boat, nudging each other gunwale to gunwale as they await an orderly flotation on the next high tide.

And the bread! How can a single nation produce so many different shapes and types? Even the fairly straightforward national symbol, the baguette, seems to be available in a staggering variety of lengths, shapes and subtle variances of constituents. Typically, being English, after commencement of sociabilities with our breezy, confident, cheerful and hopefully accurately delivered 'Bonjour Madame', we lapse into muted boggle-eyed pointing, complemented by a muttered 'un' ou 'deux' dependent on need, but more often than not, whim.

But what on earth do the French actually do with all that bread? As previously observed, it's a national institution but we've yet to witness any customer leaving a boulangerie with a solitary loaf. They seem to buy them in great quantities and – quite literally – by the yard, as they emerge clutching half-a-dozen or more baguettes, each individually wrapped in a flimsy form of wrapping, bizarrely reminiscent of Izal toilet paper.

They totter home with this vast array of bread tucked under their arms as if carrying some crusted multiple armament, seemingly ignorant of the fact that it will all become stale and inedible within about 40 minutes. So how can they use so much, so quickly? Well, if you'll indulge me, a completely fictional theory is emergent . . .

At home, when experiencing a surfeit of unwanted bread, our frugality will often cause us to blitz it into breadcrumbs, bag it up and freeze it for re-use at some point (normally Christmas) for bread sauce or some other accompaniment.

And it was this which led me to discover that the cuisine-driven French have amongst their number two historical heroes who together solved France's surplus bread issue.

In the early 18th Century, an unremarked chef-patron in a little-known village in the Loire Valley hit upon the idea of re-baking stale bread, before which he cut it into small cubes, to be crisped in the residual heat of the ovens used for the mighty cassoulets which – in those days – were a staple item on the Menu Du Jour.

Coincidentally, a French housewife in Provence, challenged by a surfeit of chicken scraps which her husband (the local Boucher) insisted on bringing home for domestic use, realised that by milling the nub-ends and dried-out leftover baguettes she could create sufficient breadcrumbs with which to coat the chicken pieces, thereby combining two otherwise redundant items into a palatable foodstuff again.

So, we must, with our tongues very firmly lodged in our cheeks, applaud the un-named chef-patron from a Loire village called Crouton, and uphold the efforts of Madame Goujon, as national, fictional and subsequently completely unacknowledged heroes of French Cuisine.

Vanity, Vanity, All Is Vanity

Trieste, Friuli Venezia Giulia, Italy

Gentle reader, I wonder what might be your position on clip-on sunglasses?

I ask, simply because I suspect that your response will be wholly dependent on your age. I, for one, have spent many years of my life to date abhorring both the look and the style of these optical appendages – belonging, as they do, to 'old people' – in much the same way of those photochromic spectacles that 'old people' also insist on wearing, the darkened colouration of which always seems to be a miserable middling-grey, imparting to the wearer the appearance of an otherwise semi-well-dressed (but still slightly ghoulish) Grim Reaper.

And yes, dear reader, you're yet again well ahead of me since you've already guessed where this is going: I – your esteemed author and hitherto dedicated follower of fashion – have acquired a pair of clip-on sunglasses, which – much to my own consternation – I have found to be A Very Good Thing Indeed.

Gone are my days of carefree youth, when – as a spectacle wearer since the age of 16 – I had always felt the need to avail of the 'two-pair' offers favoured by high street opticians. As such, I became a slave to carrying these two pairs around with me while on holiday in sunny climes. Thus, they were swopped over (with a hopelessly underdeveloped lack of dexterity) every time I came in from the sunshine – or indeed, went back out into it. Shops; museums; sea-life centres; restaurants and café-bars; underground stations; driving through tunnels – each became a challenge with which even an experienced chain-saw juggler would have struggled – as one pair had to be taken off and stowed, while the other pair was contemporaneously deployed and worn – with all the effort involved in twin-arm unfolding (dextrous tongue and nose activity often involved if hands were otherwise occupied) during which time I was given to believe that the effort was all worthwhile, as I continued to look at my trendiest best throughout.

Wrong. I just looked like a complete prat. Whereas now (thanks to a particularly large wave which rolled me and from which I emerged through the surf wondering why everyone on the beach looked suddenly very bright and very fuzzy) having lost my trendy sunglasses to the Atlantic, I am now practically equipped with a highly-cost-effective, very unprescriptive, hugely practical and functional pair of clipon sunglasses.

Now, for every tunnel; underground station; café; bar; restaurant (and yes, even badly lit public-toilets – what a boon) I simply flip 'em up and wander round, uncaring of the fact that – from a distance – I appear to have very large brown eyebrows. I clip'em or flip'em on and I clip'em or flip'em off with gay abandon, attaching them when not required to the Knumptywagen's sun-visor (trendy, eh?) or even to parts of my clothing (I think I look particularly fetching with them clipped to the placket (don't worry – it's a fashionista's word which I don't understand either) of my trendy, flower-patterned short-sleeved holiday shirts.

My only slight concern with this sublime fashion-statement of the Over-Sixty is that I am now edging ever closer to an unhealthy and premature interest in dark grey photochromics.

Summer Snow In Chamonix

Chamonix, Le Mont Blanc, France

Not having a rigid route plan on our travels means that we get to choose our waypoints as we go. So when Her Worshipful Navigating Troutess & Chief Satnav Queen studied the runes and suggested we visit Chamonix, I thought she'd lost it. Chamonix? Isn't that a ski-resort? Like, in the Alps? With deep icy snow and rutted roads? Very high up? Surely not.

But yes, there it was, lying happily slap bang on a sensible route between where we were and where we wanted to be. So, yes, let's go to Chamonix, to a small, delightful, riverside, well-wooded, friendly, family-run campsite, the poetically named Camping de la Mer de Glace, within easy cycling distance of Chamonix itself. Bright sunshine and no sign of snow greeted us – although we struggled to view anything on arrival as our eyes were still watering from having paid over 60 euros to get through the Mont Blanc tunnel – the existence of which we'd both managed to miss on the map!

In lilting English, spoken with a fascinating blend of French and Irish accents, we were welcomed by a diminutive Receptionist (who turned out to be the owner) and who – despite the fact that the whole camp was due to close for the season the day after our visit – welcomed us warmly. Included in the simple formalities was an order taken for our choice of delivered bread the following morning and the suggestion that pitch 52 would provide decent views and electric hook-up.

OMG! And that's not a reaction to the supply of electricity, valued though it always is. In the bright, mid-afternoon sunshine and profiled in majestic high-altitude splendour against yet another cloudless cobalt blue sky, Mont Blanc – royally iced with a coating of brilliant white snow – was just there, in our direct line of sight from the door of the Knumptywagen – and simply breath-taking in its scale, dominance and mountainous beauty.

And the more we looked, the more the snow-capped Alps became a huge wrap-round painted backdrop canvas glimpsed through gently swaying foreground pine-green trees – magnificently unreal in their sheer reality. Bikes are readied so let's go and experience the novelty of a ski-resort without any snow yet encircled by snowclad mountains. Out of the camp on a forested track which ran alongside a fast flowing and frost-white L'Arve, a river which was – in mid-September – already the harbinger of winter with its glacier-cold aura filling the tree-lined valley through which we cycled.

Chamonix was buzzing. A bric-a-brac street market was just wrapping up and the town was enjoying every attribute we recalled from our own fond memories of well-earned après ski sessions. Bars and pavement cafés were thriving; pedestrianised streets were thronged – although there was a strange muteness from the lack of massed clattering ski-boots tromping over cobbles. It was too early for dinner and too late for tea so we sussed out a few restaurants, decided against a beer in the fading sunlight (the temperature was beginning to drop as we were, after all, over 1,000 metres above sea-level) so we headed back to the plugged-in comfort of the Knumptywagen for yet more gazing at Mont Blanc gleaming in the gloaming.

Chamonix was too close and too enticing for us to consider cooking in the Knumptywagen so, as evening fell and having earmarked a possible eatery on our earlier visit, we dug out a couple of well-travelled padded jackets (unused on the trip until now) and set off again on our bikes alongside the now-even-colder river back into the evening buzz of this attractive Alpine town. Well, yeah – our restaurant of choice was indeed a bit touristy – it was in a prime location on the main pavement so we hadn't expected much else – but a cheerful waitress with impeccable English seated us on the front row, following which she fed and watered us well with gloopy cheese fondue and crisp mountain beers.

Replete and maybe slightly more relaxed than we should have been, we illuminated our bikes as well as ourselves (headtorches are a double-edged sword: brilliant and dynamic illumination but you do tend to look a bit of a prat wearing one) and cycled back to the camp. We both agreed our earlier recce had been well worthwhile as the return journey was conducted in an almost lightless dark-skied blackness through the forest. Which was now littered with campervans parked haphazardly wherever vehicular access could be gained. No wonder the campsite was so quiet – everyone's here avoiding a campsite fee but missing out completely on fresh bread delivered to your door in the morning as well as the incredible Alpine views, impeded here by thick-canopied forest.

Which eventually impeded us as well, since we got completely lost in the arboreal darkness, despite our advance-knowledge of the route. Having missed a bridge under the main road and then two subsequent bridges over the river, we were saved by spotting the Mountain Rescue helipad (from where, earlier in the day, we'd witnessed the arrival and departure of one of mankind's cleverest inventions.) From here we tramped our way back, wheeling our bikes through the undergrowth to find the now seemingly tiny, camouflaged path which led us back to the campsite and the electrically heated sanctuary of the Knumptywagen.

A blue-skied day; bright stars overhead; alpine freshness in the air; the sound of the nearby river; a small nightcap and a fully satisfied clamber up our little ladder to our sumptuous overcab bed on a lovely campsite in the lee of Mont Blanc. Can you think of a better way to spend a day?

PART FIVE

Heading For Montenegro

"The Gulf of Kotor is one of the most remarkable natural phenomena in Europe, the climax of the whole coast, and the most awe-inspiring entrance to Montenegro. Whether you enter it by sea or by one of the two mainland routes the sight of it will last a lifetime."

J.A. Cuddon, 1928–1996
English author, dictionary writer, teacher

One Giant Leap

Lichfield, Staffordshire, England

The annual Ritual of Resurrection, performed on our sleepy and slightly bewildered Knaus Sport Traveller as we prepared for our forthcoming Trans-European Odyssey, has become mired in a series of technical complexities equivalent in perceived scale to the launch of a manned flight to Jupiter.

Hoping for a comfortably functional round-trip, we felt that our wheezing onboard fridge should really be fixed before blast off. Similarly, our submersible (sorry, technical jargon creeping in there) water-pump had never quite performed to its full potential since it was replaced under duress in France last year, so that needed attention too.

And while I'm lying on my back under the van trying to check the condition of the spare wheel – and how one might gain access go it should the need arise, it is noticed that careless reversing into objects-unknown has smashed the rotating waste-water downpipe, so that could also do with repair to make sure we're completely ship-shape before Mission Control commences the ignition countdown.

These primary technical problems were, in the main, beyond our limited in-house DIY capabilities, so a trawl of t'internet threw up a surprisingly helpful site – the MCEA (Mobile Caravan Engineers Association) which proved instrumental in guiding a shining white knight down the narrow lane at the back of our house to attend to the needs of our malingering Knaus.

Yet I'm slipping the handbrake on the story here and rolling ahead of myself, as it wasn't all plain sailing prior to this act of mobile salvation.

During our initial search for solutions, we'd become frequently confronted (and frustrated to distraction) by the stock-response to every question we posed in relation to our problems, which was – without exception – preceded by the caveat . . . "It depends."

It depends on your voltage at the faulty unit; it depends on your leisure-battery discharge rate; it depends if you're hooked-up (another technical term) to mains electricity; it depends on the bore of your pipework; on the 12volt supply; on the phase of the moon; on your tyre pressures; on which way the wind's blowing; on the capacity of your water-tank; on your height above sea-level; on your mother's maiden-name; on the alignment of the planets (including bloody Jupiter); if the engine's running; on your fuse-ratings; whether the capacitor on the Ouija board is drawing more than eighty amperoonies and so on and on and on.

Alas then, no ideal solutions from the online cognoscenti – and thus – into a geostationary orbit alongside the Knumptywagen arrives our Redeeming Mobile Caravan Engineer in an enviably well-equipped, shiny black Transit Van, tastefully liveried along its gleaming flanks.

With refreshingly little in the way of chin-stroking or head-scratching, the fridge was quickly assessed and then carefully and multiply disconnected, every stage being photographed to ensure correct re-assembly. It was then eased gently out of its snug cocoon; extracted through the window, as there was no way it'd go out through the door (do they build these vans around their innards, we wonder?) and taken carefully away – cocooned in a blanket like a shameful prisoner, to be diligently and rigorously interrogated during a semi-distant bench-test.

Side-by-side like comrades-in arms, we then peered cautiously into the water-tank, half expecting a lurking enemy to emerge, which I guess it did, in the form of the water-pump which (in its ailing and decrepit state) was no match for the likes of us, even though our knees, backs and an elbow or two were creaking from our cramped communion with it.

And lo, a few days later, the fridge is triumphantly returned, its complex 3-way power sources (Gas, 240v and 12v) having been fully checked and pronounced working. And if it worked under interrogation, it'll work in the van. Back through the window we go; gentle grunting eases it back into place and with hearts in mouths it's rewired (via several inaccessible finger-pinching portals) and powered up . . .

Yay! Gas? Green light. Good to go. 240v? Green light. Good to go. 12v? No response. Bugger!

No green light, we do not have lift-off. No gleaming control-panel LED to denote success on the 12v front, but hey, 66% positive outcome gets our vote, especially as we had nil refrigerational functionality a week ago. (The cost of a new fridge would also have put a severe dent in our Galactic Exploration budget and delayed launch by as long as it took to acquire a replacement.)

Undaunted by this set-back, our specialist engineer had a solution. He knew a man. And that's what I love about true professionals – they don't feel compelled to suddenly become amateurs and start tinkering in the outer hemispheres of their own experience. Unlike the author, Mark knew a fellow astronaut – who had visited the mysterious planet of Twelve Volt more frequently; was therefore familiar with its geography – and would know the most effective route to a final solution.

The sub-space call was therefore made, an imploring message left, the call was returned and yes . . . you're ahead of me already, because as I explained the situation and enquired if he could help, there are absolutely no prizes whatsoever for guessing his first response . . .

Open Wide

Lichfield, Staffordshire, England

Dentists. Dentists and two conspiracy theories. About which you can make your own minds up once you've absorbed the author's laboured hypotheses which follow. Ready? Ok, here's Conspiracy Theory One.

We went to the dentist. First thing in the morning. Regular, bog-standard check-ups, OK? Coincidentally, on the day before we set off on a three-week Knumpty-van trip to Montenegro (a journey delightfully described as 'insane' by a close relative who'd just witnessed our planned route.)

A prolonged and edgy read of an aged 'Country Life' magazine in the waiting room (do properties like those advertised REALLY exist outside of our imaginations?) then a quick usher into the Surgery; recline; open mouth; probe inserted; long list of incomprehensible four letter acronyms fired like an automatic rifle at Nurse-On-Computer barely able to type fast enough; quick and vaguely uncomfortable clean ("Just raise your hand if you want me to stop" – has anyone ever?); electronically hummed to an upright position; sign a few forms then out onto the street – while The Navigator Par Excellence remains behind to pay the bill.

The author is on the street in double quick time because he has been assigned to speedily acquire something breakfasty from the newly opened Artisan Bakery directly opposite the dentist. Well, there you go - Conspiracy Theory Number One or what? You've just paid out to have your six-monthly teeth-clean and when you stumble out, all you can see are pastries. Pastries! An absolute windowful of sticky, gooey Chocolate Knots; custard-oozing Pain au raisin; muffins and – wait for it – shiny, sugary lardy cake! I ask you. What a fine way of drumming up business for this particular dentist. Clean your teeth, admonish you for eating too many sugary things, then push you into immediate temptation which no amount of flossing is ever going to resolve. ("Would you like me to book you another appointment in three weeks' time, Mr Campbell?")

And as if that's not enough, we then set off on our Epic Journey, headed south, along remarkably free-flowing motorways, headed for the Channel Tunnel via the M25 and M20. And hence along comes Conspiracy Theory Two: I believe an amalgam of Dentists (tick the box if you like the collective noun, there) must have won the contract to build specific sections of both these motorways.

I mean, who – in their right minds – would build sections of the nation's most heavily used motorways out of short, concrete sections laid at right-angles to the general direction of thundering traffic? These sections are then clearly welded together in-situ by unsupervised dental apprentices using too much bloody amalgam, so every joint is like an overfilled tooth, jarring above the bite with a quick-fire repetitive thump-thump-thump (naturally amplified by the box-like interior of the trusty Knumptywagen) until our newly-cleaned and recently pastried teeth are shaken loose in their sockets – to the point that all we can practically do is to take up that offered appointment in another three weeks to have them all cemented back in.

And for those of you tenacious enough to have read this far, our Route to Montenegro is plotted into the satnav, and you may judge for yourselves the rationality of our trip. For those keen for a glimmer of truthful reportage, we are indeed parked up in a beautifully smooth, flat and fully unseamed tarmac car park alongside an Ernie Leclerc supermarket in downtown Jonchery-sur-Vesle. And in the morning, his artisan Boucherie Patisserie opens.

And it's a drive through. Now, where did we put that dentist's phone number?

Motorway Madness

Augsberg, Bavaria, Germany

A little under a year in the planning (for which read: glancing occasionally at a roadmap and booking ourselves fixed-date crossings on Eurotunnel) we have filled our tanks and charged our batteries for another swashbuckling Knumpty tour across Europe, as the day of departure is upon us. Frenetic packing and then a late-afternoon thrash down to Kent, where a nameless Green King pub at Aylesford found itself in conflict with its own website with regards to the time they actually stopped serving food.

Ha! No matter, stout yeowoman, we shall prevail despite it being past nine p.m. – for we shall visit the neighbouring kebab house and STILL stay overnight in your manky pub carpark. And hey, while the pub doesn't deserve a mention, the neighbouring kebab shop gets a 'best ever' rating with takeaway, café, meze and grill plus an impeccably kept carpark and integrated hand-car wash - really, what's not to like?

Onward. Channel tunnel, yadda-yadda-yadda. Like a frankfurter sausage, it was quick, tube-like and efficient – without the debilitating side-effects of seasickness induced by a ferry crossing. Out into glorious French sunshine in less time than it took us to realise we'd actually set off and then foot down for another thrash along expensive but time-saving autoroutes to see just how far we could get in one day.

Chalon-en-Champagne Technical College Car Park is the correct answer. A quiet and pleasant backwater alongside a soup-green canal, we street-parked for the night, roamed the small town, dined out, drank too much beer and went 'home' to our trendy loft-bed.

Apart from an early-the-following-morning visit to our favourite retail cathedral, Ernie LeClerc to replenish stores and purchase a swimsuit (neglectfully left at home by the Navigational Quartermaster, as if she didn't have enough to think about), we just thrashed steadily onwards towards Austria – ending that day's rattling toil in the car-park of a combined museum theatre complex in what seemed to be an old prison by a river in the German city of Ulm. Amazing painted architecture from the previous century graced the city centre, standing proud between post-modernist, some-would-say brutalist glazed offices – while a towering Gothic cathedral glowed like honeycomb in the evening sunshine.

Dinner (and too much beer) was taken en plein aire outside the Rat Keller before we riverside-walked back to our carpark where – thankfully – the post-modernist and most definitely brutalist live outdoor punk-rap-band concluded their performance with Germanic efficiency on the dot of 10:00 pm and we were asleep before most of their fan-base had left the carpark.

With the first fixed rendezvous of our trip now imminent in neighbouring Austria, an early start and continued thrashing along the autoroutes of Germany did, however, almost end in tears before we reached it. Just before Augsberg a sudden noisy, alarming thudding advertised a blown rear tyre and we rolled to an ignominious halt on the hard shoulder of an autoroute junction, thankfully in the lee of the off-slip-road. No matter. With British fortitude well to the fore, we phoned our European Breakdown service and were gratified by the apparent efficiency of the response. Almost simultaneously, we were joined (from behind, of course) by an autoroute patrol car (a bit like watered-down policemen) who replaced our pathetically tiny red warning triangle with their own patrol car, hazards and blue lights flashing frenetically, while we waited for the promised rescue. And waited. And waited. And waited.

I was looking forward to a Grand Rant Of Humungous Proportions here but with due respect to both readership and blood-pressure, think it best to skip that for the time being. Our short-order frustration was simply that it took four hours for a breakdown truck to reach us. Four hours. What made this unacceptable time-lapse worse was the fact that our version of Thunderbird One had come from a depot only 20 kilometres away but hadn't been provided with any of the detailed location information we (and our guardian Watered-Down-Policemen) had provided over the phone to the Breakdown Service. Perversely, he'd also been advised that we were French and was anxious about his lack of that particular language, despite his fluent English!

Because the detailed dimensions of the Knumptywagen also hadn't been communicated onwards, his breakdown truck was too small to winch our enormous wallowing bulk on board. So, like a real-life episode of Gerry Andersons's puppet-populated Thunderbirds TV series of the mid-Sixties, he rolls out a natty, tiny, articulated, wheeled dolly – a glorified skateboard, if you like – which then doesn't fit under the blown-tyred wheel, so he can't even hitch us to his towbar and drag us off the autoroute. In his impeccable Germanic English, he politely explains he's now run out of options.

'What about the spare wheel?' we gently enquire – which seems at first to be a revelatory concept to him but he then remembers that German Health & Safety legislation prevents him from crawling under the Knumptywagen on an autoroute, citing 'danger of death' (even though Diluted Flashing Plod are still standing guard over our rear end.)

'OK' I gallantly suggest. 'What if I crawl under there and get the spare, then?' Well. That seemed to do the trick and my subconscious Brexit-based challenge was accepted. Under he went, while – Good Lord – another passing breakdown truck pulls up – seemingly out of sheer curiosity, and now both Scott and Virgil Tracy became engaged in retrieving the thankfully-still-inflated spare wheel from the Knumptywagen undercarriage.

Spare wheel fitted. Exploded tyre on road-wheel deposited into the Knumptywagen; notes of caution about onward speed acknowledged; peremptory 'dankes' are exchanged all round and we all set off into what is now rapidly becoming a sunset, now only 5 hours behind schedule for our rendezvous at our destination in Austria.

The Austrian Alpes

Obertraun, Salzkammergut, Austria

As we skirted Salzburg to enter Austria from Germany, the landscape altered considerably and we experienced a peculiar sensation as we climbed quite steeply onto what felt like a Lost World plateau. Everything seemed to be, in estate agent's parlance, "laid to lawn" as if some omnipotent deity had simply rolled green baize over gently undulating hills. Toytown roads wound across the landscape and the lack of fencing, hedging or other boundary markers around the quaintly scenic timber houses imparted a curious openness to the landscape.

It therefore felt a little odd that on this unusual verdant plateau, life appeared to be carrying on as normal – with busy villages, light industrial units and even upmarket car showrooms peppering our route. Slightly disappointed that no Conan-Doylean dinosaurs were wandering aimlessly about, we headed onwards – still metaphorically limping on our ancient spare wheel – but anticipating our not-too-distant destination.

Our closing route for the day took us past the touristic lakeside delights of Hallstatt, which we avoided as we passed through since the town is bypassed by a huge tunnel which filters most of the traffic away from its picturesque, narrow, lake-side, tourist-thronged streets.

Just over 5 hours late, we thus edged ourselves gingerly into the charmingly unpretentious village of Obertraun to find Landhaus Lily, nestling four-square and dominant within an impressive amphitheatre of towering mountains amidst the Austrian Alps. Our friends Liz & Paul, expats from the UK, were now long-established and highly-regarded hosts of this sublimely-located and welcomingly well-run B&B establishment. They were, of course, also looking forward to our (delayed) arrival as they were really quite keen for us to turn their impeccable forecourt into a downmarket travellers' encampment for a couple of nights – probably costing them two of their many preciously-earned tourist stars into the bargain.

Pub! Where else shall you be taken after a long and tedious day on the road? Their local hostelry – Gasthof-Pension Hoellwirt greeted us warmly, fed us exceptionally well with local dishes alongside which we accidentally drank too much beer, so much so that we forgot to leave them a tip – entschuldigung!

The following morning we cycled into Hallstatt – a UNESCO heritage site and tourist mecca set exquisitely on the edge of Lake Hallstatt – and seemingly already, at 10:30 am, teeming with tourists. On our arrival, we were greeted with the bizarre sight of thirty or so diminutive Asian men and women all dressed identically in what could best be described as creamy-grey rice-picking outfits: baggy trousers tucked into white ankle socks; same-colour flowing tunics; white cravats and floppy-brimmed hats – all milling around and eventually boarding a coach before we were able to turn OUR tourist cameras on them!

It's reported that Hallstatt is so popular with Asian tourists that the town has actually been replicated – building for building – on a lake-edge somewhere in China. Given that we're unlikely to get that far in the Travelling Knumptywagen, we'll make do with the Austrian version, thanks, and instead ran a gauntlet of carelessly-wielded selfie-sticks (some as long as fishing rods); found a lakeside café where we enjoyed a slightly standardised pre-packaged 'tourist breakfast' made more palatable by the addition of crisply and freshly fried eggs on top – and then got the hell out of there.

Another rendezvous with our hosts back at Landhaus Lilly was this time fulfilled on time as they finished their combined guesting duties/household chores and we set off together, they on rather flash and envy-inducing electric-bikes; us on our slightly more decrepit versions, for an exclusive trip round the locals' side of the lake.

A delightful cycle-ride allowed us more distant (and less populous) views of Hallstatt across a crystal clear lake, in which we were also able to pause-a-while-and-paddle before celebrating our achievement with coffee & kuchen at a local café. The Surprise & Delight feature of our homeward journey was revealed by loading our bikes onto a passing train which returned us with Austro-Germanic efficiency to Obertraun station, and the anticipation of a Rather Special Austrian In-Knumptywagen Supper For Four.

In fulfilment of which (and prior to drinking too much beer again) our hosts bravely joined us for a house-special corned-beef hash and baked-beans, cosily served in the Knumptywagen, parked on their drive and assumedly at the amusement of their neighbours – who will never quite get round to fully understanding those strange Brits and their very odd social habits.

Do We Feel Lucky?

Villach, Carinthia, Austria

I'm not sure how many people who know me would classify me as a pessimist but – whether it's attributable to increasing maturity or a career dicing with the rudiments of Murphy's Law – I do find myself assuming the worst in certain situations.

I also don't want to milk the blown-tyre saga reported upon previously, but blow-me-down and shiver-me-timbers, I really do want to record the sequence of events which put us back on the road again.

People more in-the-know than I advised that a spare-wheel-tyre which had lain exposed and unattended beneath our trusty Knumptywagen for its lifetime may have, in effect, passed its sell-by date. As such, it wasn't advisable to be doing a lot more miles than was strictly necessary on it, since – if it decided to expire beneath us on the next leg of our trip – then we really would be up a pneumatic creek without a paddle.

Although our quaint region of plateau'd Lost World Austria boasted much in the way of 21st century conveniences, a tyre-specialist wasn't one of them – and so we aimed ourselves as directly as possible towards the next major town on our route – Villach, just before the border with Slovenia.

Google had adjudged Villach to possess such a tyre-specialist so we dutifully therefore arrived – into the middle of a particularly agreeable, modern industrial estate – to find the dealer closed for lunch until one p.m. Surprisingly, we considered that a fine result since it was a mere ten minutes before re-opening and there was a Hofer grocery store (Austrian Aldi) where our former hosts had suggested we could acquire very decent Merlot at a bargain price, so we killed a few enjoyable minutes there stocking up our meagre travelling cellar.*

We then rolled our blown tyre proudly into the now open reception area, to be met with blank stares and a language barrier – and after some minor gesticulation and furrowed brows, Computer Said No. But Lady Behind Counter instead pointed. In fact, gesturing enthusiastically in the direction of the store from where we'd just come, she typed the name of another tyre-specialist into the Quartermaster's proffered phone, from where Google again stepped up and directed us across the carpark into another tyre-specialist's compound – not 500 yards from our initial landing site.

Young German lad at counter lapses into English at our approach (are we really THAT obvious?) and delightfully, his Computer Says Yes! "About an hour?" he says, quoting a price comparable with the UK, so yes please, young man, and please may we gnaw your arm off as it's lunchtime and we haven't even had our full-English yet. "Is there anywhere we could get some lunch?" we enquire and he points, backwards across the now well-explored carpark again and simply says "Italian".

Hand over the keys, wave goodbye to the Knumptywagen and off we amble in the searing Mad Dog heat to wander about looking for a sandwich bar or transport caff which might provide a snack or a sandwich.

Slightly bemused by the lack of specific directions, we guess on a route and stumble into an incongruous full-blown Italian restaurant, cheery with a bright-red canopied frontage providing welcome shade across the pavement; potted shrubs and greenery screening gingham-clothed tables; a buzz of atmospheric lunch-time conversation; several smart-looking cars in the car-park alongside which a couple of slick, linen-shirted business-types were clearly sealing a deal; a classically-attired waiter greeting us in a selection of languages (ha, obviously not as astute as the Tyre-Guy) and yes, a table is available for us – would we prefer inside or out? Well, forgive me, but WTF? We're in the middle of an industrial estate, ferchrissake! How is this happening to us? And why hasn't Tamworth never come up with a similar concept?

And to top it all, you'd be really, really, really hard-pressed to match the calibre of our lunch in some of London's smartest eateries. Cockles, clams, shrimp and fresh fish served up in an intense fresh tomato and basil sauce; a basket of fresh, seeded breads plus a huge bowl of dressed-mixed-side-salad, all presented with a smile and a flourish.

At some point this afternoon, we will wake-up! Until then, we might as well continue living the dream as the sun continued to shine as we took the obligatory photos to record the moment and we realised we could actually SEE our tyre-depot down the road in the distance. Paying our exceptionally reasonable bill, we ambled back, a little beyond our allocated hour, replete and probably now reeking of garlic, where the Knumptywagen stood silently sentinel, proudly boasting a brand-new tyre – for which we even gained two cents change from the quoted price.

Although they hadn't quite managed to work out how to sling the spare-wheel back under the chassis, they had instead put it into a tyre-bag for onward transportation and our own subsequent DIY technical challenge at the next overnight stop.

This wondrous sequence of events throughout the day (and, as it turns out, yet further into our journeyings) had seen Murphy and his law well and truly off the premises, leaving us with an optimistic spring in both our step and suspension as we trundled lightly onwards to our next much-anticipated destination.

**Literary license: we don't actually have a wine cellar in the Knumptywagen, OK?*

Gateway To A Land Far Beyond

Trieste, Friuli Venezia Giulia, Italy

Our journey south to Montenegro really began in earnest at Trieste, which had long figured in our minds as the gateway to Adriatic Eastern Europe and which enjoyed a certain mystique in our household since the travel writer Jan Morris wrote a whole book on the city. Despite having read it, I'm now disappointed at my inability to recall any pertinent details whatsoever (and that's more the fault of an ailing memory than any shortcoming on Jan Morris's part. I think.)

So, into Trieste we drove, a little jaded from having left a surprisingly delightful overnight stop in Bergamo, from where we'd set ourselves a slightly over-ambitious autoroute schlep across the top half of Italy. This journey was made almost perilously busy by convoys of commercial trucks, all inevitably travelling at the same speed and rudely buffeting our attempts at overtaking until most of them thankfully disappeared once we'd passed the Venice junction.

Our overnight stop in Bergamo, Italy had provided a pleasant surprise as it had been selected in the planning stage purely for its convenient location as an overnight staging post, with an 'aire' tucked unassumedly and slightly incongruously into the outskirts of the business district. Not expecting much, we were warmly greeted by a young receptionist who politely enquired as to which language we'd like to be welcomed in. The simple fenced site – with a total capacity of about 25 motorhomes – quickly grew on us, especially as we found ourselves accidentally within cycling distance of Bergamo old town, an historic hill-built, medieval fortress-like settlement boasting Roman roots.

To add to its sense of newly discovered novelty, we were also made aware (in continuing and impeccably spoken English, of course) that a funicular railway carried visitors up to the old higher town, so after a brisk and excited cycle ride, we joined a small group of intrepid funiculeers to make our way upwards in a small, modern, twin-height, standing room-only single carriage to emerge onto narrow, sun-dappled cobbled streets bustling with early-evening nightlife.

A pair of spontaneous gelatos fortified us in the Cittadella Square, then a good old mooch around attractively aged and shuttered buildings, tall and domineering, with the occasional resident peering benignly down upon us lowly, gawping tourists. After a gentle perambulation and views of Greater Bergamo below us, a corner bar caught our attention, where we enjoyed pasta fortified with octopus and potatoes, so an agreeable double whammy on the carbs-front.

Back down the funicular in the dusk (this being Italy, no timetable information available anywhere, so no idea what time the last 'train' departed) and an exhilarating downhill cycle back to the campsite, for a nightcap and bed at a decent hour.

So, yes, eventually, Trieste. Our arrival was made more dramatic by a tympanic thunderstorm coupled with an approach which descended steeply via a series of hairpin bends running through suburbia, so the houses and apartments seemed to be clinging to the edge of the storm-slicked tarmac, each gasping for breath under streamingly heavy rainfall. Thankfully, we found ourselves in a small convoy led by a cautious passenger bus and our now trusty satnav glowed reassuringly from the windscreen, so we found ourselves safely guided to sea-level at the City's tidy little marina. Here we found a front-line already populated by a range of motorhomes interesting for their collective ages and scale, amidst which we shouldered our middling way to claim a pitch for the night, despite the signage which threatened we'd be towed away after nine p.m.

The thunderstorm passed, the pavements steamed as the evening sun quickly warmed them again, so we unhooked the bikes and cycled about three kilometres along the main road into the waterfront centre of Trieste. Imposing civic buildings – old and new – presented a grand and pleasing prospect as we cycled onto the large main square and into the hinterland, finding well-earned refreshment at a waterside café-bar, where, amongst other delightful misunderstandings, we were served glasses of Hoegaarden beer in glasses so large we needed both hands to lift them.

A dusky return to our peaceful, waterfront pitch ensued – with an overnight accompanied by the lulling sounds of halyards gently tapping against yacht-masts – and thankfully no winch-clanking intrusion from the City council's tow-truck.

We Cross The Border Into Eastern Europe

Njivice, Primorje-Gosrski-Kotar, Croatia

After a short, commuter-busy drive out through the straggled University campus of Trieste, our crossing from Italy into Slovenia was marked solely with abandoned border-control buildings artfully lit by low-level and glorious morning sunshine.

Beyond this slightly underwhelming but uninterrupted entry into another world, rolling hills layered to the wide horizon, all covered with a peculiar verdant close-knit forest, a bit like footballer Kevin Keegan's 1979 permed hairstyle – just a lot tighter and – well - obviously a hell of a lot greener.

There then followed another seemingly very short thirty-minute drive across country where Slovenia's main fascination became the number of roadside restaurants offering outdoor hog-roasts. At the time of morning we sailed past, these were being diligently tended by moustachioed and ragged-aproned chefs, whose comedically rotund bellies were clear testament to the simple rustic fare they were preparing – as tantalising aromas of barbecuing pork and hot herbs drifted through our open windows.

Back out of Slovenia and into Croatia through a cursory border check by a bored Customs official who waved us through as we waved our passports, without us ever needing to come to a halt, so our passage into Croatia was unimpeded, unremarked and therefore again slightly underwhelming (in marked contrast to our eventual exit from the country, about which more another time.)

Well, shout hurrah for Croatia, but more importantly, hats in the air please and three rousing cheers for the Reader Of The Satnav Runes; Navigator Par Excellence; Part-time Weather Girl and Chief Finder Of Excellent Locations Where We Might Possibly Stay The Night. The island (Otok) of Krk lay a little way off our intended route but a detour to a previously noted beach-side campsite seemed worth the effort, so after safe passage over an impressively arched and clearly recently-constructed toll-road bridge, we arrived at Njivice Resort – a combined hotel and large-scale, highly agreeable campsite complex.

Cheerful, welcoming English-speaking receptionists offered us a selection of plots dotted around the shady site, which, in exchange for holding one of our Passports (we let them choose the best-looking one and I lost) we were allowed to trundle around the site to pick the location we liked best. Easily done as site reference IP 208 was a mere 150m from a delightfully compact beach – with plenty of mature trees providing dappling shade and which was already bustling with happy families ranged around the lapping edge of a wondrously clear azure-blue Adriatic Sea.

Knumptywagen parked up; electric umbilical plugged in; reclining chairs deployed . . . yadda yadda yadda, you get the picture (we're becoming such a well-oiled machine at this campsite lark.) On the olive- and fig-tree shaded walk back up to reclaim the Good-Looker's Passport, we pass an onsite supermarket, a bakery and a colourful fruit & vegetable stall plus a Beach Toy Purveyor who had on display China's entire inflatable-plastics-manufacturing output from about 2007 to present day.

Judging by the plethora of 'D'-marked number plates on the vehicles parked-up around us, our neighbours were mostly German (a comparatively easy drive, we guessed) and indeed, we were soon engaged in conversation with Heidi (and husband) from Stuttgart, who spoke English well enough for us to understand that they had been encamped for four weeks and were visited occasionally during this sojourn by grown-up grandchildren who popped over to join Groβmutter und Groβvater for a few days am meer.

Bliss. A swim in the clear sea. Freshly baked bread and pastries. Sunbathing. At last, it seemed the wheels could be left unturned for a while as we transformed ourselves from travellers to holidaymakers, albeit (and slightly sadly) just for the one day. As such, further discretionary expenditure on dinner 'out' became wholly justifiable, as we unhooked the bikes and cycled a short, winding and gently pedestrianised coastal path around our swimming bay to the local village of Njivice for a waterfront dinner of freshly cooked fresh fish followed by outlandish ice-creams from the next-door parlour, as the sun set on us from across the Adriatic.

Fishing For Trout – With A Bucket

Camp Klin, Lepena, Slovenia

The Soca (pronounced Socha) River is one of Slovenia's finest, unspoilt natural attractions, known primarily for its gin-clear yet ultramarine water colouration; it's fast-flowing, gorge-routing power and its reputation as a major trout river - along with other leisure pursuits such as rafting and cycling/trekking along its 138 km length from its source in the Julian Alps in north-western Slovenia to its communion with the Adriatic Sea near Montfalcone in northern
Italy.

Somewhat bizarrely, Number One Daughter had it first drawn to her attention in Manchester, England by a work colleague to whom she just happened to mention that her parents fly-fished for trout. We were subsequently recommended to a fishing guide –whose website had whetted our appetite many months prior, in the dull grey days of an English spring.

Coincidentally perhaps, Her Navigational Highness The Trout Meister Of All She Surveyed was soon to celebrate A Rather Auspicious Birthday and as such, it therefore came to pass that Lovely Daughters Three bestowed upon her a gift voucher for a day's guided fishing on the Soca River, as a very considerate birthday gift.

Incredibly, our recommended Guide was already fully booked for our anticipated dates but instead recommended us onwards to another local guide, clearly a member of the local river-guiding community. So it was that we wound our way across the border out of Austria and along a gently hair-raising, hair-pinned route into Slovenia and the spectacular Soca valley – thence to the recommended Kamp site of Klim, nestling in a confluence of the Soca and Lepena Rivers.

On the rare occasion that we actually use an official campsite, I always find myself mildly amused by benchmarking our arrival experience against that of the official Camping & Caravanning Club's lakeside facility on Derwentwater at Keswick in the English Lakes. Here, well-honed efficiencies, proficiencies and procedures are to be rigorously adhered to, as the arriving camper diligently queues in line behind the barrier; to then be greeted by a team of uniformed camp-site staff, any one of which – following your satisfactory suitability assessment and registration – is assigned to the task of escorting you to your allocated, numbered pitch, on a bicycle, which you are to diligently follow, please, without exceeding the camp speed limit, to park as directed in an orderly and considered fashion, thank-you-very-much and enjoy-your-stay.

Kamp Klin? Well, hey, yeah, just let me finish up serving this guy his beer and that group out there with all these coffees, and how many nights? Yeah, well just drop your passports in when you've found a pitch. Where? Oh, well anywhere you fancy really, just use this tag to get you through the barrier and – yeah, well, just – sort of anywhere you like really. Oh – and just pay when you leave, OK?

Which is why the camp is laid out in such wonderfully relaxed random chaos, with absolutely no wardens on bikes leading us onwards. Cars – numberplated from throughout Europe – with oversized tents as roof-racks – are just dumped haphazardly between trees; tiny canvas shelters rub shoulders with hulking great Germanic motorhomes where the occupants of each just glare at each other disapprovingly; classic VW camper vans have disgorged at least four times their volume of camping paraphernalia across swathes of riverside grass, making it impossible to pitch anything else within 100m of prime riverside site; smoke is curling from random barbecues; washing lines are slung at throttlingly dangerous heights between trees, shrubs and telegraph poles; mist is beginning to swirl from the rivers into low-lying areas so campers emerge, ghost-like, yet also on electric scooters; giant oversized Hummer-type 4x4s with bizarre and impenetrable graphics painted on both the vehicles and their owners line up proudly for photographs; small, seemingly parentless children sporting half-shaved heads and the occasional glint of a body-piercing or two just tazz noisily about, invading what until then you'd considered to be your personal space and just stare at you provocatively; then . . . you begin to gain some insight into what could become a post-Brexit apocalyptic version of Keswick-On-Speed and – tbh – we know which we prefer.

But trout! You want to know about the trout! And what's with the bucket of the title? Well, if you haven't already guessed, fly-fishing the Soca River in the dog-days of August with a knowledgeable, experienced and personable guide – should be on everyone's Bucket List, regardless of whether fishing is your bag or not. The experience was exquisite. "Meet at 08:00hrs with Gregor, your (Slovenian) guide, at Kamp Reception, where he'll help you with the requisite licenses", was our only emailed instruction. So we did.

And by 9:00 o'clock, we'd been whisked to an upriver location in Gregor's car; were donning our waders (a new and challenging experience in itself) at the edge of a deserted, mistily beautiful river's edge and - with rods in hand - were led into the shallow but surprisingly powerfully flowing, clear blue waters of the Soca River.

Neither of us had ever fished a proper river before, let alone one as unspoilt, crystal clear or fast-flowing as this one. That was part of the gifted experience – to raise our experience above the often-muddy still waters of the UK, where it was usual that nothing would be seen beneath the water's surface, least of all any hungry trout.

Here, it was a revelation. Cossetted from the nullifyingly cold mountain water by our hi-tech, breathable chest-high waders and hefty boots, standing knee-deep on what tends to be called a 'freestone' riverbed, not five metres in front of us, sinuously holding station with the merest of body-flexing in the powerful current, lay some very beautiful fish. Feeding on minute water-borne insects, both larval and hatching river flies, our task was to mimic these tiny creatures, casting our weighted fly-lines upstream of the waiting fish and immediately having to adjust or 'mend' the floating fly-line as the current dragged it unnaturally downriver, while the artificial fly sank to a depth viewable by the waiting trout. The accelerated speed imparted by the drag of fly line on the surface made the art of presenting our flies even more of a challenge and whilst it took me quite a while to get the hang of 'mending' my cast line, wouldn't you know it, The Honourable Navigating Troutess hooks into her first fish of the day within five minutes of setting wadered-foot into water.

And such was the pattern of the day set. We fished in several different locations throughout the morning, with Gregor quietly spotting and pointing out waiting, feeding fish, so much so that – with the aid of polarised sunglasses, we also began to spot the hitherto unrecognisable shapes of fish – either rainbow or marbled trout – hanging on the edge of gently swirling eddies or perhaps lying – with subconsciously primaeval instinct – in the lee of a big boulder and moving with such economic energy only to intercept a passing morsel of food – or our artfully tied artificial flies – sometimes taken immediately with surprising speed and energy and sometimes studiously ignored for cast-after-cast until Gregor's experience suggested we change the type, colour, patter or size of fly – and cast again.

The sun having dispelled the morning mists, it reached its zenith and – whilst the water swirling round our lower limbs remained numbingly cold – its rays penetrated the steeply sided river gorge to the point where we decided to retire for a languid and shady outdoor lunch back at the campsite. Here, in the strict tradition of fishermen the world over, we talked absolute bollocks to each other for a couple of hours (Gregor's excellent command of colloquial English standing him in good stead amongst strong competition from the 'away' team) and then off we set again for a further round of abject delight.

Strangely, as we fished into the afternoon, out of a clear blue sky above us, rain began to fall, initially pockmarking the river surface, turning thunderous and then just gushing down to soak us thoroughly while we fished gamely on. The rain passed, the sun re-emerged and although we steam-dried to a point, the temperature had fallen and by six-thirty p.m., we decided to call it a day.

The final tally - typically - was Head Navigatoress & Chief High Trouting Priestess – 5; Lowly Author – 2. But what the hell! We've both now enjoyably part-filled our Buckets.

Footnote: It's not a cheap exercise, this trout-fishing malarkey – at the time, the fishing licenses alone cost circa £60.00 per head per day, but this revenue contributes to preserving the river environment and fish-stocks. The marble trout, a species indigenous to the Soca River system, was almost wiped out through lack of any sustainable water-management, so although we catch them, the fish are all returned alive with great care to the water and our licence fees support the ecological balance and continuing purity of the river itself.

Overwater Underwater

Kamp Klin, Rovinj And Environs, Croatia

Two separate water-based experiences stand out during our trip: one on the mightily beautiful Soca River in Slovenia (supplementary to our day's fishing, reported elsewhere) and the other just offshore from an also previously reported rocky coast a mere jink around the corner from Rovinj in Croatia.

So, which would you prefer first? The Soca river? Well, that's serendipitously handy, since that's what you're getting – in the form of a spontaneous rafting trip, advertised during our stay at Kamp Klin and hey, the beauty of our rambling lifestyle is that we don't need to be anywhere particular tomorrow – and 10% off – so why the hell not?

A short trip up the green-wooded, steep-sided, river-carved valley to a delightful pull-off from the snaking main road, and a warm greeting at the imaginatively-named 'Top Rafting' where we could join a downriver raft at one-o-clock and yes, it'd be fine to hang around (literally) until then as the surrounding stream-bordered gardens boasted a number of hammocks which we, as Pioneers Of A Certain Age And Now Questionable Agility fully avoided, brewing tea in the Knumptywagen instead, as-you-do.

It being end-of-season-mid-week, it turned out that only two other crew members would join our boat, a twin-hulled inflatable to be piloted by Ziga, a Slovenian student who'd spent his summer paddling tourists to their anticipated doom on a fast-flowing and boulder-strewn stretch of the Soca – which appeared to have been designed and built for the purpose. We therefore joined two young cycling, travelling, camping millennial ladies from Antwerp to be driven up-river in a rattling minibus towing our little Minion-coloured raft. This was then manhandled into a particularly wide, slow-flowing and innocuous-looking stretch of water, while we donned our wet-suits, lifejackets and helmets, so as to look especially fetching for our Don't Fall Out Of The Boat safety briefing from Ziga.

And off we serenely set. Scenery? 10/10. Gently unfolding river-canyon? 10/10. Unspoilt, gloriously sun-splashed tree-lined valley? 10/10. Guide & company? 10/10. Oh Lord, bloody great boulders in the middle of a curvy stretch causing water to foam and churn narrowly past on either side? 10/10. "Forward!" "Back!" "Stop!" shouts Ziga variously from his commanding position perched at the rear of the raft, manfully leaning into his paddle to steer his now-expert and responsive crew safely through the boiling rapids and over the jaw dropping transparent green depths of this forever-surprising river.

As a diversionary entertainment from all this intrepid pioneering, we paused half-way to join a couple of other rafts, one of which had been upturned and pulled up onto one of the numerous giant rocks to create a novel water-slide – from which (your author became alarmed to realise) we were each expected to launch ourselves (for fun, apparently) into the flowing depths, which proved just a little on the c-c-c-c-cold side. This however didn't deter the Navigating Troutess, who then led the charge by delivering herself in several athletic postures down the slide until we were recalled to duty and set off on the next leg of our waterborne adventure.

"Safety!" shouts Ziga, at a point where our raft becomes jammed sideways by the current against a house-sized boulder and – like the crack, highly-trained team of Marines that we'd been become in the past forty minutes – we responded as instructed by all piling into the rear-base of the raft, in the process knocking our brave Captain Ziga from his perch, off the back of the raft and into the swirling waters. Thankfully, this can't have been either a unique nor surprising experience for him since, within seconds, like a cartoon character, somehow he was back in the boat.

Oh, how we laughed! Although I'm not so sure he was that amused, since the photos of this particular episode from his helmet-mounted Go-Pro never made the cut into our album of photos supplied (for a small extra fee) at the end of the trip.

And having experienced a surface session, we then we went sub-aqua. Or at least her Esteemed Worshipfulness The Peerless Knumptying Navigator And Chief Troutess did as we move the narrative briskly away from rafting on the Soca and on to the Istrian coast where the aforementioned EWPTKNACT dons her snorkel and takes to the warm(ish) shoreline waters of the Adriatic, just south of Rovinj.

It should be noted here that your esteemed (and surely, by now, most favourite) author - having worn spectacles since his early teens - struggles on the rare occasion when snorkelling appears on any trip itinerary, since facemasks tend to leak avidly when worn atop any form of prescription eyewear. (I did see fit, on one family holiday on the Turkish coast several millennia ago, to pro-actively equip myself with a pair of contact lenses instead. However, the abject stress caused by three members of my immediate family all simultaneously attempting to help me fit miniscule transparent suction-cups to the surfaces of both eyeballs proved too much for my constitution and I decided that sitting on the shoreline watching everyone else's snorkels circulate gently around the bay was a far more relaxing activity.)

So, when the Navigating Amphibian emerged from her lone immersive experience, she was positively bursting with excitement at what she'd seen, recounted here with as much journalistic skill as a complete amateur can muster. It appears that, having swum around in about four metres depth of clear water and observing a few starfish and sea-urchins, our heroine decides to simply float in neutral, so to speak. And as she became immobile, sea creatures began to emerge below her. Hermit crabs and blennies appear and bustle about, and then a fish swam by. And then another. And then several more. Within seconds, these few fish – each about the size of a decent herring – had turned into a fast-moving, silvered shoal, heading out towards the open sea, at speed.

Passing swiftly around our passive snorkeller like a burst from a sparkling Sodastream, not one fish touched her or collided with its companions as they avoided the floating obstacle (sorry, dear). Transfixed at this sudden spectacle and in awe of the experience, she reckons it can have lasted no more than a few seconds and must have involved over a hundred fish. Any attempt she may have made to give chase was deemed pointless as these streamlined, shining creatures had collectively disappeared into the wide blue green yonder. In the stillwater vacuum of their wake, however, her eyes regained their focus on a magnificent jellyfish – similarly passively floating, sub-surface, not two metres away.

Well, David Attenborough would have been proud of her as – realising the jellyfish had no integral motive capabilities – she could swim around it at a safe distance and observe at leisure. Almost half-a-metre across its 'skirt', and with a peculiarly vivid colour-scheme, this true denizen turned out to be a Fried Egg Jellyfish, a native to the Adriatic and Mediterranean, and reported to be "very beautiful and very scary" all at the same time. Having missed all of this unique and stimulating submarine spectacle, when we got back to the Knumptywagen, I googled prescription facemasks.

We Discover Signs Of Conflict And Visit Busy Waterfalls

Skradin, Šibenik-Knin, Croatia

An early rising at Michael's roadside Auto Kamp, a brisk service of the van's more necessary facilities (including the directed and unusual draining of our waste/grey water into a gravelled depression by the water-tap) and then back onto the breath-taking Croatian coast road, inexorably southbound, zigzagging our route around the mountainous scenery until we reached Zadar, a large and modern-looking city which was reputed to contain a recently installed tourist attraction.

This 'wave-organ' – an architect-designed set of seaside steps – apparently produces variable musical notes as water movement forces air through a series of installed vents. However, it was already very hot; the outskirts of the city-centre were busy; road-signage was confusing; we hadn't told Satnav exactly where we wanted to go; we don't really 'do' big modern cities and so it came to pass that instead of checking out the organ (if you'll forgive the expression), we completed a quick, unstopping circuit of a shopping-centre car-park and used this orbital inertia to propel ourselves out of Zadar and onwards.

Earlier (and very cursory) guidebook reading had highlighted that Krka National Park was within passing reach of Zadar, so it was to Skradin that we now headed, along a route which took us inland and through some surprising scenery. With a brief roadside stop to repair a suddenly flapping over-cab sealing trim (too much sun appeared to have dried and shrunk it) we were suddenly aware that roadside structures were showing signs of the 1991-1995 civil war. Randomly, buildings were pock-marked with identifiable bullet-holes (or at least clearly visible indentations in brick and plaster work) which provided a stark reminder of the bitter struggle for independence which tore Yugoslavia apart.

In the UK, while it happened, we seemed to have absorbed the news by a sort of distance-learning process, a media-based osmosis, if you like, from a safe, impartial (and probably indifferent) distance on our comparatively unconflicted little island. Today, however, as we drove past road-signs for Zagreb; collapsed houses (which could have been attributable to bombing, explosions or post-war cowboy builders) as well as a pock-marked military barracks, the enforced dissolution of a country into several hostile component parts all became very visible, very real and very chilling in its proximity.

At Skradin, our approach was welcomed with open arms as a series of T-shirted young parking touts beckoned us in to roadside fields. Uncertain at that stage of what we were expecting to find, we pressed on into Skradin itself, a large village reminiscent of Grasmere in the Lake District, where our ongoing curiosity was rewarded by an empty parking field almost adjacent to the village centre. Here we were roundly fleeced of 100 kuna (about £12.00) but were then fulfilled by a very short walk to a modern, mirror-glassed tourist office rather incongruously adjacent to a more historic church in the little beating heart of Skradin. A brief wander around imparted the lie of the land and the sight of a queue of people rapidly forming alongside a riverside quay prompted us into the tourist office to acquire two 'tour' tickets to see the Krka waterfalls.

This exercise involved joining the lengthening queue and eventually boarding a large National Park river boat, which then took us on a 20-minute shuttle-like trip upriver towards the falls. Onboard, we had the pleasure of Steve's company; a fellow-passenger and well travelled Australian with whom we could at least converse in native language. Although he appeared to be travelling alone, it transpired his wife had taken up position on the opposite side of the boat, a tactic they had adopted during their travels to ensure they covered two separate photographic angles.

Disembarking along with about 100 other passengers, it became immediately clear that the waterfalls and park area surrounding them were going to be A Busy Place, confirmed after a short boardwalk to an enormous picnic and café area which was positively teeming with human life. We wandered through this area along with the general pedestrian flow and found ourselves on a wooden bridge which provided a great (if somewhat cluttered) view of both the falls and the pools below them. Here, surprisingly, many visitors were either swimming or cavorting in the shallow water above a curiously folded limestone riverbed clearly visible through the clear, flowing water.

How to describe the waterfalls? Well, they looked as if film-director Peter Jackson (of 'Lord Of The Rings' fame) had conceived, created and installed them after he'd done with his trilogy of box-office successes. In essence, it was difficult to believe they were a natural phenomenon. Low level, boulder-like outcrops were almost entirely covered with moss-like vegetation and rose gently in ordered layers so the water flowed and cascaded over and around them while sparkling through the greenery. Hordes of us jostled for suitable 'selfie' positions on the bridge before wandering further along the designated pathways and up into a jungle-like interior where amazingly clear flowing water simply poured and flowed everywhere you looked, seemingly in every direction.

A wide wooden boardwalk carried a thinning crowd into the depths of the park, where every pool and every slowing bend contained languid shoals of fish, just lazily holding station against the water's gentle flow – to provide much intrigue and beautifully sunlit photo opportunities. Guides could be heard telling their tours that these fish were trout, but closer inspection revealed that – unlike trout – they all sported a well-defined diamond-pattern to their scales – and when a later signboard identified them as Adriatic Dace, then who were we to disagree?

Full with wonder and amazement at this whole natural spectacle, we continued on a two kilometre circular walk around the boardwalks, eventually returning past some more traditional waterfalls, beneath which swim-suited people were dousing either themselves or their children amidst screams of excitement and cold-shocked laughter. A brief queue for one of the return shuttle-boats and a cruise back to the dock at Skradin brought our visit to the falls to an end; we extricated the van from its expensive rest-stop and set off back towards the coast at Sibenik, in search of a place to rest our own weary selves overnight.

Storm Over Otok Brac

Omis, Dalmatia, Croatia

We'd left the waterfalls of Krka National Park behind us and returned to the Croatian coast at Sibenik from where we headed for Split, which we bypassed along with a lot of Friday afternoon traffic. We enjoyed a brief hooted altercation with a crazy woman, assumedly driving an unfamiliar Mercedes as she was clearly incapable of controlling the vehicle and its progress through rush-hour traffic. She seemed determined to get the most out of her vehicle's horn, so our humble Knumptywagen gave voice in return – and then some, much to the embarrassed disgust of the Onboard Map Reading Sat Nav Rune Reading Queen.

Our optimistic and impulsive arrival at a large family campsite on the outskirts of Split was greeted with the kind offer of a U-turn on their premises since they were smilingly fully booked on this busy Friday afternoon. Further campsites were available about 30 km south, we were told. 30km? At this stage of our energetic day, that sounded a bit like the other side of the world, but off we dutifully set, to marvel at yet more incredible Croatian coastline. We kept our eyes open for any possible 'wild' camping spots, semi-aware that this wasn't technically legal in Croatia, and fully aware that the road existed solely to facilitate onward travel with very few suitable 'off-road' locations anyway.

However, at a small settlement called Omis just beyond the amusingly named Dugi Rat, there was suddenly a rash of small 'auto camps', each adjacent to its neighbour and each clearly fronting the sea. We pulled into one which was dotted with shade-giving trees and a few motorhomes already resident, but as we ruminated about the best spot to choose, we noticed a beach-side pitch on the other side of the fence in the adjoining site. There was no sign of anyone who could have booked us in anyway, so out we went again, covering at least 10 metres of road before pulling into the next site, where we simply helped ourselves to pitch number 6, right against the low wall which separated us from a narrow beach and the sea beyond.

Delight! From a narrow and inhospitably small boiler room which clearly doubled as the site office, there emerged a young man who booked us in, took our passport details plus 18 euros fee and then promptly left us to fend for ourselves, since four very enthusiastic Polish lads had just rolled in, popping small 'pup' tents out of a crammed people-carrier almost before their wheels had come to a stop. Before we'd even got our levelling ramps out, their camp was set up around a small table, which flexed (as campsite tables tend to do) under the weight, volume and variety of Tinned Beers Of The World (but probably mostly Of Poland.)

A walk along the water's edge, a swim (for at least one of us) and an in-Knumptywagen dinner of pork-loin with shallots, served with a very agreeable pasta, rocket & cream-cheese accompaniment, inspired by the Ready-Steady-Cook School of Culinary Masterclasses. The horizon of our view out to sea was impeded by the presence of Otok Brac, an offshore island beyond which, as dusk fell, it became apparent that a huge – and so far eerily silent – storm was raging out to sea. The sky darkened prematurely as we tried unsuccessfully to photograph both the sheet and forked lightning which silhouetted the island and illuminated the distant sky with an impressive display of nature's wrath.

We had retired to our bed by the time the storm arrived on our own shore, delivering torrential rain which hammered onto the acoustically tuned Knumptywagen roof. Overwhelmingly loud thunder accompanied this percussive attack directly overhead and spectacular lightning now illuminated the quickly-flooding campsite – as well as the poor sodden Polish pup tents. 4:00 a.m. saw us struggling to fully close the Knumptywagen's windows and roof-vents as a wild wind whipped in to complete the performance and then everything abated, seemingly instantaneously. The water-logged campsite had drained itself before we were back in bed and the following morning there was little evidence of the maelstrom that we'd lived through. The Poles' pup tents were drying on an improvised washing-line while they were already drinking on the beach and testing the temperature of the sea by simply wrestling each other into it.

Onwards. Off we went back onto the coast road which shortly led us inland into a fascinating, very wide and very flat arable region, where a large river formed the artery to many branching veins, all clearly canalised to provide irrigation for a patchwork of different crops, including trees, shrubs and indeterminate ground-level plants. A long five kilometre sweep of road took us through and around this magnificent arable floodplain, which ended in a run of roadside stalls at Opuzen, each displaying a vibrant paint box of coloured vegetables, fruits, melons and bottled products, all racked and displayed for our delectation as we sailed past. We did in fact stop, taste and purchase an array of products, much to our and the salelady's delight as we gallantly parted with about 15 quid for salad. Waitrose would have been far cheaper in comparison, but apparently that wasn't the point.

Over the mountains and out of the Fruit Bowl heading for Dubrovnik, which we planned to visit fully on the return leg so we passed swiftly through, with only a minor diversion to the much publicised Camp Solitudo, where we enquired about booking a pitch for the following Sunday. A smiling assistant pointed us to a site-plan on the wall, which demonstrated exactly how vast the camp was, and explained we had no need to pre-book as he had plenty of space. Apart from the sheer scale of the place, it further transpired that Camp Solitudo was not only expansive but also the most expensive campsite in all of Croatia. Needless to say, we found an alternative and contrasting overnight location in Dubrovnik on our return journey, which provided both the most disturbed night and early-start of the whole trip.

Cavtat had been earmarked as our next port-of-call, but as we wound our way down into the harboured town, it became apparent that motorhomes weren't favoured here, as explained by the quayside car-park attendant who wanted the equivalent of 70 euros for us to park for two hours. Another swift abuse of a turning-circle and off up the hairpin bends, through the modern hotel belt and back onto the main road again.

It was at this stage that the Chief Navigating Campsite Procurement Officer revealed she had cunningly already prepared a Plan B and promptly directed us towards another lesser known coastal village which, I'm ashamed to say, I'm minded not to name in print, as when we reached it, it was very quietly charming, unspoilt, non-touristy and therefore quite idyllic.

A small campsite revealed itself, into which we pulled, impressing a resident German as we parked the Knumptywagen unknowingly with just a couple of inches roof clearance beneath a large, metal framed and vine-clad shade-shelter. Our view of a small, enclosed bay with an array of small boats bobbing at anchor reminded us of both Borth-y-Gest near Porthmadog in Wales as well as a delightful place called Oyster Bay on the west coast of Ireland. So entranced were we at the location, the view and our good fortune that we failed to notice British numberplates on an adjacent motorhome, so were taken aback to be warmly greeted in our own language and were soon engaged in typical campsite chit-chat with Jill and Ken, our new neighbours.

We enjoyed a quick wander around the functionally pretty harbour to get the lie of the land, after which the Chief Navigator took her snorkel into the sea, as is her newly acquired custom on these occasions. Sitting out admiring the view was soon followed by a saunter up to the local, recommended (and apparently only) restaurant within walking distance. No booking? No problem, explained the Patron, hulking an extra table from we-know-not-where and plonking it down on the patio. An hour may need to elapse before we could eat, he explained, but have a drink while you wait, please. So, we did. An unlabelled litre bottle of house-red appeared and, true to his word, our amazing seafood platter for two arrived an hour later, by which time we were completely pissed. (Not strictly true but you needed a bit of light relief – it can be heavy going, this plain reportage.)

A memorable meal, a stunning location, a dash back to the Knumptywagen pre-main course for the anti-mosquito spray and then some voluble and amusing chat with another British couple – Adelaide & Alan (hello again if you're reading this!) on the next table, eventually walking each other home unsteadily and promising to be best friends forever.

The following morning, we arose early and bought a boat. Well, a canoe. Oh, OK, an inflatable single-seater kayak with all the trimmings. An impulse purchase, being sold by a Belgian gentleman whose perfect English allowed for a spot of good-natured negotiation before we handed over hard cash; pulled the plugs on his inflated but under-used vessel; stuffed it into the Knumptywagen and set off with mounting anticipation for the final leg of our journey to Montenegro.

At The Sign Of The Wild Boar

Dobrota, Kotor, Montenegro

Most of Croatia is behind us, its amazing coastline almost totally consumed by our rolling tyres and aging but unfaltering Fiat Ducato 2.3 litre diesel engine lugging 3.5 tonnes of wallowing motorhome behind it.

Here, at Croatia's southernmost finger, neighbouring Bosnia-Herzogovina is separated from the sea by a tantalisingly thin crust of land, almost as if it had just had its picnic lunch and its Mummy wouldn't allow it to go anywhere near the closely lapping Adriatic Ocean (for at least an hour) in case it got tummy-cramps.

It's also interesting to note that almost all of Bosnia-Herzogovina is landlocked, apart from a tiny weeny little insignificant stretch of coastal frontage which can't be more than five kilometres across, and with which they've done absolutely bugger-all. You'd have thought they'd have built a huge sea-port in order to access the trade routes of the world but not a bit of it. Just rolling green countryside; unspoilt natural coastline; a few scattered hotels and an endearing lack of commercial opportunism, which we have to wholeheartedly applaud.

The general topography didn't really change as we headed towards Montenegro although one of the new, hitherto unseen and unusual road-signs – that of a wild boar (which we excitedly assumed would be wandering into our path anytime soon) – did tend to add a certain expectation to the continuing journey. (It didn't, just in case you were wondering. We assume they'd all been spit-roasted in Slovenia.)

Instead, clusters of Italianate cypress trees spiked themselves skywards like a speleothem (liking that one, eh?) of pencil-thin, dark-green stalagmites – each straining upwards to give glorious, pointy-fingered praise to the cloudless blue sky. Orchestras of roadside cicadas continually shook their noisy maracas at us as we trundled by, so much so that the continual percussion became an intrinsic part of the general road noise filtering its way through our gloriously wide-open cab windows.

Our border crossings on the journey so far had been unremarkable, cursory affairs – and the roads had been traffic-free, so it was a slight shock to find ourselves joining a slow moving queue of vehicles at the south-bound Croatian border. Although the passport check was eventually a brisk formality, we had to queue for about 20 minutes to pass through. Elated to be released into what we thought was Montenegro, our expectations were thrown again when a further queue appeared just around the next bend. Here, it appeared, was the Montenegrin border and the previous delay was simply to exit Croatia. If that was the case, we asked ourselves, were we now queueing in an indeterminate No Mans' Land between the two countries? Lacking sufficient (for which read 'any') local language capability, we decided it best not to question this geopolitical fault line as we sat in another slow-moving queue to eventually reach an impassive, uniformed Border Guard sitting in his mirror-windowed booth.

Passports seemed to be in order, but vehicle documentation was required. Here you go, Sir. No? No good. Insurance? Green Card? That was the sum total of our grunted, almost primaeval communication and since we didn't actually possess a Green Card (but instead could wave DVLA's impressive-looking V5C document as proof of vehicle ownership) our passports were duly withheld and we were pointed peremptorily to another mirrored booth, where a similarly impassive (and maybe just slightly grumpy) woman pointed us towards an industrial-looking office. Here, Slobodan Milosevic's younger (and obviously smarter) brother sold us a scrappy piece of white paper (which was therefore neither Green nor made of Card) for the 20 euro note I was inadvertently holding – which may or may not have been the actual fee, who knows?

So, now in possession of an official Scrappy White Paper, we reclaimed our passports, boarded the van and did indeed pass into the land of Montenegro.

A now comparatively short hour's journey to Kotor Bay. Onerously described as a fjord, it is apparently a gulf (and don't ask, as we have no clue about the difference) but it is very big and interestingly shapely. Impressively huge tree-clad and grey-topped mountains encircle the whole enclosed seawater bay – where the surface was as calm as a lake and the sun seemed to intensify as we trundled gently around the lengthy perimeter road. We spurned the ferry across the throat of the bay (which our beloved Satnav insisted was a road) and carried on, the finishing line now almost in our sight.

Excitement mounted as we progressed towards our final destination, the small water's-edge town of Dobrota, just west of Kotor – the main town which gave this beautiful bay / gulf / fjord (you decide) its name. It was just past noon on Sunday 10 June that we pulled up outside a modern-looking villa-with-sea-view, having added an impressive 1,723 miles to the trusty Knumptywagen's mileometer since leaving home.

Our holiday rep – who greeted us on the steps – was clearly startled by our premature arrival in a bug-spattered, UK-plated motorhome which now must have resembled a giant, shop-soiled fridge-on-wheels dumped on the villa's forecourt. His spoken English was impeccable as he politely explained that we couldn't leave the van there, as he was expecting another group to arrive from the airport very shortly. "We know" we said. "They're our children."

And the holiday began.

The Croatian Coast Road Goes Ever On

Starigrad Paklenica, Zadar, Croatia

Michael (or at least his well-signposted 'auto-camp') beckoned us in off the dusty Croatian road for our night's travelling stop-over, with Germany still clearly dominating the semi-transitory population of this small, tree-shaded, sea-edged site. So much so that our host simply greeted us in a monologue of rapid-fire German, sadly none of which (being English) did we understand any better or any worse than any similar welcome delivered in Croatian.

We were quickly allocated a tiered pitch, looking down on what appeared to be a slightly disgruntled German-couple-mit-hund, and set about our one-night-only campsite deployment duties, to avail of a tree-restricted view of a small patch of sea, wherein The Navigating Rune Reader quickly immersed herself by way of journey's-end refreshment.

Our chance arrival at Michael's had been happily preceded by totting up yet more mileage on our south-bound trajectory, having travelled an almost deserted and sweetly surfaced road which hugged every topographical crease, dimple, curve and hairpin-bended inlet of the mid-Croatian coast. Views out to sea along the route were limited by the continuing low-lying presence of arid-looking offshore islands comprising bare limestone slopes which our limited research suggested were called 'karst landscapes' – where 'karst' – in some slightly onomatopoeic way – seemed as apt a description as is necessary.

On our left, huge domineering grey folded limestone mountains rose up immediately from the very edge of the road which had been carved into them, each peak climbing behind another to impossible heights, some of which even on this bright-skied and sunny day, had snagged a few passing clouds and clung onto them, seemingly to retain welcome shade for their balding, sun-bleached peaks.

Tiny hamlets of stone cottages, each topped with bright-orange pan-tiled rooves, littered each precarious inlet we circumnavigated, where a muddled collection of one-man wooden fishing boats bobbed like flotsam or rode out the gentle swell tucked against tiny stone-built quays. Each inlet boasted what the paint-manufacturers might describe as a Relaxable Turquoise colour-scheme, with rapidly Shallowing Water emerging from Obscure Obsidian and Deep-Water Dark through a stepped range of Adriatic Azure right up to Paddly Daddly as Gentle Waves lapped onto narrow and erratic strips of Gravelly Beach. (And all of this while I was supposed to be keeping my eyes on the road, I thank you.)

Onwards, ever-onwards, with our trusty not-so-low-mileage-anymore Knumptywagen issuing not one single audible squeak, moan of lassitude or cough of uncertainty as it climbed steep inclines, only to free-wheel in a high-pitched low-geared whine down any number of other-sides – continually consuming still-empty, sun-baked roads.

Michael (a local mountaineer, judging by the photos adorning the walls of his small bar-cum-site-office) had chosen the location of his site wisely, as it saved us from travelling too far and accidentally stumbling into Zadar (which subsequently turned out to be in our favour.) With a little of the afternoon left for our (and the van's) well-deserved relaxations, we brewed tea (you can take the English out of England); we lolled around a bit while being passively entertained by a local Small-Lizards-Dashing-Busily-About Show – performed exclusively for us on the border stones of our pitch; one of us swam in the sea (obviously not the Van and even more obviously, not your favourite author) and then we took a short walk along a straggling seaside footpath to the larger village of what we think was called Starigrad, (but subsequently believe this may just mean 'Old Town', as road-signage bearing this name seems to be popping up with frequent regularity.) Old Town or not, a modern snorkel-and-mask were here procured -and then tested on the return leg, to be excitedly pronounced acceptable.

We dined in-van and under-awning with the delightful smell of hot pine trees adding spice and aroma to our culinary efforts – producing a supper involving much delightful local salad produce, bolstered by a sensibly-sized chunk of smoked filet-mignon steak, previously procured.

Finally, the day's heat refused to dissipate even as the sun went down, so we spent our first uncomfortably hot night in our over-cab bed with no refreshing breeze at all to be had through our widely open, mosquito-netted windows.

Sun, Sea And . . . Sand?

Val Vidal Camp, Rovinj, Croatia

We've discovered that a four-week trip has a very different dynamic from a two-week trip in the Knumptywagen. Granted that a lot of motorhomers set off with far-more ambitious timescales than ours – but aging and expanding family, stop-at-home pets (when last investigated, you couldn't get passports for chickens and goldfish) and grass that insists on growing exponentially while we're away – are all valid reasons for limiting our self-indulgent excesses to just four weeks.

Two weeks in, we've discovered that we're beginning to relax into a slightly unreal, itinerant lifestyle where we have no pre-defined travel plan and – for the first time in four years of motorhome ownership – we really think we've joined the fraternity and understand a little about the true 'freedom of the road'.

It's also a completely different dynamic when travelling abroad. For a start, motorhomes on the 'continent' are almost as numerous as cars so there's none of this (go on, admit it – tedious) waving acknowledgement of each other in which we seem to be obliged to indulge on the tiny little island we class as home. Jeez – if we waved to very motorhome we've passed on this trip, our arms would have worn down to tiny little stumps, rendering steering and gear-changes impossible and resulting in hunched immobile shoulders for weeks. Do you see car-drivers waving as they pass each other, just because they're in similar vehicles? Nope. So, let's drop it, guys, and assume we just all like each other, OK? It'll really make for far happier journeys all round, honestly.

So, here we are, on a delightful, small (say, what, 30 pitch max?) family-run campsite just south of Rovinj in Istrian Croatia, a country where 'wild' camping isn't allowed – and (we understand) can be subject to heavy fines – consolidated by the very unequivocal road-signs which slash demonic red bands through graphic depictions of motorhomes, caravans and tents – and then advertise the '112' telephone number beneath, so miscreants can be immediately reported to the Police.

The downside of this is that the bit of Croatia we've experienced on this trip so far seems to have become homogenised into huge, sophisticated camping complexes (often incorporating a resort Hotel or two) where individual camping pitches can run into hundreds (the one we've just left boasted 577 separate pitches.) The occupants are nearly all German motorhomes, with a genteel smattering of Dutch caravans – and the sites boast upmarket toilet and shower blocks; bars; restaurants; exclusive sea frontages; beach-club style amenities including tennis courts and jet-ski hire – all accompanied with rates to match. We're not complaining – having just indulged ourselves on one such site for a couple of nights. It's just that – like so much of commerce-driven 21st century life – it's still delightful to stumble across a site which isn't guarded 24/7 by automatic barriers and a sun-wrinkled Security Guard in a hut.

And here we are. En route, we've managed to avoid similar locations in Slovenia – where two separate lakeside sites were just stuffed to absolute capacity – and as a result appeared to the casual bystander (us, on the wrong side of the barrier and the hut) to be seethingly and chaotically claustrophobic – so it can't just be a Croatian peculiarity.

So, do we identify our 'Best-Of-Trip-So-Far' site, at risk of it also becoming over-run; absorbed and amalgamated to the point that we can't find it on our next visit? Yes, we do, since we ourselves may also need to refer back to these pages at some point in the future if we want to revisit. Seemingly unpublicised, Val Vidal was just metres inland from another seemingly rammed sea-edged site – Mon Paradis, which thankfully was full when we speculatively arrived. Val Vidal instead took us in (it was getting late) and found us a spot – proving to be well-established; owner-managed; quiet; unassuming; shaded; friendly; clean and delightful, even down to the doughnut-man going door-to-door in the mornings - and having a genteel bar where they'd even let you set up a tab!

Despite naming the site, we may venture beyond Istria on future trips as the one major downside of the Istrian coast isn't widely reported: almost all of the coast has no beaches. Meaning, there's no sand – just narrow strips of pebbles and/or rocks and/or stone built jetties so it's not a hugely comfortable experience bedding down for the day by the seaside. Even diligently-laid towels can't protect pierceable flesh from sticky-out rocks – and your inflatable lilo will last minutes. So, if you've come for sun, sea and sand – the Istrian offer isn't quite as alliterative despite the warm, clear blue and almost non-tidal sea.

Croatian Camping And A Visit To The Launderette

Novigrad & Rovinj, Istria, Croatia

Heading south along the coast from Slovenia and into Croatia, we experienced a minor queue at the border (which thankfully was nothing compared to the two to three miles of traffic headed in the opposite direction) and then began to hunt for a suitable coastal campsite where we could rest our rolling tyres for a couple of days and begin to enjoy a seaside holiday.

At the first site we thus stumbled across, our innocent enquiry of a smartly-dressed Receptionist in a smartly-presented Reception was met with a smartly-wry smile (he clearly enjoyed this bit of his job) as he suggested we could indeed enjoy a pitch for a couple of nights – if we were nudists. Which we weren't. And still aren't, despite the temptation of a waterfront pitch in the shade of lofty, resinous pine trees. Onwards. As reported elsewhere, the camping sites all seemed vast, with no sign of the smaller, less sophisticated and therefore more intimate 'autokamps' of our previous experience, so we just trundled on along the coast, peering without enthusiasm through perimeter fences at acres of massed caravans; chalets and motor-homes – until, worn down by their frequency, we pulled into just such a site marginally south of Novigrad.

The Aminess Sirena Campsite had no less than 577 numbered pitches; 24-hour Reception; a resort hotel; two bar-restaurants; water sports; a tennis centre; bakery and newsagents, as well as hundreds of German-plated motorhomes and caravans. After a spot of bilingual negotiation and reassurances about dress-code, it also had us. For two nights please. For two people. No, no pets. No children. By the sea. With electricity. Clothed. Yes please. Thank-you. Hvala.

And so it was we took up camping, Croatian-style. The sun shone and it was hot. We had immediate access to the site's private beach (albeit all stone, rock and concrete underfoot); the sea was crystal-clear and full of snorkellable aquatic life; our pitch provided mottled shade and foreign neighbours all round (so no-one felt awkward about not being able to talk inconsequential bollocks to each other for ages over the perimeter hedging.)

The nearby 'miniature' walled town of Novigrad is described as a gem of the Istrian coast, but – without wanting to sound too tiresome here – almost all of them obviously are. Not quite a case of "seen one, seen 'em all" but our initial inspection of the town inspired marginal interest, as opposed to full-on, let-us-at-it enthusiasm. It was an agreeable town, compact and easily navigated, with no crucifying climb to a dominant church on a hill. We'd also espied a gently unassuming backstreet Konoba (Tavern), the Gatto Nero (Black Cat) which was just setting out tables as we cycled past and we therefore logged its existence for a possible subsequent visit.

Both campsite and Novigrad grew on us during our brief stay and we did in fact enjoy a typically Croatian meal with friendly staff on our subsequent return to Konobo Gatto Nero where rustic, slow-cooked and deeply flavoursome beef-cheeks were served with mashed potato and a rich, wine-dark gravy; goulash and gnocchi – all rounded off with a digestif of choice (as long as your choice was grappa.)

Despite the premium costs, the site was well-serviced and maintained; our pitch was perfect and we enjoyed the environment, the atmosphere and the ease of accessibility to this miniature gem on the Istrian coast - before moving onwards, ever onwards - towards Rovinj.

And is there much to say about Rovinj? Well, yes, in that it again represented a Venetian-style, maritime town – aspects of which were indeed very similar to Venice with three-storey pastel-painted terraced villas seemingly rising out of the sea, standing dominant and picturesque on the edge of the town centre. We'd initially been excited to have discovered an 'aire' within easy walking distance of the port, and even more delighted to find it had sufficient free spaces for us to park up under a bit of tree-shade, as we'd planned to remain here overnight and explore Rovinj.

It was hot. Although Rovinj was delightful, it was overly busy and very touristic with a lot of souvenir-stalls ranged alongside the harbour, so we climbed a steep path to visit the now classic Church (of St Euphemia, just in case you wanted to know) which – yes – you guessed it – dominated the town from its lofty position up a steep hill. And it really was very hot. A languid, shady lunch was the only antidote – which we enjoyed at a small pavement café on our way back down, (alarmingly on perilously slippery polished pavements where more than just us almost took a tumble) and well away from the teeming waterfront. At some point during this romantic, culinary indulgence we must have decided to do some laundry (can you tell how long we've been married, I wonder?) and thus ambled back to the Knumptywagen, via some very expensive fruit-stalls where our relaxed disposition led us to accidentally acquire some very expensive fruit.

Having somehow gleaned the location of a local launderette, we decided we'd 'done' Rovinj so moved on to the outskirts where we spent an enforced hour's wash and forty minute's tumble-drying – in the company of an Anglicised German Biker from East Grinstead, who was also 'running his smalls' and clearly hadn't been married to anyone for any time at all and, as such, just wanted to talk. He did, however, seem to understand how the launderette worked so we pretended to be his friends for as long as it took us to get our laundry done.

Prior to all this, on our route south from Novigrad to Rovinj, we'd been forced inland to circumnavigate the Limski Kanal – an impressive fjord-type natural intrusion into the coastline – where we'd also found classic road-side stalls competing to sell expensive olive oils; grappa and truffle-based products – which of course, with our still fervently relaxed disposition, we also had to purchase. This experience of the Istrian interior – coupled with the slightly disappointing lack of any sandy beaches – prompted a decision to cross the surprisingly lush and verdant landmass and see what the less-developed east coast might offer on t'other side.

This Is Where We Live!

Valamar, Otok Krk, Croatia

We shout it a lot to ourselves as we travel (as if attempting to justify and condone our extreme good fortune): "This is where we live!" which is, in essence, anywhere we choose to pull on the handbrake for more than a traffic-light's pause.

And as such, we're now sitting in the Knumptywagen, seemingly in the eye of a tremendous Croatian storm, which continues to roll around us – firing off bolts of magnesium bright flares into the sky – yet not one drop of rain has fallen – although our in-Knumptywagen Deezer music selection has been underpinned – if not actually overwhelmed – by thumping, rumbling, thunderous, sky-delivered bass-notes for the past two hours.

We're also experiencing a certain valedictory sense of fulfilment since we've found our Journey's End. Otok Krk is one of the more accessible islands making up an archipelago (had to get it in somewhere) nestled in the gulf of the Adriatic between the hanging triangle which is Istria and Croatia's 'mainland'. A chance encounter led us here, since we had no ultimate destination in mind, but a visit to a promising-looking but then disappointingly tired, end-of-season, litter-strewn campsite on the eastern shore of Istria resulted in the recommendation, so here we are.

Here? Oh, go on then. These pages – as previously mentioned – are probably the best place to record such detail, as we can then refer when we need to, without the need to wade laboriously through pages of handwritten journal notes (oh yes, we do those too!) when we need to remind ourselves for any subsequent visit. So, Skrila Sunny Camping by Camping

Adriatic out of Valamar can be found here: 45°1′7.77″N : 14°34′0.43″E

There you go. Those are the needlessly complex traditional co-ordinates for where we currently live.

Or, if you've caught up with a brilliantly simple, entertaining and ultimately very clever, potentially life-saving App, then we can be found instead at whistling.testing.undertones. The free What3Words app which generated that specific location-identifier is based on overlaying a 3m x 3m gridded framework across the entire planet's surface (I think I read that equates to 57 trillion x 3m squares) and then allocates a unique three-word identifier (from a vocabulary of only 40,000 words) to each square – thereby providing a means by which anyone with the app can locate anyone who's published their three-word location – anywhere in the world. Just thinking about the possible applications gives me a headache but also – be warned - excites me sufficiently to become a W3W bore in social situations.

So, a 'chain' campsite but a superb beachside location. Fresh; new; well-designed and laid out; thriving; virtually full; spotlessly clean; staffed by multilingual, motivated, helpful, friendly, enthusiastic staff; a beach bar; a restaurant; a supermarket; a greengrocery stall; biweekly fresh-fish van visit; a superb pitch with a view of the ocean - plus electric hook-up and even our own personal water-tap - (important features for us Knumptyers) – and all with only three weeks to go before the end of their season. Tell me, what's not to like?

And a walk of – ooh, what? 150 metres to the beach and a crystal clear, cobalt, placid sea? The beach – from a distance and in the brochure photographs – looks like bleached sand, but as you set foot on it, you realise it's pebbled. Not in the chunky way of cobble-type, anklet urning, lilo-puncturing pebbles but tiny, white stones – a bit like raw haricot and pinto beans mixed with fossilised Sugar Puffs, topped by a liberal sprinkling of real pebbles, just to allay any sense that the entire beach might be edible.

We shall stay here for many days. Well, at least until Wednesday (it's now Saturday), since we then need to head for the UK again, for appointments with excited young children who've been promised an overnight in the Knumptywagen; to celebrate both 30th and 90th birthdays in two separate locations with family and – oh yes – Calamitous, Dick-Headed-Cameron-Induced Brexit, allegedly in about six weeks' time. See – you just can't stay away from home too long.

But, just for the record, we've never stayed anywhere for more than three days – barely enough time to deploy the awning, never mind two never-used underslung scissor jack-like thingies at the rear of the vehicle, which, we understand, are called 'steadies' – designed to stop us rocking on our suspension while we live in the Knumptywagen – and which are probably so rusted from non-use, we'd never get them retracted even if we did decide to deploy. (You really needed to know all that, didn't you?)

So, we've now survived the inbound apocalyptic thunderstorm – which did indeed decide to visit its not-inconsiderable wrath upon us – in the form of marble-sized hailstones. (How can they have even fallen from the sky when the ambient temperature remains in the low-20s?) The thunder and lightning are now no longer very-very-frightening-me, although heavy rain continues to thrash noisily against the Knumptywagen roof and is forecast to continue all night – so I guess it's bedtime. Earplugs in. Night night.

The Hurrier I Go, The Behinder I Get

Srednja Vas, Bohinj, Slovenia

We realise that tomorrow we must begin the homeward leg of our Croatian Odyssey, yet the story of our trip so far still feels barely nascent. Our visit to the 'must-see' locations of Bohinj (and subsequently Bled) Lake in Slovenia had led us, by fortuitous accident, to the most wonderful motorhome 'aire' on the outskirts of a tiny village called Srednja Vas. This not only provided spectacular views up and down a verdant, mountain-edged U-shaped valley, but hard-standing; electric hook-up and a free Park & Ride minibus service back into the Windermeresque tourist resort of Bohinj. Being pioneers, we chose instead to cycle this four-point-eight kilometre winding road, getting caught on our way back in a torrential downpour which did nothing to amuse the taciturn proprietor of the village store, as we dripped our way around her tiny aisles in search of provisions for an in-Knumptywagen dinner.

We'd already dined out the night previously by walking (in gathering dusk) a short and fascinating route – flanked by tall, narrow, vertical, rustic timber-built hayracks set in open fields – to stumble upon a bustling, atmospheric outdoor restaurant ('Gostilna Pri Hrvatu', just for the record) - where we were served welcome beers, wild boar and exquisite raspberry pancakes. "5-star" it says in our journal notes and indeed, was well worthy of that accolade since we'd found it by complete accident nestling beneath the local church in a tiny, agricultural village where no other form of hospitality appeared to exist. Indeed, a couple subsequently seated within earshot of us proudly proclaimed that they'd made a special journey (from Lake Bled, some 31km distant) to sample its fare, having read about it in a guidebook. So how clever were we?

Lake Bled is also one of Slovenia's primary go-to tourist destinations (an atmospheric photograph of its undoubtedly picturesque island-church graces the cover of our Lonely Planet Guide) although we found Lake Bohinj marginally less over-developed, despite the rammed campsites from which we were turned away, clearly demonstrating the popularity of this 'lesser' destination. Our magnificently scenic inland drive from Soca to Bohinj provided steep ascents and descents; soaring mountain tops; harvested fields filling the cab with the smell of freshly cut grass (still being hand-scythed in some locations); hairpin bends aplenty and a throat-lumpingly narrow, steep-sided river gorge running alongside most of it.

Although our motorhome-specific satnav provides the confidence we lack on these sort of routes, it also reminded us to exercise a little caution when it led us from our two-night stopover at Srednja Vas. Both it (and we) were completely ignorant about a couple of temporary road signs which encroached half-way across our carriageway on the way out of the village, so we weaved past them to promptly discover they indicated that the tiny rural road ahead was closed for resurfacing. No matter, as we were swiftly offered an alternative route from our colour-keyed dash-mounted screen, which we – plus another couple of local motorists – duly followed.

As our fellow-motorists disappeared ahead of us, the cloud of dust we espied in the distance should really have alerted us as the tarmac surface suddenly gave way to a gravelled track. Satnav continued to display a route forward so on we trekked, assuming we would soon be returned to solid ground, but – of course – not a bit of it. Rounding a bend, the track suddenly climbed steeply towards a tree-flanked Y-junction and as we approached, our lumbering 3.5 tonne bulk lost traction and we slithered to an ignominious, handbrake-creaking halt. The expedition's Intrepid Navigating Troutess alighted the vehicle to see what lay ahead, only to manage (just) to flag down a speeding pick-up-trucked local about to hurtle around the junction from the opposite direction – and straight into our now groaning, anchored position.

Oh my, was he not impressed. (And who could blame him really? Suddenly finding a UK-plated Knumptywagen jammed half-way up a gravelled farm-track, miles from bloody anywhere, would be enough to have any right-minded citizen tapping the side of their head) but he was at least gracious enough to reverse off the junction, where, now witnessed by an unimpressed and impatient audience of one, we had no option but to roll backwards; take a run-up and hurtle as best we could up the track in an attempt to reach one arm of the 'Y'. Here, we'd ascertained we might then conceivably allow gravity to roll us backwards into the other of its arms, whence we could turn around and head back down the hill – back to tarmac and away from this infernal, tight-lipped and very British embarrassment.

Tyre-smoke, mud, exhaust fumes and rocks spewed into the air around us for what seemed like an eternity but we managed to reach the arm of the 'Y' – whence our audience immediately accelerated onto the track we'd just cleared and disappeared at contemptuous speed over the distant horizon. "Well, up yours too, mate" we thought, as we gently edged our now cooling tyres back towards safe haven on tarmac. Our ignominy deserved one further outing however, as – having waved a friendly farewell to our camping compatriots about 45 minutes previously – they were now to witness our mud-spattered bulk pass by the campsite again, in the same direction as previous, our eyes now studiously fixed on the road – and journey – ahead.

We didn't wave this time.

Painted Ceilings And Getting Lost On Bicycles

Ljubljana, Slovenia

We'd timed our arrival in Ljubljana, Slovenia's capital city, to coincide with their regular Friday-night summer food festival. As so often happens with large cities, we'd found an 'aire' – a simple, no frills, motorhome stopover – just within the city limits, where – for the sum of 12 euros – we could add ourselves to five allocated motorhome spaces, considerately provided (we assume) by the city council. And we were the sixth to arrive. Undaunted as we have become by this type of unfortunate circumstance, we just parked up anyway since the location was a municipal carpark with plenty of spaces – the occupants of the surrounding offices and light industrial units having clearly all pushed off early to fill their faces at the food festival.

We were greeted almost immediately by an English-speaking fellow camper, reeking of alcohol and tobacco, who stumbled out of an aged Belgian-plated motorhome, to suggest we had parked too far away from the thoughtfully-provided, municipal electric hook-up – to which, he slurred in impeccable English, 'we were bloody entitled to' as part of our fee.

Staying for one night doesn't necessitate such an umbilical, so we graciously declined his suggestion that we just park transversely across three spaces in front of what were evidently roller-shutter doors to one of the surrounding industrial units. Our considerate English reserve was subsequently thus rewarded by a huge German-plated motorhome which arrived soon after and simply did exactly that, with little apparent consideration for any potential consequences – but enabled them to plug-in and draw down on their share of valuable, all-inclusive Slovenian electricity.

Anyway. To market. Bikes were speedily unracked; a passing native provided pointed directions to the city-centre and off we set; a swift and busy cycle-laned trip (mostly on segregated pavements) into the beating heart of Ljubljana. Leaving our bikes on the threshold, having weaved our way along pedestrianised riverbanks we found the food-festival in full swing, thronged to immovability with rows of steaming food stalls creating narrow alleys of enthusiastic foodies.

Given our 45-plus years of soon-to-be-curtailed Europeanisation, it shouldn't have been surprising that the types of food on offer didn't really differ greatly from that experienced back in the UK so – apart from the fascination that was the horse-burger stand (from which your favourite author was – some would say – ignominiously dragged away), we decided to seek alternative sustenance elsewhere in the capital.

En-route, we paid a visit to the Cathedral, intrigued by hordes of guided tour groups gathered outside formidably huge, closed doors, carved and embellished with saintly scenes. As such, the Cathedral itself appeared closed but just around the corner, another set of doors – this time bearing a startlingly powerful bas-relief of a cluster of priestly faces all seemingly cast in burnished metal – opened at the tentative touch of a probing pilgrim, so we followed suit.

Painted interiors spread from wall-murals up across the domed and vaulted ceilings where the depiction of heavenly goings-on was so ornate that the shrouded garbs of the fervent participants had the appearance of twisted seaweed – and was absolutely transfixing. Which I guess was its worthy purpose when it was conceived and painted, in the early eighteenth century. Gothic Baroque would perhaps best describe the ornate interior, belied by its fairly uninspiring exterior (apart from the doors).

We guessed that the Sistine Chapel might need to up its game a little since – despite it attracting the weight of global painted-ceiling publicity – the Cathedral Church of Saint Nicholas, Ljubljana gets our vote in that particular category.

We enjoyed a beer at a pavement café; were turned away from several pavement restaurants (it's Friday night – do you not have a reservation?) until one middle-of-the-road location (literally in the middle of the road) – Güjžina – found us a table from where we enjoyed more beer coupled with Slovenian specialities based on goulash and calf's liver to sustain our ride home.

Dark had fallen in the meantime but we were well-lit and knew where we'd parked, so our cycle back through still-thrumming streets shouldn't really have got us that lost, should it? Google Maps saved us from ourselves as we cycled through a busy bus-station for the second time and we eventually reached the security and safety of the Knumptywagen, patiently awaiting our return like a bored but faithful dog.

Thankfully, we were able to get the bikes quietly re-racked on the back of the Knumptywagen without attracting the attention of Drunken Smoky Belgian across the way and thus retired silently to our carpark bed, having felt we'd done justice to Ljubljana or - at the very least - to most of its outskirts.

The Slovenian Coast

Koper, Fiesa & Piran, Istria, Slovenia

Having now travelled what we considered to be a goodly chunk of interior, our plan had always been to travel the Slovenian coast - which beckoned in the form of a short strip of seaboard just 27 miles long. Koper (renamed in Slovenian from the far-more poetically Italian 'Capodistria') was a 65-mile journey from Ljubljana and lay just south of Trieste. It commanded a position of seemingly no strategic worth whatsoever as Slovenia's northernmost coastal city but having found a large car-park on the outskirts of what turned out to be its rock-strewn sea-side, we cycled in to explore an unpromoted 'old town' interior. It was very hot. The Old Town was very small. We took some photos. We cycled back. And then drove on.

Now, Piran was a slightly different platter of seafood. Much publicised as being a well preserved, historic, Venetian-styled coastal port and well worth our time, we felt a visit necessary but couldn't find – despite copious research – any Piran-based motorhome friendly sites. What did pop up was the nearby small resort of Fiesa, where a campsite appeared to exist and towards which we made due haste.

Our timing was perfect as – not having booked a pitch – we arrived at one p.m. to accidentally coincide with a 12 noon check-out time, so a warm and friendly welcome awaited us; we were ushered through a locked barrier and assumed prime position in a small campsite of about twelve motorhomes, with a view to the sea across a couple of hundred metres of grassy parkland, already littered with sun-bathing families. A couple of café-bars, a beach volleyball court and a small, unobtrusive shower-block added to the jumbled people-watching opportunity, so we deployed our awning; laid out the reclining chairs;

hung out a newly acquired drying line (every good motorhome should have one) and declared ourselves ensconced and established for as long as we wanted to be there. With the sun still shining bright, we then strolled across to a narrow shingle beach and plunged ourselves into the surprisingly warm(ish) waters of the Adriatic.

It turned out that Piran was but a short walk on a coastal path around a promontory immediately accessible from our beach, so the following day – having lazed assiduously for most of it – we 'dressed for dinner' (meaning a change of shorts and T-shirts) and ambled around the point. Well, yes, Piran is indeed an attractive little town, with a classic, central harbour; narrow rambling alleys and lanes dotted with interesting, bohemian shops and a rather strikingly large central square (allegedly created by filling in the former harbour.) Above all this, a gurt big church stood sentinel, not really noticed until our journey home, when it provided a spectacular illuminated backdrop to the thriving town square.

A refreshing beer in still-strong early-evening sunshine was taken at the Theatre Bar on the harbourside before tracking down a restaurant "tucked a little away from the main tourist drag" where "this fine little place doesn't mess with the basics . . . fresh seafood . . . nicely cooked and served with a smile." Which it was. Although displayed photographic images of the dishes on offer can be a bit of a turn-off, in this particular instance, the mixed seafood platter looked (and sounded) well worth our attention. With the rocking prows of moored vessels nodding gently not fifty yards away down a side-street, who were we to argue with the journalistic might of the Lonely Planet Guide to Slovenia, or indeed with the chef of the slightly uninspiringly named Gostilna Park restaurant.

A gentle stroll led us back to the Knumptywagen through the bustling town and along the coastal path but in the dark now so thankfully avoiding our earlier bizarre viewing of a completely naked elderly gentleman enjoying the impetus given to a certain part of his anatomy by throwing small pebbles into the sea – presumably as a perverse form of local entertainment (mainly for him, we guessed.) And so to bed.

Baleful Grey And A Dose Of Sunshine

Bale, Istria, Croatia

The Croatian village of Bale wasn't on our main tourist map – although there's no doubt of its rise through the league tables to become so, despite its near proximity to absolutely no part of the coast. In fact, as a metaphorical pencilled note in a margin, it sits 14 kilometres inland from Rovinj and therefore accidentally lay on our route eastwards across Istria towards Tunarica campsite at Ra'a.

It had a large, almost-empty surface carpark with easy access so we stopped. It was mid-morning, the day's heat hadn't taken hold so we wandered into the village centre, via a church into which, as is our wont, we entered. In the cool, warm grey sandstone interior a meek-looking tattooed woman greeted us although it was some moments before we realised we were expected to pay an entry fee, despite a complete lack of any signage to that effect. Given that the fee per head amounted to about 50p, we paid it, still not sure if our tattooed verger was genuine or had just hit on a clever, indoor revenue-generating scheme from which to fund a second forearm or perhaps a spot of inking-in.

Whatever. A fascinating yet seemingly un-curated array of ancient stonework was gently illuminated to provide a delightful but incomprehensible display of vernacular religious architecture. Fragmentary pieces of presumed medieval arch were positioned to represent the whole while chunks of truncated fluted pillars stood sentinel around the perimeter. Upstairs, a full-blown church offered itself as further evidence of an earlier era's commitment to Christianity – ornately carved dark-timbered confessionals echoing the stone pillars below.

The village itself continued the warm-grey stone theme with gentle alleyways offering up intriguing views into other people's lives, their homes laid open through front doors left beguilingly ajar or to be glimpsed through netted windows. A small pavement café seemed to provide the only hospitality and we squeezed our way in to a tiny, wobbly table where refreshments were duly provided. Bale's indefinable spell was eventually broken by a bunch of English cyclists chatting amicably but noisily on the next table and with due regards, we retraced our steps past the church to the patient Knumptywagen and continued our journey across Istria.

Our targeted campsite at Tunarica suffered a little in our initial appraisal since our arrival coincided with a torrential thunderstorm accompanied with a drop in temperature and a dark grey clouding of the sky. Even after our welcome at Reception (and relief that we could remain clothed during our stay) the site failed to pick itself up from an end-of-season, down-at-heel, slightly uncared-for look and feel. Litter speckled the perimeter of several pitches and our view of the sea through tall, carousing pine trees was a disappointment as a wind-whipped bay vacillated with moored pleasure boats and not much else.

Swimming from the small, untidy beach was out of the question and our attempted walk along a rocky shoreline path proved a dead-end, which imposed a retrace of our steps to an uncharacteristic afternoon spent in the company of Tim Robbins and Morgan Freeman, who joined us in our gale-rocked Knumptywagen for a spell in Shawshank prison, which became a bit of a metaphor for our slight sense of weather-induced despondency.

The campsite restaurant also boasted an end-of-term tiredness, with a surfeit of bored waiting staff serving up mediocre fare, of which we partook that evening with as much enthusiasm as it deserved – and resolved that tomorrow we'd move onwards, rather than yet turn towards home.

And so we did. Settling our bill the following morning, whilst bemoaning the unexpected bad weather (as only Brits on holiday can do), the Receptionist offered a suggestion about a 'sister' site, some way distant on the Croatian island of Krk, which she thought would still be open and was, she'd heard, in an idyllic beachside location – with better weather.

It was.

Skrila Sunny Camping, lodged discreetly on the Krk coastline between Punat and Stari Baska has already featured elsewhere in these tales, but elements of it needed a little more reflection, mainly because it provided a sought-after 'holiday by the sea' and – in contrast to the Tunarica site – offered lively, agreeable and enjoyable facilities. Live music in the beachside bar; a thriving restaurant offering seafoods served by just one bustling, committed and enthusiastic waiter; a delightful pitch with a view of the bay and not 150 metres walk to the beach. It was here we enjoyed delicious, stolen, finger-tingling, creamy afternoon dozes in the sunshine and where overhead, in the middle of the brightest of sun-seared days, the sky was so densely azure-blue, you believed you could see ephemeral stars in it – reproducing the optical intrigue of an optician's field test.

The early-afternoon heat also created air thin enough for the engine noise from jet aircraft passing stratospherically overhead to scythe its way earthwards like a skein of sound falling through a shimmering nothingness to our slumbering ears, as we dozed; relaxed; read; swam and sun-bathed for four glorious days.

And so it was, that by happy accident, this delightful campsite became our turnaround point, when we eventually packed up our spread-eagled outdoor chairs and table, rewound the awning and set off back north across the spectacular island bridge onto the Croatian mainland.

GSBT 1: Sveti Rok 4

Zadar/Zagreb, Dalmatia, Croatia

The prospect of travelling via the Grand St. Bernard Tunnel through the European Alps had always appealed and although this ambition became viable on the outbound leg of our trip to Montenegro, I'm embarrassed to admit that – as we travelled on our homebound journey through Croatia northwards from Zadar towards Zagreb – our tunnelling experiences far outshone any romanticised notion of the GSBT.

Having effectively bypassed Zadar, our route continued on an all-new, barely unwrapped and very shiny A1/E65 dual carriageway which began climbing towards the awe-inspiring mountains of the Velebit range, honeycombed with road-tunnels, each of which appeared after almost every sweeping, inclined bend. And as if Croatia's finest civil engineers were keen to prove a point, these impressive tunnels were accompanied by similarly jaw-dropping viaducts of scare-inducing height.

Our intrepid journey along this particular stretch of motorway was made even more so by the quickly developing gale-force wind which had sprung up as we climbed higher. Gantry signs flashed graphic warnings at our high-sided vehicle as we emerged from one tunnel onto a huge, arcing and perilously high viaduct which crossed the neck of a wide, white wave flecked sea-strait and lagoon below us.

The motorway's indicator windsock bulged and buckled at its post – almost tearing from its mounting as we passed – by which time we were down to 30-k.p.h., having to wrestle with the Knumptywagen's seemingly-possessed steering wheel. Plucky caravanners and all those lucky motorists towing oversized powerboats were forced to crawl in jittery convoy in the (very) slow lane, as their expensive appendages swayed alarmingly and alternately inwards towards the concrete parapet and then outwards again as we edged past.

Respite from the wind was only achieved once inside a tunnel, each of which was individually named (alongside undoubtedly proud Constructor's branding) but the most telling attribute to the engineers' skills were the signboards announcing each tunnel's length. GSBT, eat your heart out! We actually lost count of the number of tunnels which were either its equal – or indeed longer – in terms of kilometres travelled underground. Even the Sveti Rok tunnel pipped the GSBT by a couple of hundred metres in length and (we later noted) was far better value since the road-toll had cost much less – and we'd enjoyed a whole lot of smooth extra miles plus lots of crosswind induced nerve-twisting excitement thrown in for free.

Dubrovnik Welcomes Us

Dubrovnik, Dalmatia, Croatia

We reach Dubrovnik having crossed the Croatian border with sufficient passengers on board to justify a raised eyebrow or two in the Customs shed.

With a family holiday in Montenegro now sadly behind us, we had agreed to give four adult family members a lift to their extended stay in Dubrovnik as we headed north on our route homewards. So it was that from our small Knumptywagen passenger window, the Chief Navigating Officer leaned out to hand a bemused Border guard a wad of six passports.

"These people are all with you?" he enquired, thankfully in English, then went on to ask if we were all staying in the van – which could clearly only just seat the bulky six of us, let alone accommodate us all for a fortnight's holiday.

"Yes" we glibly replied, the lie acknowledging that it would take far too long to explain the true reasons - and through we sailed, leaving our Border guard bemused and most likely astonished at the claustrophobic living conditions these English must endure.

Our passengers are thus delivered to an out-of-town self-catering location which enjoyed no vehicular access whatsoever. With little option, we park precariously on a fearsome adverse camber at the side of what appears to be a major through-route; disgorge our passengers, manhandling their bulky luggage out through the toilet window, this unlikely area having provided the only available storage area for four grown-up suitcases.

Waving fond farewells, we re-join the flowing traffic and head back towards Dubrovnik's walled old town where we manage to parallel-park on a side-street and set off to explore.

The relatively recent reality of the Yugoslavian conflict in the early nineties, in which this UNESCO World Heritage city became an embattled strategic centrepiece, is starkly represented by a large wall-mounted graphic plan which identifies the individual location and type of damage caused by the explosive conflict between the resident Croatians and the Yugoslav Peoples' Army – noting where each bomb or missile landed; the damage caused and the subsequent rebuilding which restored the city to its current status.

This jewel in the Adriatic Mediterranean is now overrun with warriors of a different type: tourists, many of whom disembark en-masse from the bowels of humungous cruise liners and storm the narrow streets, pillaging the gift-shops and overwhelming the field kitchens – now masquerading as restaurants and cafes – and whose only defence against this swarming tide of nationalities seemed to be to charge extortionate prices for their fare. Joining the melee, we are provided with a striking and memorable walk through narrow streets, rammed with restaurants, bars and boutique-style shops. As such, it wasn't until we paid our 150 Croatian kunas and clambered up onto the high, wide and defensive ramparts above the chaotic and close-crammed terracotta rooftops that we gained any true form of perspective of this historic Balkan stronghold.

As we ourselves became part of the multi-national throng marvelling at the complexity of rooftop views from our walled circuit, an American family strolled by, gaping (as we all were) in amazement at the pan-tiled panorama. As they passed, one of the children could be heard, with astute political incorrectness, enquiring of his parents "Hey, is this part of Trump's wall?"

Despite the wonders and marvels of this mediaeval city, our Knumptywagen experience of Dubrovnik left a little to be desired, but it is a bustling city so we counted ourselves lucky when we eventually found a semi-dubious overnight parking spot under an inner-city flyover. Falling just short of this was a small, ramshackle industrial estate where we eventually decided to claim what felt like a slightly safer car-parking space – it being Sunday and the offices were clearly not occupied. However, we'd overlooked the enthusiasm of working Croatians when we were woken from fitful slumbers at five a.m. by the sound of slamming car-doors. And as someone tried to shoehorn their car into the adjacent space reduced in width by our bulky overhang, we decided we'd had our fill of Dubrovnik and, with blinds still drawn, we did a very swift pyjamaed flit out of the car-park and onto the open road again, northbound in soft, very early-morning light.

Malfeasance In Austria's Second City

Graz, Styria, Austria

In Graz, between the hours of 18:00 – 23:00 hrs on any weekday, it's a prosecutable offence to be seen on the streets if you're not in visible possession of either an oversize ice cream cornet or a bicycle.

Thankfully, the offence is very rarely enforced so we felt confident enough to break this particular European Union Directive as we wandered around Austria's second largest city in excited and wondrous amazement. And if we had to recommend a motorhome-friendly campsite to facilitate such a visit, then Reisemobil-Stellplatz Graz must be at the top of our list.

As highly qualified (but obviously not fully paid-up) cheapskates, we'd originally planned to stopover in an 'aire' catalogued as being close to Graz city centre. Our plans were thwarted when this turned out to be a down-at-heel industrial estate better suited as a TV location for a Scandi-noir gangland showdown. Onward then to our fall-back selection, a little way out of town which turned out to be extremely agreeable.

This beautiful, well-established, tree-shaded site was adjoined by a huge, attractive outdoor swimming pool – to which we would be granted free admission once we signed in for our one-night stopover. Access to the City centre? Yes, a bus ride away, from a stop within a short walk of the site. Just pick your spot, park up and let me know which one you've chosen, our genial gentleman receptionist informed us, in clipped but otherwise perfectly colloquial English.

So, we did. Due to our newly adopted regime of travelling during the mornings, we'd arrived as the sun was casting welcome shadows into the early afternoon's heat and our selected herb-fringed pitch provided both welcome shade and a view of the gently bustling swimming pool. With little hesitation we collected swimming gear and set off through the site towards the pool, grappling with both a keen sense of anticipation and a matched pair of cumbersome sun-loungers.

Lawned surrounds; a poolside café; ice-cream pavilion; toddlers' pool and a liberal scattering of sun-tanning bodies distracted us momentarily from the artificial islands, the wooden walkways and the distant diving platform all set in the informal, infinity-edged clearwater pool. What amazed us even more was the bottom of the pool itself, which was completely pebbled to provide a delightful finishing touch to this very stylish lido.

We also realised that the indistinct trail of specks in the middle-distance of the main pool were actually newly post-natal mallards, navigating their broods of bumble-bee-costumed ducklings between the earnest, rubber-capped lengthers and the eagerly-thrashing pubescent youths, besporting themselves for the benefit of laughing companions.

The sun shone. We harvested envious glances as we gracefully reclined in our sun loungers, our toned* bodies glistening with sun-lotion. We swam (yes, even your esteemed author deigned to enter the water – I've never swum with ducklings before); we lazed; we read our books and generally unwound (although from what, I've really no idea, as we'd been far too relaxed for the past three weeks, but it does sound busily impressive, does it not?)

And in between hazed bouts of dozing through the glorious weekday afternoon, we sketchily planned an evening bus ride into the lawless centre of Graz, where the cyclists and ice-cream shops were assumedly already doing their bit to challenge wholly fictional EU law enforcement.

**not necessarily*

The Number 32 To Graz

Graz, Styria, Austria

I guess I had a sheltered and privileged upbringing, as bus travel never really featured in my childhood development – and neither has it much since. That's probably the main reason for the anxiety I feel when the prospect of bus travel arises. Whether and when it would turn up; how to know which bus would take you to your destination; how to know when to get off; what ticket to ask for; what loose change is needed to placate the driver; what happens if I get the wrong one? There were always too many variables for my liking – and it made for uneasy travel.

Such was the case as we stood at a bus-stop outside our campsite, it being too far to cycle into the city of Graz itself – although the camp receptionist (surely that doesn't sound quite right?) had given us full instructions – so it shouldn't be that difficult, should it?

At 7-p.m., the only other occupant of the bus-shelter was an interestingly proportioned woman with a fag on, who very pointedly turned her back on us (but thankfully didn't waggle her Brexit foot) and we were gradually joined by a growing queue of other passengers, shuffling not into line to gain the best seats but instead trying to find patches of shade to avoid the blinding and still hot evening sun lowering in a cloudless sky. Our anxious anticipation was that Bus Number 32 would transport us cleanly and simply straight into the centre of Graz and despite the first one sailing ignorantly past us, the next soon arrived onto which we gratefully clambered.

Seemingly the only passengers paying a cash fare (all of two euros each), we were delighted to find that the trip was indeed a straightforward linear journey with active monitors in the bus ceiling displaying both the whole route as well as each stop (also pre-announced by a Siri soundalike) so we realised we would therefore be transported to our chosen destination with no fear of never being seen again.

So it was that we alighted (excuse the bus jargon, feeling quite an expert now) onto Jacobinski Platz in the centre of Austria's second city, Graz, where we were immediately handed a well-written tourist guide and city map by a uniformed bus-marshall. (How did she know to give us the English version – was it the rather fetching shorts we're wearing, perhaps?) and off we wandered into the heart of Graz. Thankfully, our disassociation with giant ice-cream cones or bicycles went unnoticed by law-enforcement, and we therefore avoided arrest.)

Graz was delightful. We wandered undulating streets, one minute flat pavement, the next precipitous cobbles with plein-air dining on cleverly-stepped wooden decks running down (or up) the middle of these narrow thoroughfares. A calm bustle of busyness prevailed; patient parents gently force-feeding alien pasta into the recalcitrant mouths of suspicious toddlers; young couples staring over menu-tops into each other's eyes, him agitated with nerves as tonight was clearly the night to pop the question (or maybe he was just engineering a less-committed late night preceded by coffee back at hers); middle-aged marrieds eating disinterestedly and looking diligently past each other between every mouthful; dating, tattooed same-sex couples not sure who should pick up the tab – and old people (like us) trying not to stare while stealthily watching for any signs of imminent bill-payment so we could bag a table and feed our own faces.

We wandered the old town. A large church of cathedralesque proportions was locked against us while stylish classy shops selling handbags and fashion rubbed shoulders with grocery, nougat, ice-cream and bicycle hire outlets. Café-bars and restaurants proliferated, each seeming too busy for us to even enquire about a table, until suddenly everything became quiet, green and open-spaced, as if we'd walked across an invisible border into upmarket parkland. As we stopped to consult our very obvious 'Look, We're Tourists – Mug Us or Offer Directions, You Choose' map, a lovely lady towing two small children on scooters stopped and tried to mug us. (Only kidding. She clearly wasn't Brexit-conscious, so was unaware what dicks our slim democratic majority had been and therefore instead treated us with an amiable, patronising kindness.) Witnessing our emaciated faces and bloated, starvation-evident bellies, she directed us back towards a bit of the old town we hadn't yet discovered, and with 'Glockenspiel Square' ringing in our ears, we wandered back the way we had come, past the Church-Maybe-Cathedral and turned, as directed, down another cobbled incline beside it.

Had we opted to consult our beautifully produced Dorling Kindersley Guide To Almost All Of Europe prior to setting out (a wonderful tome but just a little too bulky to cart about on a romantic evening in Graz) we'd have already been aware of the existence of this delightful restauranted square. Fortuitously, our later arrival meant that an outdoor table was immediately available and so we sat, ordered beer and savoured both the atmosphere and our expectations.

Our waiter – wearing regulation braced leather shorts and an associated beard – recommended a couple of typical Austrian dishes from the menu which we were quickly to enjoy: breast of pork stuffed with potato and apple, served with a light caraway jus and shredded cabbage salad, while my companion enjoyed skillet-served chicken thigh fillets in a powerful paprika, tomato and white-bean sauce accompanied with baked potato and sour cream. Oh my! Now hopelessly overfull, we were sadly unable to even consider the giant ice creams we'd promised ourselves.

Unfortunately, the giant Glockenspiel clock above us was silenced after six p.m., so we weren't able to witness the emergence of the two automated figurines from little arched doors, who – assumedly on the hour – would have approached each other in a shy, clockworky sort of way; looked wordlessly over each other's shoulders and then retired, each silently wishing they'd either popped the question or picked up the bill.

Bus 32 duly returned us from whence we came, where we loaded our fat little tummies into the Knumptywagen, clambered our nursery-like ladder up-above-the-cab-so-high and slept the sleep of renegades, dreaming of running from the law, sans ice-creams or bicycles.

Good Morning Awning

Winzer, Deggendorf, Germany

We're so often 'on the move' and rarely stay in any one location long enough to 'make camp' – so the Omnistor wind-out awning attached to the side of the Knumptywagen doesn't often get to see the light of day.

It was therefore a rare treat to wind it out and enjoy a warm summer's evening during a one-night-stand at a small site close to Winzer in the parish of Deggendorf, Germany. A morning's worth of travelling meant we could enjoy a full afternoon exploring the surrounding wide arable valley of the River Danube, which flowed close by, as we were told by our motorhoming British neighbours. They knew this because they'd spent the last nine years cycling along it – not (as I'm sure you've realised) – continuously, but as an ongoing year-on-year retirement project, moving onwards every summer as their annual journeys progressed.

In passing conversation, they also pointed us towards a hidden but highly agreeable swimming lake, where we enjoyed a refreshing dip during our exploratory cycle ride, before returning to the Knumptywagen – where we set about enjoying an evening under the awning.

It was here, in the gloaming, that we were also visited by a newly arrived and socially gregarious German neighbour, who had spotted our GB numberplate and consolidated our national stereotype by arriving with three cups of freshly-brewed tea as a means of introduction. Again, our lack of any language-skills (other than Brummy-with-a-taint-of-Scouse) would have been embarrassing - had we found any gap in the 'conversation' into which we might have interjected. In perfect English, our new visitor, Linda, volubly explained how she and her husband had been travelling for 12 hours non-stop (from which we could only deduce that they'd clearly not spoken to each other for the last 11) and she had tales to tell. Tea was slurped; a pair of small dogs was fetched for our admiration; family history was expounded and stories of past visits to the UK were retold.

At one point, husband sheepishly came to find her; was universally ignored and eventually roamed off again, excusing himself by saying he had to dry his hair. So, by the time Linda and her dogs took their leave, night had fallen and we opted to pack up as best we could to facilitate another of our speedy early-morning flits onward to pastures new.

Table and chairs were cleared, cycles were racked – all in a swift, efficient and now well-practiced waltz, which sadly ground to an unexpected halt when we tried to retract the awning.

Click, click, click. Lots of winding-type noises accompanied very little in the way of winding -type action, as the damn thing stubbornly refused to be wound back in. It would happily continue to wind out with ease but when we tried to retract it, it continued to click as if it was slipping a cog.

Cursory inspection exposed nothing – other than my sad delight in being able to don a headtorch, kept onboard for just such an emergency (and used about as often as the neglected awning) so we optimistically decided it would have sorted itself out by morning and retired to bed. Here we were able to contemplate the irony of our situation, where – after almost 3,000 miles of travelling – during which the mechanical and myriad complexities of our 10-year-old Fiat Ducato engine faltered not once – we were now rendered completely immobile by a failed sunshade.

The following morning, the camp-site's wobbly aluminium stepladder was extracted from a nearby hedge and closer inspection of the winding mechanism ensued. With very little in the way of visible mechanics, we tried various methods of retraction, until the Engineering Navigating Chief Petty Officer suggested I apply screwdriver leverage while she wound the winding handle. Click, stop, click, grunt, click and little by little the awning disappeared back into its casing. Stifling an overwhelmingly British desire to cheer loudly (not done at this time of the morning, old boy) we celebrated by taking breakfast under an open sky, packed up and slipped our moorings to get back on the road.

Further investigation once home resulted in the whole 3m-long awning being removed from the Knumptywagen (2-man job, unwieldy and surprisingly heavy – that's the awning, not us); the business-end being thereby dismantled and a new, nifty-looking, solids state manual gearbox ordered off t'internet. Fully exposed awning fabric laboriously scrubbed on the lawn (until we discovered a highly effective bleach-mould spray which will simply add to the sorry state of our parched grass as it's rinsed off) and a glimmer of hope that it'll all go back on again in the right order.

We Taste Some (More) Wine And Cycle Around Sangatte

Sangatte, Pas-de-Calais, France

It should be noted that during our homebound journey northwards, we did actually stop overnight at a small campsite at Val-de-Vesle, near-enough midway between Dijon and Calais. It too was supposed to be flanked by a river which turned out to be a disappointingly fluid free and over-brambled ditch.

There was nearby, in its stead, a dirty-great industrial-sized canal as straight as a very dull accountant, along the side of which we cycled, with massive grain-stores as the only landmarks in this featureless agricultural prairie. We were quietly in search of (as – it has been whispered – we always are) a quiet, thirst-slaking hostelry, tavern, bar or pub. Since this was rural France, none of these options were forthcoming and we instead returned unfulfilled by any hint of hospitality (or indeed humanity) to the Knumptywagen. Here we allowed ourselves a peaceful night and set off northbound again, feeling holier-than-thou for having indulged in some semi-strenuous exercise. (On the bikes, thank you, and not during the peaceful night, OK?)

Yet again, with our new-found, emergent campsite confidence, we'd researched a site at Sangatte, just outside Calais – and it was to this we were headed for our final overnight stop on foreign soil. Beforehand, in amongst the fervent camp-site research, we'd also accidentally identified a potential wine-hypermarket in Calais which we felt duty-bound to visit, never having indulged in any form of 'booze-cruise' experience before.

The most striking feature of our chosen outlet – the imaginatively and memorably named Calais Wine Superstore – was the large Tasting Room into which we initially wandered, somewhat in awe at how such a facility could be so devoid of supervision nor any form of access control whatsoever. The owners, it appeared, were similarly from our Sceptred Isle (which might also explain the Northern Irish accent cashing us out on departure) and they had seen fit to install a large circular standing-height table on which was provided a wide range of opened wines, all available for help-yourself, free, DIY tasting. Which we began to do.

"Oh, my word, you're English" spoke an authoritarian, well-educated and vaguely tobaccoed voice from the other side of the table. "Where are you from?" Slightly bemused by our response of "Croatia" we engaged in conversation with this benign gentlemen, who was accompanying his Gastro-Pub-In-Surrey-Owning-Son to buy "wines for the business. We do it about 10 times a year" he pronounces, proprietorially pouring himself yet another very large glass of red and waving the bottle hospitably in our direction. "My wife really enjoys this one. Look, it's £4.99 a bottle – marvellous value!" he proffers, his now slightly dubious pouring technique evidencing just how much tasting he'd actually done. We back gracefully out into the main store in search of anything under £3.99 – just for a sense of one-upmanship.

Less than fifteen minutes up the road, Sangatte surprised us. With a dubious reputation gained from the installation of a refugee camp here in 1999, it was a pleasing, sleepy-looking and innocent little town with many similarities to the small, unassuming coastal towns on the opposite shore of La Manche. Our campsite was a mix of residential chalets and a wind-blown handful of European campers, presumably also 'in transit' and thankfully without refugee status. Yet.

The beach was also surprisingly inspiring of our awe. Wide, flat and tide-washed sand was backed by a benign sea upon which plied many ferries, glinting like beacons in the light of a still-bright lowering sun. Tall denuded forested groynes stood in silent patient rows right along the beach, in an eerie homage to the lines of troops who must have awaited anxious evacuation from similarly wide, sandy beaches a little further to the east of our current position – over 75 years previous.

On a lesser road through the town and indeed, almost on its outer edge, a little local (and entertainingly named) restaurant – Le Blanc Nez – appeared to be open, through whose dingly-belled door we tentatively entered. "Bonsoir Monsieurdame, une table pour deux?" to which we mutely nodded, swallowing our previously rehearsed opening gambit in the face of impressive local linguistic capabilities. Comfortably full of smiling regulars, many of whom nodded an international greeting (weighted with pity for our Brexit-induced sense of awkwardness), we were efficiently seated and menus presented.

"Excuse-moi, erm, Madame, s'il vous plait? Quelle est le plat du jour?" enquires your favourite wordsmith, as a result of which we smiled and nodded innocently as our matronly, bustling waitress machine-gunned us with what was, no doubt, a mouth-watering description of the finest dish to have ever emerged from her table de cuisine. Not one sound, not one syllable, not one word was either recognisable or intelligible to us and while fellow diners smirked with Gallic discretion into their napkins at our amusing plight, we reverted to type and pointed at stuff we thought sounded edible from the menu.

Joking apart, the food was wonderful; very French, stylistically presented but unpretentiously homely in both its flavours and portion size. Un coupe de champagne celebrated our last night 'on the continent' and then a huge black enamelled pot of steaming Moule Mariniere avec les frites for my companion while a decent slab of beautifully cooked cod in a shellfish sauce graced my side of the table complete with mixed vegetables steamed to al dente perfection. A wonderfully pallid and therefore clearly home-made crème caramel was shared between us, while the lady on our neighbouring table grappled with an 'ooh-lala' énorme plat du profiteroles which were, collectively, very definitely bigger than her head. 'Very tres bonne' say our subsequent journal notes and indeed it all very was. A short cycle ride back to the Knumptywagen for a nightcap followed by an undisturbed night on a campsite in Sangatte prior to our return to the UK – where we are doubtless soon to become European outcasts in our own right.

PART SIX

A Game of Three Halves – Italy, France, Italy

"Day after day, day after day,
we stuck nor breath nor motion
As idle as a painted ship upon a painted ocean
Water, water everywhere
and all the boards did shrink
Water, water everywhere
nor any drop to drink."

Samuel Taylor Coleridge
1772 – 1834
The Rime Of The Ancient Mariner

Searching For Stanley

Lichfield, Staffordshire, England – and beyond

If you haven't yet come across Stanley Tucci, American-Italian actor, director, writer, presenter, amateur chef and Londoner, you'd best strap-in because you're about to become acquainted.

His BBC TV series, Searching for Italy, is a sumptuous foody tour of Italy's 20 regions, from Piedmont in the north, where the country's thickest bit (geographically speaking) melds itself to France and Switzerland; borders with Germany, Liechenstein, Austria and Slovenia and then heads all the way down to the Puglian heel and across to the Mediterranean islands of Sicily and Sardinia.

And we had a Knumptywagen lying idle.

Our plan? We didn't really have one. We thought we'd try to retrace at least some of Stanley's visits to various Italian eateries, necessitating a repeat-wallow in his TV series on iPlayer, ostensibly to make notes of those locations but instead discovering that a fellow author – one Melanie Renzulli (guising as italofile.com) – had already done all the legwork.

Your humble author had also recently enjoyed an exceptional evening in His company at Kensington's Royal Albert Hall, no less, where Stanley delivered an amusingly entertaining chat with friend and fellow actor Hayley Atwell live on stage. Admittedly, it might have been a slightly oversized venue for such a performance, but an audience of 4,000 people didn't diminish the sense of intimacy and insight into a life less ordinary.

So now a tunnel crossing is booked; France will be gently traversed in the general direction of Nice where we hope to turn left; negotiate a sunny and reassuringly expensive Cote d'Azur and penetrate our objective through Menton on the coastal border.

Once in Italy, our world will hopefully become our very own edible marine bivalve and we shall trundle semi-aimlessly along meandering coastlines; through sun-warmed olive groves and vineyards; visit artful cities and mediaeval walls; beaches; markets; galleries; rolling countryside and witness speleothems of backlit poplars spiking distant horizons.

There is, however, a developing navigational plot that an approach from Lyon towards Turin may be a better tactic, leading us through Bra (oh joy!); Alba; Alessandria and Piacenza towards Parma, Modena and Bologna to the Adriatic coast at Rimini, then backtracking through Florence to Pisa and up the Mediterranean seaboard via Genoa as we head for home again. And therein lies the true beauty of Knumptydom – we can decide where and how we go, as we go, and do as much or as little as we damn well please.

Advance preparations for the trip? Well, your optimistic author signed up for a beginner's course in conversational Italian – 10 live online lessons which simply reminded me that I had aptitude for neither educational retention nor any language-skills beyond my native own. A long-suffering local tutor, Mariagrazia, bore my ineptitude with startling patience and forza d'animo (look it up, I'm afraid I had to) although I can now greet her proficiently when we meet. In English, mostly.

We studied roadmaps and a charity-shop Italian Guidebook from 2019, with neither any great dedication nor seriousness. We also signed up to what we hope will become our 'go-to' destination management services: Agricamper Italy and ACSI Europe, the former of which provides guidance to rural enterprises such as farms and vineyards, where we can park up overnight in exchange for a purchase or two of whatever local produce they may be producing. The latter is an almost internationally recognised camping club card, affording us discounted rates at campsites across Europe, providing we visit in the 'off' season, which we thankfully are.

Finally, local mobile motorhome electrician Gary was summoned to the premises to install a new reversing (and secretly-Stanley-seeking) camera which he did with alacrity, skill, fortitude and professionalism, providing us with an hitherto unattainable technicolour rear view beamed through a nifty screen strapped to the otherwise redundant driving mirror.

And then, off we go. Bikes are strapped, gas canisters are full, fridge is on and our much-used Checklist has more ticks than a rabid dog. Please feel free to follow our journey through the following chapters and yeah, well, wish us a belated buon viaggio!

Bugs On The Windscreen

Villefranche-Sur-Saône, Auvergne-Rhone-Alpes, France

Where many gather in my name, the queues shall be long, the rolls shall be dry, the bacon overcrisped and a lot of smoke shall emanate from the kitchen area.

Thus spake St. Wulgun, the nearest we have to a patron saint of the English Channel, who's observation rang true as we entered the Eurotunnel terminal in search of a swift coffee and Earl Grey. The place teemed with various groups of blokes, queuing at every one of the limited number of fast-food outlets.

These groups included edgy-looking gangs of aged motorcyclists clustered in their leathers, (some sporting sweet little white bootees, about which we wondered deeply), cluttering every available surface with their battle-scarred crash helmets – as if preparing for a latter-day crusade.

The outlet we chose was indeed churning out bacon-rolls in industrial quantities but since (as observed by St Wulgun) demand was considerably exceeding supply, the burnt offerings weren't enticing enough for us to indulge. Free ketchup, we observed, was also being applied in volumes sufficient to render the items palatable, whence we repaired to the waiting Knumptywagen clutching our trophy refreshments.

We'd arrived at the terminal in good order, having overnighted less than 20 minutes away, in the village of Smeeth, where The Woolpack pub had welcomed us with the threat of both a Quiz Night and a 'reduced menu' clearly instigated to deal with the surprising influx of locals keen to flex their collective grey cells. We availed of both, failed to make the cut in the Quiz and went to bed with indigestion in the carpark.

And now we're a long way into France – opting for toll-roads where our constant speed deposited us firstly at a riverside overnight at Chalon en Champagne and subsequently close to Villefranche-sur-Saône, where it's pissed down continually since we parked up in a campsite unsurprisingly devoid of other human habitation.

A bizarre (and very wet) cycle-trip into the local village has introduced us to yet another Saint – the venerable Jean-Marie Vianney, a former parish-priest of Ars-sur-Formans and – for his abject dedication to the Eucharist; the poor of the village and sinful men in general – the patron saint of all parish priests.

Saint Jean-Marie, whose arrival in the village during the eighteenth century apparently spawned (is that a word I can use in connection with religious celibacy, I wonder?) a large basilica; statues; effigies and a convent (from which speedily cycling nuns have emanated at amusing intervals); a church; a multi-lingual video installation and several souvenir shops selling religious items.

These items included the most bizarre little models of the Nativity, set in architectural representations of famous cities around the world, which even featured a Joseph character dressed up as a leprechaun posed before the cliffs of Moher on the island of Ireland. As we marvel with amusement, the torrential rain eases off, and a sudden increase in temperature is apparent, despite the diminishing late-afternoon daylight.

Which hopefully presages the arrival of warmer weather. As we've travelled across France, we've actually spattered quite a few unsuspectingly suicidal insects across our windscreen, which should portend great hope and optimism for a future which might include – at long last – a warming summer.

We live in hope – and might just say a few prayers to Saint Jean-Marie while we're at it.

Jagged Mountains, Jagged Tooth

Bardonecchia & Bra, Piedmont, Italy

We're en-route to Alba in Italy, allegedly Piedmont's foody capital and – whaddyaknow – there's a place called Bra just before we get there. So we (for which please read "I") just have to pay a visit. Which we do. And it's a singularly average Italian town, semi-industrial, population circa 30,000 and pleasant enough to drive through in the uncharacteristic sunshine we're experiencing today.

But no sign of anything remotely Benny Hill which might generate enough puerile humour suggested by its name and somehow essential for this particular tale. I had thought (nay, hoped) that the town would be graced with two unfeasibly large hills, or that we might have got lost, or crashed the Knumptywagen, or run over a policeman – whence the title of this piece could then have justifiably been "Pair Of Tits Cause Havoc In Bra". Sadly, it was not to be.

So I am reduced, dear reader, to simply highlighting the sign which greeted us as we entered Bra, displaying, as it does, a list of twinned (geddit?) towns around the globe, the last of which was listed as Corral De Bustos. Fnaar fnaar.

Enough. We have other experiences to report – the most critical of which has been an unplanned visit to an Italian dentist. Due to an unfortunate entanglement with a particularly crusty chunk of bread, the High Priestess of Navigation, Devices & Small Cigars fractured a molar, which she firstly seemed stoically capable of enduring but then decided that a serrated tongue might not be conducive to full enjoyment of our allegedly gastronomic tour in Stanley's footsteps.

Hence we phone our insurers, who – it transpires – use Google just like the rest of us to find exactly the same Dentist as we had, not five minutes before placing our 'emergency' call. A strangely unclinical address in a condominium block not five minutes from our illicit overnight location in snow tipped Bardonecchia results in an appointment being made just two hours hence. Amused by having to ring a doorbell to gain access to a residential flat which housed a dentist's surgery, the HP endures a 45-minute procedure at the hands of a dashing Italian dentist, keen to practise his English-speaking capabilities upon her, while her own means of verbal response and encouragement was clankingly full of surgical metal.

We emerge, having paid a bill which is – of course – just five euros less than the excess on our insurance policy, so there's another eighteen-digit claim reference number which Aviva will consign to their no-doubt heavily overloaded 'Pending' files.

And then we went to Alba (via Bra, of course) to find it a highly agreeable place to park up illegally in a car-park for the night and wander its streets in search of softly-palatable food and drink.

The Fusina Ferry Takes Us To Venice

Venice, Veneto, Italy

Although we've travelled across the top of Italy a couple of times, we'd been heading elsewhere and it had therefore never occurred to us that we should visit Venice, en passant, so to speak. The presumed hassle of finding a suitable campsite or just somewhere to park the Knumptywagen while we visited had just discouraged us from thinking that such a visit was for the likes of us.

However, on this occasion, we had the time to spare and that prospect stirred thoughts that we should make the effort. Uncharacteristically, we turned to one of the many online motorhome forums (which we'd only ever passively consumed before) and requested suggestions on where we might find safe harbour to undertake such a visit.

Well, the responses were almost overwhelming. We had about 95 replies in total, all from helpful people we'd never met, many of whom suggested a campsite at Fusina which appeared to be 'across the lagoon' from Venice itself. The prospect of a regular waterbus which could be taken from the campsite directly into Venice certainly appealed so with satnav primed, we headed west along an unnervingly busy, truck-infested E55 autostrade towards we-knew-not-what.

A couple of online recommendations had also warned us not to be put off by the approach to the Fusina campsite but even so, the peculiarly wide, dusty concrete roads through strange post-apocalyptic industrial areas and a small village unnervingly named 'Malcontenta' proved a challenge to our resolve. On arrival, however, the site was clearly well-managed, welcoming and well-wooded with a 'suit-yourself' pitching policy which provided a grassy patch with a view of a very distant Venice through the trees and across the lagoon. It quickly became apparent that this entire green and pleasing site was immediately neighboured by a massive commercial port, with huge tankers and container ships coming and going with the frequency of London buses, and an alarming proximity to the 'premium rate' front-line pitches of the campsite, so we were quite pleased that this area was fully booked when we enquired on arrival, so we couldn't have paid the hefty supplement even if we'd wanted to.

The following morning, slathered with sun-tan lotion and wearing comfortable shoes, we were ferried across an other-worldly lagoon – studded with strange triangular timber shipping lane markers – to disembark at the Zattere landing stage where we were immediately and totally immersed in this unique, amazing and awe-inspiring city.

Brief iPad research the evening prior had advised, above all else, that we should expect to get lost in the city, suggesting that this was part of Venice's endearing charm. Our expectation that we'd be able to stroll alongside the edge of the Grand Canal quickly evaporated in the rising heat of the day, as we realised that the streets were mostly little more than alleyways – and that lapping water instead of pavement fronted many of the fine façades, forcing us to route our meanderings away from the water's edge and along these alleyways. And yes, you guessed, we not only got completely lost but also hopelessly disorientated in the process.

It mattered not one jot. Venice was just bloody wonderful. Yes, of course it was busy – even though we were almost 'out of season' but – with an estimated 20 million visitors annually – the hustle, jostle and occasional people-jams were all part of the atmosphere and experience. We walked and walked and walked. And stared and stared. And then walked some more. Every corner turned presented a new and unique viewpoint packed with fascinating features and architecture. Even the doorbells on the apartment buildings were intriguingly detailed and entertaining, each push-button represented by a quirky gremlin seemingly poised to say 'Ciao'. Dream-like views emerged as narrow canals gave onto wide waterways, churned with the apparent chaos of launches, gondolas, ferries, motorboats and water-taxis all purposefully headed in every conceivable direction. The sun shone, the sky stayed blue, we continued to be amazed and enthralled.

Despite an unremarkable coffee and uninspiringly touristic cheese-toasty taken earlier in the day, by mid-afternoon we found ourselves in need of more substantive sustenance. We'd already completely mislaid an attractive-looking waterside restaurant earmarked earlier and were similarly unable to locate any of the eateries recommended by family and friends. After considered debate (and yet more walking about) we eventually rested aching legs beneath the table of a long, languid, late and satisfyingly expensive lunch in the lee of Accademia Bridge – surprisingly one of only four which crossed the Grand Canal.

Up until that point, the view from our table had only ever been informed through mediocre reproductions of Canalatto oil paintings so the real-life animated scenes of Venice going about its business in the bright sunshine left us open-mouthed with amazement – making it a bit of a challenge to actually consume our well-deserved lunch.

In retrospect, we probably also missed a trick by not taking one of the numerous Grand Canal waterbuses on our arrival, which would have helped us gain a better sense of the geography of this ludicrously lovely city. Gathering our thoughts about the remainder of the day, and with the waterbuses plying continually through our view, we decided that late was always going to be better than never so, heaving our corpulent little tummies from their resting places under fine linen napkins, we waddled to a nearby jetty and crammed ourselves aboard for a trip along the Grand Canal.

Yet more views unfolded adding further perspective. Spirally-striped barbers poles stuck out at jaunty angles from the petulant water; gondolas nodded crazily at their moorings; low-sterned water-taxis burbled their way alongside as if challenging for a race; liveried hotel porters unloaded precarious luggage onto sea-weeded jetties; seagulls wheeled silently between the closely-packed spires and domes of churches and civic buildings – and we jostled for position on the standing-room-only open decks of our waterbus.

With time-limited tickets and feet which were now beginning to protest, we disembarked and decided our aged frames probably couldn't take an extension into Venice's undoubtedly entertaining night-life. Getting lost yet again, we managed to walk ourselves back to the Zattere landing stage in time to squeeze in a refreshingly costly gelato before boarding a return ferry which navigated us back to the familiar respite of the Knumptywagen moored amidst the trees on an opposite shore.

As a memento of an amazing day, our sole souvenir amuses us every time we get the bicycles out, since it was a much-needed puncture repair outfit, discovered amidst bed-sheets and flowerpots in the depths of an off-piste, ridiculously incongruous general hardware store tucked away in the heart of this most astounding of Italian cities. And no, we wouldn't be able to find it again, even if you paid us a million euros.

The Interview Panel Will See You Now

Peschiera Del Garda, Veneto, Italy

In the same way as we realised we could pop into Venice on our way home, we decided we could also say hello to Lake Garda. In line with our new campsite regimen, we even preselected a location; phoned ahead; booked a pitch and rolled up feeling like VIPs – instead of our normal arrival as unexpected awkward relatives seeking last-minute hospitality.

Now, you probably don't need me to tell you that Lake Garda is A Very Large Lake Indeed. In fact, at 34 miles long and between two and 11 miles wide, it's the largest body of fresh water in Italy. With a surface area of approximately 143 square miles, that makes it 25 times larger than Windermere, so it's no wonder that everything on the other side looked Very Small Indeed.

Our pre-selected campsite, San Benedetto, was on the southernmost edge of the Lake – close to the bustling tourist town of Peschiera Del Garda, about which more later. This time we were not only allocated a numbered pitch but also a pair of natty plastic wristbands which were to be worn 'at all times' to denote our official residency of the site – so we were a little disappointed to realise there wasn't a theme park beyond the barrier.

As we rolled to a halt on pitch number 58, we felt very much the new kids on the block, as almost all our immediate neighbours looked as though they'd been there all summer. Which is why you've got to be on your game when you begin to establish your domain, as it's a little like attending an interview. Neighbours of all nationalities will normally wave or nod a greeting as they stroll past, but that's only to disguise the fact that they're surreptitiously judging you.

That smiling German couple sitting on the opposite pitch are actually the Chief Executives of the Main Evaluation Panel, seemingly immersed in their magazine and paperback, but in reality assessing your level of experience, competence and the degree of slickness with which you mount your vehicle on its levelling ramps; deploy your awning and roll out your multi-coloured PVC floormat. In fact, the shrewdest of them will also be calculating the orientation of your vehicle relative to the sun's current position vis-a-vis your morning or afternoon doses of sunshine and the degree of midday shade cast by surrounding shrubs and trees.

Taking your bicycles off the rear rack? Make it look good, guys, as if you've done it a hundred times before. One of you to the front; one to the rear; 1-2-3 and lift. Kick those stands out as you align them side by side to the rear of your vehicle, and don't forget to retract the bike rack and stow your chevroned warning sign safely before completing the manoeuvre, because you're still being judged.

But delightfully, you too can enjoy playing the game, as you only need to have established yourselves for five minutes ahead of new arrivals to look as if you too have been here all summer. And – oh my word – you surely don't want to be parking-up facing that way! And, whoops-a-daisy, but you also surely don't want to drive your vehicle onto its levelling ramps that way round. Oh, you do! Well then, that's never going to work. See, you've just overshot and dropped your nearside wheels off them both. Oh dear. And your wife really doesn't need to be standing just there while trying to direct your reversing attempts. If she windmills her arms like that, you're: a) never going to be able to see her in either your rear view mirror or reversing camera and b) going to end up with an inaccessible LPG locker door as you've parked too close to the hedge and won't be able to turn your gas on. Oh my!

Anyway. Having witnessed our well-oiled, professional deployment, we are judged to be deeply experienced despite our youthful good looks and our passing audience lose interest but now feel compelled to make that completely unnecessary visit to the shower block, solely to preserve the camp-wide Truman Show subterfuge in which we've all secretly engaged.

For the supplementary benefit of the Interview Panel, we also subsequently invent (on the spur-of-the-moment) a clever method of transporting our bulky reclining chairs down to the lakeside beach by slickly strapping them to the sides of our bikes and coolly wheeling them through the camp looking, for all the world, as if this ingenious technique was just an everyday occurrence for us.

Flushed from our now successful induction, we promoted ourselves and went out for lunch. At a trendy lakeside bistro. And then a lakeside picnic the following day. And hired ourselves a pedalo for an hour just so we could boast on Facebook that we have a boat on Lake Garda. (One of us swam from it. Lots. And it wasn't me.) And then a fantastic dinner in Pescheria Del Garda, at a waterside pavement restaurant we had to queue to get into, so we knew we'd made the grade. And when we explored further, we discovered this bustling, heavily trafficked riverside town had somehow managed to blend its historic, fortified architecture with a spanking new town square, all squirty fountains and wide-open marble paved spaces. And it was all thoroughly agreeable, if not downright enjoyable.

And being the wholly approved, fully vetted accomplished executive campsite rebels that we were, we wore our theme-park residential wristbands not once very much at all.

And Still Falls The Rain

Parma & Modena, Emilia-Romagna, Italy

Despite our best efforts at remaining positive and enthusiastic about our homage to Stanley Tucci (a journey which has already prompted a failed attempt at gastronomy in Alba and a 'farm-stay' in the most unimaginably beautiful and serene location perched on a 'colle' in amidst impossibly sloping vineyards) we sadly remain overwhelmed by almost incessant pissing Italian rain.

Rain which – despite our idyllic, bucolic surroundings – was overfilling many of Emilia-Romagna's rivers to generate international news stories of extensive flooding, evacuations and even deaths in the region through which we were passing. Not that we had any specific plans, but our vague direction of travel towards the eastern Adriatic coast of Italy was now confounded by a pre-selected campsite at Bologna being underwater, as well as the increasingly frenetic news reports of major flooding everywhere east of our current position.

On the bright side, that's almost the entire raison d'etre of a Knumptywagen, so in it we sat over coffee, Earl Grey, maps and bowls of granola to reroute our vague travel plans. Parma was close. We should do Parma and at the very least find some prosciutto.

So, in we trolled, parked up and wandered into the centre, (sporting a very gay umbrella which hadn't seen active service since middle-daughter's wedding) to visit the sights and seek out a restaurant recommended by a near-relative who'd lived in Parma and knew where to send us.

In our headlong enthusiasm for all-things-Stanley Tucci, we'd naively overlooked the indifference which can sometimes be shown by Italian waiting-staff. Having been seated at a thankfully covered pavement table in a charming Parma side-street, and having ordered our bottle of still water, we were absolutely and universally ignored by 'our' waiter. We perused an impenetrable luncheon menu (which even confounded Google Translate) and – after a increasingly frustrating 15 minutes where eye-contact was definitely not being served – we gathered our belongings and walked out again – to thankfully find an unassuming takeaway sandwich shop where we couldn't have been treated better. Grazie mille.

A campsite allegedly close to Modena had proffered availability for the night but as we approached, our hearts sank to find its location was sandwiched in a patch of indifferent scrubland between a truck-park and two autostradas. We were, however, aghast yet perversely entertained to note a plethora of British numberplates, many belonging to caravans which looked as if they'd pitched for a fortnight, God help them. From over a green fabric perimeter fence, continuous hooting from Italian truckers seemingly stuck behind yet more hapless Brits in the wrong toll-booth lanes was clearly going to be our soundtrack for the night.

Just outside the muddied gates of International Camping Modena, there was an inauspicious 'Ristorante Turismo' – probably best described as a 'roadhouse' in the American genre, which looked closed, miserable and massively avoidable when we recced it in the late afternoon. "Open at 7pm" proclaimed the yellowing sign in a murky door, and so we resolved (Lord alone knows why) to check it out thereafter – both of us fully disbelieving that it would be open at all.

Well. Neither of us could recall having eaten out so well in a long time. Steaks were cooked to perfection; delightful green salads as accompaniments; olive-oil, balsamic vinegar and chilli-oil on each table. A carafe of wine. Tiramisu to die for. Sensible prices. The place was rammed. Truckers rubbed shoulders with families, singles,

Germans, Dutch (in wooden clogs, really), Italians, Us – the evening confounded all our expectations and Stanley Tucci would do well to add it into Series Three of his gastronomic tours of his homeland, please take note.

And with our newly-derived Flood Avoidance Plan now firmly engineered, we'll wake up sharpish tomorrow; retrace our route to Parma (sadly sans any souvenir Modena Balsamic vinegar), turn left and head for the comparative safety of the Mediterranean coast at La Spezia – and a possible sojourn by the sea.

Gotta love a Knumptywagen!

Expletives (Many, Varied & Ripe) Deleted

Massa, Liguria, Italy

What was the sign-off from the previous chapter? "Gotta love a Knumptywagen"?

Hmm . . . maybe not today, eh? In fact, today, for the first time since we took possession over eight years ago, we fell out of love with our beloved Knumptywagen.

Our overnight on a friendly, almost-seaside campsite at Massa on the Ligurian coast, just south of La Spezia, was disturbed throughout by incessant brushed-snare-drumming of precipitation on our roof, accompanied by the continual bass-drum thump of consolidated rain dropping off the trees under which we had parked up.

On awakening, our infrequent and occasionally problematic water-supply-out-of-taps made itself known, and – despite helpful advice about resolving possible airlocks from our English neighbours – any potential alternatives to us abluting out of a bucket for the rest of the trip were clearly rapidly receding.

As a result, it would be fair to say that we found ourselves at possibly our most despondent ebb since we began our travels. The apparently simple issue of a lack of a water supply to several taps (as well as the all-important loo) were simultaneously involved; myriad; complex and inter-reliant. Testing any one part of the system presented a complex web of 'what-ifs' which included power-supply failures; water-pump investigations; leaking hoses; failed water-heating boiler; fuses; trip-switches; 12-volt versus 230-volt electricity; the aforementioned airlocks and the continually pissing rain.

Despite mounting odds and my as-yet-unspoken thoughts that we should just pack it all in and head for home (some 1,000+ miles northward) the High Priestess dug deep and suggested we enquire about professional assistance at Campsite Reception. In the pleasantly surprised resultant preparation for a motorhome mechanic arriving on site, we type our predicament into Google Translate, God bless it and await his arrival.

It's astounding to relate that – on arrival – we show the mechanic our Google Italian translation of the problem – to quietly realise that he won't (or maybe even can't?) read it. Instead, he leaps forward, multi-meter in hand and pronounces our water-pump is 'live' – of which we're already well aware.

Over the next politely awkward and uncommunicative fifteen minutes, he checks everything we've already checked; shrugs as only Italians (and maybe the French) can do; suggests he can do nothing else; produces an electronic credit-card reader (which miraculously does work, of course), takes his call-out payment and buggers off.

The rain continues, reassuring us that our anticipated daytrip to visit the nearby and allegedly more-than-picturesque Cinque Terre would have been wasted under this grey, glowering sky and continually pissing rain. So instead, the High Priestess diligently surfs the internet seeking further local motorhome servicing while I simply sulk and ponder exactly how long it would take us to throw in the towel and just run for home.

Well. After cursing several blind alleys, Her Supreme Holiness discovers a motorhome rental business, which appears to offer servicing, twenty-five minutes' drive away. Their phone rings out unanswered but with nothing else to distract us, off we trek, eventually to find a locked gate and no sign of any life. Of course! It's Friday afternoon. We're in Italy. Absolutely fuck-all is going to happen here today, and our collective despondency instantaneously plummets to unchartered depths.

Then a little man in a little Fiat arrives, queries in broken English why we're peering forlornly through his fence and welcomes us into his repository of aged, faded and clearly failed 'rental' motorhomes. His raggazzi are summonsed (go on, look it up, I had to, despite learning the bloody word about a hundred times over) and we spend the next three hours just standing around, while enthusiastic diligence, then frustration, then uplift, then scowling, then cheerfulness, then screwdrivers are applied to various internal components of the Knumptywagen, none of which had never seen natural daylight before today.

Signore! Success! Yay! But then confusion as part of the chain vehemently declines to perform. More expletives (probably); more elation; more furrowed brows. A trickle of water here, a suspicious leak there. We just stand alongside and wait, while ants crawl over our feet.

And eventually, at five p.m. on a rainy Italian Friday, a compromise success is declared where we all agree enough has been done; we have a vague flow of water and other vital components (such as the fridge) are working again. Our spirits are lifted and we pat our ragazzi enthusiastically on their shoulders (because even Google Translate can't cope with 'thank-you, thank you but enough is enough').

And how might we pay you, stout fellows? Cash? Ah! We have no cash. Card? No. No card. OK. "Ou est le nearest cash-machine, por favor?" (See. I bloody knew those Italian lessons would pay-off) and I go whirling off with our raggazo in his car into a bizarre Friday rush-hour hinterland where every cash-machine we visit is out of order, until we find one which spews forth crisp Euros and we return triumphant to hand-over the stated fee plus almost double that in deeply gratuitous tips.

And hence back to the campsite we trundle – to celebrate with long-overdue food and too-much-drink in the camp restaurant, return to the Knumptywagen to test everything again – and find ourselves in the same dubiously erratic situation we were in before any of this tedious malarkey started.

Gotta love a Knumptywagen? Jury's still out.

Let Toodling Commence

Bordighera, Savona, Italy

We have now been in Italy for a whole week and for the first time since we arrived, it has not rained for over twelve hours.

We are therefore in a better – if not quite celebratory – mood and can reassure our avid readership that the tumult reported in the previous piece is now behind us. How so? For a start, we have running water; a loo that flushes and a fridge that cools! And whilst the water flow through our taps hasn't been fully resolved, it has proved fun guessing out of which tap the supply will be delivered – since both kitchen-sink and hand-basin taps need to be opened in order to encourage a flow out of just one of them.

We are further dilemmarised (good, eh? Just made it up. Spellcheck is not happy) by the fortunate circumstances that have befallen us from around midday today, in that – not only did it stop raining, but the sun has shone for almost a whole Sunday afternoon – and it was hot! As such, we have taken so many celebratory photographs that it's proved impossible to select just the one or two which we'd normally send home to illustrate both our travels and travails. (See – I'm on fire tonight – might be the combined effect of running water – and maybe brandy.)

But just afore ye go, I need to backtrack a tad, since you need to know we had planned to strap two e-bikes to the back of the Knumptywagen prior to our departure. Frustratingly, mine had developed a fault which no amount of pleading with local cycle shops could cure. After a cascading sequence of phone calls, we were lucky enough to track down a freelance cycle-repair tag-team who between them had volunteered to see if they could sort out the issue before we set off.

Despite best efforts (and the impenetrability of Chinese electronics) the bike was not cured, so we were really touched when we were simply offered the loan of a spare bike for the trip. We duly collected what has turned out to be the Wolf-in-Sheep's-Clothing of the ebike world – and just for a change it was the High Priestess who trailed in my dust-cloud this morning as we toured the fascinating floriculture of last night's Agricamper stopover.

Indeed, as an inexperienced user of this high-powered, custom-built e-bike, I couldn't make the damn thing go slow enough and have spent more time braking than pedalling. (I simply daren't open it up to its full potential – I'd be wheelying into Montenegro before it ran out of juice.)

Suffice it to say that we have again enjoyed an afternoon's trip – and well-deserved lunch – on the prom alongside the Mediterranean, on the Italian Riviera, under blazing hot sun and with smiles again on our little Knumptying faces.

Foreground Noise

Olivetta San Michele, Liguria, Italy

In the hills of Italy, we discover a spectacularly located wilderness – sourced, of course by the ever-diligent High Priestess Of Spectacularly Located Wilderness Campsites, which this undoubtedly was.

The site – if such it could be called – rambled, nay, tumbled amidst an aged terrace of olive trees (one of which, our French Italian bilingual host was keen to point out, was over 1,000 years old.) The setting was idyllic. Blue skies (the first since we'd arrived in Italy over a week prior); warmth; views across a precipitous tree-clad valley while the steely-green leaved olive trees provided shade and tranquillity to possibly the most peaceful spot we'd ever encountered. As added value, the site straddled the border betwixt Italy and France, with a ragged line demarcating the difference set in concrete and celebratorily straddled for yet more photos home.

'Pick some cherries' our host urged, providing wobbly step-ladders to the High Priestess, with whom – and only whom – he had chosen to engage. So we picked some cherries and then retraced our arrival route (this time on foot) along hair-pin bends to explore the visually agreeable hamlet of Olivetta San Michele.

Amongst its unsung fascinations, we discover a walled graveyard, set high on a colle overlooking the village and packed full of surprisingly substantial family mausoleums, lesser graves and intermittent mounds of dry, stony earth. Vignetted photographs of occupants adorned almost every tombstone; faces and hairstyles so stern as to make their gender indeterminate, with ages ranging from eighteen to eighty and many with fresh cut-flowers clearly evidencing regular pilgrimages from more able family members up the steep hill.

As we roamed the isolated, seemingly depopulated village it was both entertaining and saddening to realise that every idyllic vista worthy of an artistically composed landscape photograph was foregrounded by heaps of discarded, random crap. Old cars; tyres; rusted agricultural equipment; tangles of barbed wire; fencing poles; plastic garden chairs; coils of tubing; a motorbike; an ancient weed-infested Saab; electrical cables; solidified bags of cement; field drainage; pots; tiles; paving stones – they were all there as evidential reminders that the practicalities of human life went on – no matter how high up, nor how remote the location – our intrinsic need to discard and waste so much over-produced stuff prevails.

On our return to site, we smile benignly at the slumped, ragged old caravan which functions as the camp's washroom facilities – containing, as it does, a freestanding, slightly wobbly toilet; a shower cubicle the plastic curtain of which physically crumbles to the touch; a hand-basin; a washing machine and a population of spiders which likely outnumbers the local villagers. "Washing machine only at night" our host has advised us, a fact which we test once he departs to find that it certainly does not appear to be working during the afternoon, when we felt we might have gained most benefit.

All is revealed at dusk, however, as the caravan and its contained electrical appliances all automatically spring to illuminated life – absolutely coincidentally with the roadside street lighting further up the hill – thus perhaps explaining our previous suspicions about the hefty, amateur-looking – and obviously unauthorised – power-cables which trail throughout the site.

Arrivederci, Italia. Bonjour France

Nice, Alpes-Maritimes, France

It was never our intention to give up so easily on Italy but the incessant rain, mortally dangerous regional flooding and temperatures lower than Eastbourne forced our hand and we've now replanned both our homage to Stanley Tucci and our itinerary.

With the benefit of experience, perhaps our attempt to retrace his culinary tours of Italy was a little over-ambitious, given that he had the backing of experienced and professional CNN TV production crews; probably months of intense pre-production and on location research; wranglers; drivers; drone-pilots; local guides; Michelin-starred chefs and fixers, while we just had – well, ourselves and a Knumptywagen, which – on reflection – was probably not the best vehicle in which to penetrate off-road agricultural hinterlands or indeed, busily trafficked Italian city-centres.

Both of which we actually managed, to our credit, although the continually pissing rain put a damper on most of the anticipated pleasure.

But let's just draw breath a moment and reflect on where we did actually get to in Italy: A dentist's parlour in Bardonecchia; a municipal car-park in Alba; an isolated vineyard at the end of a perilous farm track in Castell D'Arquato; a muddied truck-stop outside Modena; a motorhome repair-shop in Massa; a visit to the very heart of Parma; a floral farmyard in Albenga; a swim in the Mediterranean (not me, obviously) at Vallecroise; an epic cycle ride to botanical gardens just outside Menton and a final Italian 'hurrah' in an isolated and fairly vertiginous mountain village way up behind Ventimiglia.

And now we are welcomed into Nice at an inauspicious road junction by a bizarre but impactful sculpture – a massive human head encased almost entirely in a cube of concrete - and whilst I could go off-piste here to conduct some in-depth online research into it, I really can't be bothered. It is mentioned en passant here, in order to announce our successful penetration of France, through Menton (where the Gendarmes on the now teeny-tiny-border were too busy checking out the clearly suspicious contents of the campervan just in front of us to even warrant us a Gallic second glance).

The sun was shining, cab windows were open and we progressed in an agreeably buzzy flow of traffic onto Le Promenade des Anglais, thereby fulfilling one of the rather eccentrically amusing ambitions of our venture – equal in stature, we feel, to our earlier trip through Bra.

My Editor (all the best authors have one, dahling!) back in England was keen to point out that the epithet 'des Anglais' may not necessarily relate to us Brits doing our usual colonial cloning of overseas territories, but again, I'm afraid the Gallic indolence which has recently taken hold results in absolutely nil research being undertaken on this otherwise distinctive distinction. Sorry.

Anyway, the point is, we have driven our embarrassingly decrepit Knumptywagen the entire length of the promenade at Nice. Faded, over-wide, bug-spattered, aged, moss greened and downright awkward (and that's just the occupants) we belched diesel fumes along narrow, traffic-clogged lanes alongside soft- and open-topped Bentleys, Porsches, Ferraris, Maybachs and other feats of automotive engineering that were clearly too expensive to warrant identifying badges. And to add to our perverse sense of one-upmanship, we sucked on Werthers for the duration. So there.

And – despite a challenge issued by a family member, we did actually manage to park up! Not for long, admittedly, but sufficient for us to record the moment for posterity, which instigated yet more WhatsApped photobombing home.

And having arrived at an acceptable beachside campsite dans la plage du Gaillarde, a few kilometres south of St. Aygulf, on our first 'date-night' meal out of the whole trip so far; with our feet scrunching in the sand; red wine that actually had a label and wasn't fizzy; two beach fishermen reassuringly catching bugger-all (as is the way of these things) and ultimately the first reassuringly expensive restaurant bill for a meal we ate, appropriately enough, with coutellerie d'Azur.

Elvis

Port Grimaud, Provence-Alpes-Côte-d'Azur, France

Camping de la Plage Grimaud is a very large site. We know this because Elvis has been resurrected for a special 'one night only' performance in the Campsite bar-restaurant. And there isn't a spare seat in the house. As dusk falls, He is giving his Americanised all; campers are eating, drinking and applauding and a lone couple are rock-and-rolling (gently) around each other, she smiling gleefully, he looking sheepish and avoiding eye-contact with his enthusiastic dancing partner.

The site – with almost 500 pitches – straddles the main coastal road, St. Tropez signposted 9.5km to the west; St. Maxime 6.5km to the east, while we enjoy cyclable proximity to the fascinating waterside, Italianate construct which is Port Grimaud.

We find ourselves pitched au bord de la mer pour deux nuits, s'il vous plait, having expended just thirty minutes on our journey here from our previous stopover, but then an hour standing – each of us in a separate queue – to check-in at Site Reception (hoping for this entire and tedious duration) that a pitch on this popular site might be available.

No such thing as advance booking; no Advance Passenger Information completed online; nothing efficient about the process whatsoever, as we diligently await our turn at the desk. Once there we carefully biro all our details onto two pages of an A4 Booking Form and then wait at the counter while our multilingual Receptionist repeats the exercise by keying it all into a desktop computer. Thankfully, we realise that as many people queuing to get in are also queuing to pay their bills and get out, so pitches are becoming available. The poor lady queuing in front of us reached the counter to find she'd already paid-by-card in full on arrival and was free to go. She looked a little shell-shocked when she realised that was an hour of her life she wasn't going to get back. Très fastidieux pour toute les personnes impliquées, n'est-ce pas?

It has also become separately apparent that we seem to be the only people touring the entire reach of the south coast of France without a bloody dog on board. Or two. Or three. In most cases, Campsite Receptions want to know how many petite chiens are travelling with us before they'll even take our names – or our Euros.

Now, we have absolutely nothing against dogs and our many good friends own and enjoy them. But what are these tiny, cat-sized, pointy-snouted and often snarling creatures for? A four-legged wasp-equivalent, they seem to be carried absolutely everywhere, tucked under arms like furry, bulgy-eyed clutch bags – or, if let loose on the ground, zut alors, then they're on invisibly thin retractable leads, always played out at full stretch thus representing trip-hazards aplenty, especially since the people attached to the other end are always engaged in immersive conversations with other dog-owners, each of whom are inevitably looking the other way.

Indeed, while we queued at Campsite Reception, with nothing much else to distract us, we witness the arrival of an older couple in their overlong 'camping-car' which they simply abandon outside Reception, blocking the campsite entrance to further traffic, while they take their dog for a crap in the grass. Just stopped. Opened the door; hoicked the ugly bat-faced creature under an arm; carried it to a grass verge; stood staring at trees while it performed; scooped it (and thankfully its little gift) up again and then sauntered back to their camping car, completely oblivious to the traffic-jam they'd initiated.

Ah, c'est une vie de chien!

As I Reach For A Peach

San Tropez, Provence-Alpes-Côte-d'Azur, France

Ok, hands up! Who recognises the lyric in the title?

And more to the point, who's already subconsciously carried it onwards in their heads, as the rest of the iconic words flood out of otherwise vacuous spaces in our brains where we unknowingly store all this stuff? Or at least the brains of those of us who matured in the 70's and would count Pink Floyd's "Meddle" amongst the many trophies which made up their prized album collections.

So, come on – along with me . . . "Slide a rind down behind, the sofa in St Tropez. Breaking a stick with a brick in the sand, Ridin' a wave in the wake of an old sedan." No-one's entirely sure about the meaning of the song – love lost, love regained, an ennui-ridden sojourn in the south of France, maybe? Only lyricist Roger Waters may know and – as far as I'm aware, he's declined to comment and probably wouldn't as – by all accounts (especially Dave Gilmour's) – he's allegedly of an artistic temperament and best not approached. So, we are sadly none the wiser, suffice it to report that it's a bloody lovely and very emotive track, even if you've never been to St Tropez.

Which we just have! (See, you knew I'd get round to it eventually!) And we've not only been, but we cycled there. And back again. And what a delight it was. The sun shone and an extremely civilised cycle-lane ran the whole distance between our campsite and aforesaid seaside town. Interrupted, we were pleased to discover, by an overwhelmingly attractive roadside Boulangerie Patisserie at which we had to stop for a spot of petit dejeuner, donchaknow.

Boats. Everywhere. Big boats. And surprisingly, Big Black Boats, all awaiting a call-up by central casting for the next James Bond movie. Sleek, radar-invisible black boats, the equivalent, we figured, to the recent fashion for white cars. Where a plethora of black automotives existed before, now the moneyed cognoscenti favour black boats over white. Their hull shapes had changed too – solid, bulky and upright, three storeys high, unpunctuated by portholes and looking more like polished coalfaces than water-carving hulls.

And we swear that at least one of them, as we espied it cruising out of the harbour towards open water, had its anchor encased behind a glazed picture-window in its recessed hull, a work of combined art and marine engineering in itself.

We lock-up the bikes, we wander amidst our fellow tourists of all nationalities, along the harbour's edge gawping at the scale and conspicuous, unembarrassed wealth on display all around us. Bathing-platformed sterns are lettered with ports of origin: Valletta, Cowes, Georgetown, Southampton, Nice, London with many also flying the Red Ensign. Small crowds of onlookers gather should any movement be spotted onboard, although most of this seems to be crew either polishing stuff or stowing wholesale pallets of Coke Zero in a hold somewhere. No-one recognisably famous is espied.

It is thankfully not yet crawlingly busy and as such a pleasure to perambulate, alongside the shaded, tiny restaurants which spill onto narrow pavements alongside boutique shops, chandlery and inevitable hairdressers. Competitive pétanque is underway in the town square above the harbour, with many uniformed teams and bespectacled umpires all adding the necessary je ne sais quoi.

Sadly, our earlier petit dejeuner has done for us and our disinclination to dine expensively en plein aire is offset by un glace a deux, before we unlock, saddle-up and head for home, quite possibly to reach for a peach or two.

Bread And Chocolate

Montelimar, Auvergne-Rhône-Alpes, France

We're headed north. Admittedly, not quite 'on the way home' just yet, but turning our backs on the sunny Mediterranean, which we've enjoyed very much. And we find ourselves on a site just outside Montelimar, being famous both for its nougat and seeming to be – well – very normal.

We found the lakeside Camping L'Ille Blanc via Google, as our go-to ACSI site directory didn't seem to have anything we liked the look of in this neck of the woods. Yet, when we arrived mid-afternoon (after a dull autoroute slog of a tad over three-and-a-half hours) it seemed closed. Off the beaten track; locked gates; tired, faded murals of cartoon happy campers; no directional signage; no sign of life. But then, just as we were about to move on (we knew not to where) un personne appeared, keyed in a gate-code and we were admitted with a shake of the hand, a simple, smiley 'help yourself to wherever you fancy' gesture and in we rolled.

Do you recall the banjo scene from the 1972 Burt Reynolds film 'Deliverance'? We parked up in a seemingly empty campsite, well off the beaten track. Surrounded by natural beauty, birds singing, lake glistening in the afternoon sun. A handful of unoccupied static caravans dotted the perimeter. A couple of shouty, shirtless labourers wandering round with a chainsaw and a noisy brush-cutter. Who knows we're here? What if we're never seen again? Dang-a-dang-dang-dang.

The setting was idyllic. A peaceful, swimmable lake (not for me, obvs) trimmed with mature woodland; frogs; small fry flitting about in the warm shallow margins; herons; kites; cherry-trees; a pitch right on the water's edge – we really couldn't think of anywhere better to be murdered in our beds. But then, lo, we awake the following morning and it's still idyllic and as far as we can tell, we've spilled no blood whatsoever. A lazy titular breakfast and we enquire at Reception if there is a river nearby. "There is no river. Only the Rhone. Just over there" is the informative response and after a brief recce of what is indeed a very big non river, we decide to cycle into Montelimar, where we know they sell nougat, and where Google believes there's a fishing-tackle shop.

In the interim, three young German lads have arrived on bicycles and pitched up nearby, and to tell the truth, they look far more wholesome than we do, so maybe they'll be eaten first? Then another guy turns up – again on a bike, then a couple more with a little tent, so we figure we're safe, lock the Knumptywagen – and cycle into Montelimar.

Which seemed very comfortable in its own skin. No touristy pretence; no great fortified basilica set on an insurmountable mound; no ostentation. In fact, in parts, it seemed a little down-at-heel, with empty retail units and a scattering of down-and-outs populating those frontages. And yet, classy designer-clothes outlets seemed also to proliferate, with pedestrianised streets also featuring shoes, hats, pharmacies, cafes and yes, the very occasional nougat emporium. The local market hall was shut and there was no sign of any other food stores, delicatessens, bakeries or boucheries. We locked the bikes up close to the Hotel de Ville, found an agreeable small gallery showing the work of local artists and then a delightfully pure French Brasserie, where we refreshed ourselves before cycling 'home' again, an exploratory walkabout and acquisition of nougat having been fulfilled.

On the way back, our fishing-tackle shop had raised its lunchtime shutters and was the most populated shop we'd entered so far, in all of France, ever. And with just cause as it stocked absolutely everything an outdoorsyperson might have required, including a lot of rather alarming hunting kit, meaning racks of hefty-looking knives, pistols, rifles and shotguns alongside our arguably more passive hooks, monofilament and worms.

On return, our laundry had satisfactorily line-dried, hanging as it now did almost over yet another little pup tent occupied by a further newly-arrived solo cyclist, who seemed to care not one jot as we unpegged our beautifully arrayed and sweet-smelling underwear from around him.

Wine Bluffs

Mâcon, Bourgogne-France-Comté, France

We are in Mâcon.

Well, just downriver from said French town in a delightfully unprepared early-season campsite on the banks of the River Saône. We arrived in the heat of the day to find Reception closed, but a Dutch caravanner ahead of us was negotiating with an intercom, so when the barrier was raised for him we simply tailgated in, drove around a fairly empty site and bagged an empty pitch right on the edge of a very wide river. The sun shone and we smiled and nodded at distant neighbours, separated from each other by modestly high beech hedges, which could easily have been used to hide-but-hint at Barbara Windsor's assets in Carry On Camping.

Mâcon. Bourgogne. Beaujolais. Bordeaux. Aah, wine country. And I'm already way out of my depth. Increasing maturity brings with it the emergent realisation that the world of wine is likely to remain as impenetrable to me as my Italian lessons became. Why, for instance, did the French choose to initialise many of their main wine-producing regions with the letter 'B' – even though they're spread across a very wide country?

And as Basil Fawlty snobbishly fawned, "I can certainly see you know your wine. Most of our guests wouldn't know the difference between Bordeaux and Claret" – a comedic and unknowing idiocy to which I can fully relate – wherein lies the rub – I also haven't a bloody clue. Which brings about that key moment of social embarrassment whenever a Sommelier (we patronise all the best places) invites you to taste the wine you've just selected. Well, yes, OK, I will, but I'm afraid I won't have a clue if it's good, bad, indifferent, corked or worth the price we're about to be charged for it.

And, while Wine Buffs may bluff, the Chief Navigating Officer knowingly pronounces that any wine tastes good after the third glass, and in my book, she's more than likely right. We therefore think our best bet on the wine-tasting front is suggested by a friendly and distant relative from Canada who respectfully suggests we seek out the safety and reassurance of the Orangina Vineyard, where we would likely find something more suited to our uneducated palates.

Anyway. Mâcon. Into which we proudly cycled, mainly along half-constructed riverbank paths, thus arriving alongside a large riverside quay. Here, we espy three moored river-cruisers – like giant floating harmonicas, with rigidly arranged double rows of cabins along their low-slung length and shiny tops, peppered with floppy-hatted tourists, clearly enjoying their shoulder-season river-cruise discounts. The passengers are thankfully all onboard, lunching on their all-inclusive menus and not engulfing the town with their overwhelming ant-like exploration.

On our own brief and slightly saddle-sore visit to the always-smiling Office de Tourism, we ritually collect our free town map but are then distracted by an impressive array of leaflets for the many available local Chateaux, vineyards, wineries, tours and degustations. One particularly caught my eye, for the quaint monotone photograph of the clearly most important male members of the family in their cellars, each smiling at the camera, and each delicately holding a glass of what we presume is their finest vintage.

The leaflet designer had obviously decided to adopt a monotone photo to imply an historic setting, and then to highlight the product by colouring it a bright yellow – the net effect - to my perverse eyes - being to imply the gathered trio were drinking their own urine.

Now, I may not be a wine buff, but even I know that's not the right colour for white wine, and as such, we'll be avoiding any degustation at their particular establishment, merci beaucoup.

Bonne santé!

Le Van Du Pain

Seraucourt-le-Grand, Hauts-de-France, France

It feels a little like a throw-back to a slow-paced era, now long gone, but our campsite's just had a visit from the Bread Lady. What a delightful indulgence! A hoity-toity tooty-tootle on the horn (along with a continually chugging diesel engine – just like Mr Whippy) announced her arrival – and even before she'd come to a standstill, we'd unfolded ourselves from our tents, camping-cars and caravans – almost all the nations of Northern Europe represented – and gathered, nay, flocked to her – clutching purses laden with loose foreign change.

A little sliding side-window displayed her wares. Apple turnovers; croissants; pain-aux-raisins; pains chocolat and of course, a deep paper sack, from the top of which the crusty tops of golden baguettes peeped out, like a nest full of open-beaked fledglings.

"Bonjour Madam" we all take it in turns to practise, "Nous voudrions un baguette, s'il vous plait, et un pain au raisin and one of those apple-turnover things which I'm now pointing at hopefully through your little side window, merci beaucoup." And back to our temporary homes we all trooped, to settle in and enjoy le petit-déjeuner en plein aire, while the Bread Lady served crumbs to a secondary queue of ducks.

By the time we reach Sangatte, a fresh breeze is blowing off La Manche and long trousers are sadly contemplated for the first time in over three weeks. Madame welcomes us to her functional campsite, where we reckon the majority of occupants are in transit, either headed south or north, identifiable by either a spring-like gait or a slight dragging of sandals-and-socks (and one couple – Belgians, probably – in wellies and shorts, we know not why). Our one oversight in the entire trip then comes to light, as we realise it's a Monday afternoon and our restaurant of choice (and main raison d'être for using this campsite) is actually not open this evening. What fools we are.

Whilst an in-Knumptywagen wilted-spring-onion omelette will certainly sustain us, that's hardly the point of our last night away, and we set about finding an alternative which is ouvert. And indeed we do – in the next village along the coast at Escalles, where a restaurant is open and will take us in. Madam advises against the 25-minute cycle ride as the road is hilly; it's already blusterous; getting just a bit English-chilly – and we've only one set of clip-on bike lights between us. A taxi! We'll splash out and get a taxi! Why the hell not? On our behalf, Madam graciously makes several phone calls in machine-gun French, whence we discover the nearest taxi is in Calais and a round trip to our now-booked restaurant will set us back close to 80 quid!

So we tidy-up, lock-down, unplug and drive. And it's a delightful 10-minute trip, over lush rolling downland on an empty road with glimpses of the sea, as if we were in Sussex. And it turns out that Restaurant Les Falaises is slap-bang at the entrance to a gently undulating and very agreeable-looking campsite we'd never have discovered otherwise. We dine well, with a bit of local art and presumably local campers creating a very decent Monday-evening atmosphere and return home accompanied by an energetic deer which thankfully bounds alongside us in a field adjacent to the wandering road. Earmarking the site – Camping Le Blanc Nez – for future visits, we trundle back – crossing over the Channel Tunnel, as depicted by satnav – to our own now rather mundane site and reclaim our pitch – with full tummies and none the worse for our exploratory last-night adventure.

A Taste Of Tuscany

Montecatini Terme, Tuscany, Italy

Although it feels slightly disloyal to admit it, we should report we are just returned from a revisit to Tuscany – without the Knumptywagen!

Uncharacteristically, a newspaper advert had piqued our curiosity – offering a Taste of Tuscany and promising new-fangled methods of travel such as aeroplanes; airconditioned coaches; upgradable hotels; guided excursions and the dedicated services of a Tour Manager. Promotional discounts were on offer; dates were available; weather looked agreeably hot and sunny; airports were accessible; luggage was permitted and it was clear that the stars had aligned in our favour.

So, feeling slightly outrageous, we booked. And off we went, arriving after dark at our upgraded four-star hotel in Montecatino Terme, Tuscany, on a delightfully sultry September evening.

Our first 'surprise & delight' feature of this particular Hotel was the disgruntled lack of interest provided at Check-in from a surly and harassed-looking Night Manager, even though he appeared to have absolutely nothing else to do. Having clanked our own way up to the fourth floor with our luggage – and being inexperienced hotel-users – we were then interested to discover that one of the primary delights of a four-star hotel in Italy is that certain rooms are graced with holes in their bedroom floors.

The ankle-breaking position, depth and size of our complimentary hole was clearly a welcome supplement to the hospitable warmth of our arrival, only then to be enhanced by a similar degree of loquaciousness once we reached the bar, having prised self-same Night Manager from his self-absorption at a glowing computer screen in an exposed and cluttered back-office which had clearly been organised by a passing hurricane.

Buffet breakfast the following morning was laid out in a semi-palatial, pillared yet tiredly decorated suite, serviced by an incongruously dinner-suited, bow-tied waiter who directed his similarly slightly under-trained and under-staffed staff to assist us with cornflakes and other low-cost buffet delights.

It became clear from this first foray that we were now considered a 'group' and as such we joined a similarly bemused gathering of fellow arrivals at a long table, laid for ten and at which we were directed to take our seats. Having all arrived from Blighty the night before – (via the same 'Taste of Tuscany' advertisements from a plethora of popular British journals) we all immediately set-to and compared gossip on our individual arrival experiences and the state of our various accommodations.

Breakfast queried and then consumed, we are then bustlingly ushered into the Hotel lounge, a curiously darkened repository of mixed, disarrayed and uncomfortable furnishings wherein was promised our group introduction to Tuscany, about to be breathlessly delivered to her newly acquired family by our dedicated Tour Manager and self-proclaimed Mama Mia.

Non andare via!

Leanings

Pisa, Tuscany, Italy

Pisa was a sight to behold. Or, at least, the Campo dei Miracoli – that famous cluster of impressive marble-white religious edifices – was. Crisply and cleanly lit by fresh autumnal sunlight, we viewed the spectacle across vibrant green, unpopulated lawns which carpet the surrounding area.

While the Torre Pedente was obviously the star attraction, it became quickly apparent that its associated buildings in this spectacular arena were also slightly inclined from the perpendicular – due, we are informed – to shallow foundations set in sandy silty subsoil by eleventh-century builders, who probably weren't fully up-to-speed on the old subsidence lark.

The global fascination with the Leaning Tower, over and above its neighbouring acolytes, was immediately obvious even at this comparatively early hour in the tourist day. We were already shoaling in large numbers and gathering at limited vantage points for the now-ubiquitous perspective-tricked photographs of ourselves pushing against the lean of one of the world's most famous towers.

This entertaining spectacle – once perceptively described as a bizarre mime convention by Italy's very own Minister For Tourism – became even more amusing as we witnessed phone-squinting tourists struggling to art-direct both the angle and position of their subject's outstretched limbs, when it was clearly far simpler just to position the subject and then move with the camera to achieve the best-angled shots.

Always keen to approach from a different angle, your humble author thus cajoled the Chief Navigating Officer & Expedition Photographer to shun the populist approach and instead seek alternative viewpoints, which of course, we managed at great personal effort, including pointing miserably at "No drones" signs affixed to nearby lampposts; leaning into a fibreglass ice-cream cone outside a pavement café and finger-pointing at tiny fridge magnets arrayed outside almost every souvenir shop.

Our week's itinerary is before us, and we're going to be busy. It's delightfully hot and sunny out there, so we're also going to be exhausted. Montecatini Terme and its higher grandparent, Alto. A thermal spa; Pisa & Lucca; Florence; Siena & San Gimignano; Chianti region; hill-top villages; butcher's shops; gelaterias; giant penises; bars; lunch in a castle; dinner on high; wine-tasting; walking tours; guided tours; coach trips – we're cramming in huge, tasty mouthfuls of Tuscany – and it's all very digestible.

So, apart from our shambolic, down-market hotel, we've had a blast. And if you were diligent enough to spot the giant penis buried in the previous paragraph, then you'll be gaining your own flavour of the humour that's emerged from our little coterie of Fellow Four Star Guests. (Although you'll need to stay tuned if it's piqued your interest!)

For yes, we were The Group Who Opted To Pay An Upgrade Supplement for a four-star hotel, only to discover that the three-star offering, just around the corner, was in every respect far better than ours. Sporting such luxuries as an agreeable residents' lounge; quality fixtures, fittings and décor; a peaceful location; non-leaking plumbing; a Reception desk staffed by professionals with hospitality skills; an inviting swimming pool which wasn't rimmed with pigeon-droppings or an adjacent building site; a mixed bag of various sun loungers, deck-chairs and parasols that weren't broken or held together with string and you'll begin to get an impression of our upgraded disgruntlement.

And probably best not to mention the safes. Safes, can you believe? It became clear from our spritz-fuelled, after-hours, outdoor patio gossip that our Hotel room décor was as diverse as the east end of London during the blitz. Classic sun-shading shutters hung precariously off their hinges four floors above the carpark; bathrooms were either "belle epoque" or uber-modern; paint and wallpapers were peeling or scuffed (no doubt by mishandled steamer trunks from a previous era) and whilst every room seemed equipped with a safe, there didn't seem to be a usable one in the whole building.

Keys were missing (I mean, from which prehistoric era did hotel safes ever operate with keys?) because "guests have taken them, so (shrug) it's not our problem". Digital safes were pre-locked with unsmiling indifference to any knowledge of the code which might reopen them. When we were eventually moved to a room without a complimentary hole, our safe was so laughably small it only just accommodated two passports, with a stupidly hefty key worthy of Broadmoor Prison which, of course, we then felt obliged to store safely in the drawer immediately underneath it.

"Tomorrow (shrug)" became the catchphrase and stage-direction oft delivered when queries were repeatedly made at Reception – until a back-stage scriptwriter changed the riposte to "It won't be fixed (shrug) while you're here" delivered with the same deadpan indifference as that served up alongside the gallons of Aperol Spritz* we were ordering from the very Italian-paced bar.

**Footnote: Can't resist adding an observation from a passing Scots guest, who wanted to know what was all that "Irn Bru Fizz yer al'drinkin there?"*

The Four-Star Fellowship

Montecatini Terme & Environs, Tuscany, Italy

Our 'Taste of Tuscany' holiday is already sadly at an end, and it was indeed a full-on Tuscan experience – introducing us to this unique and exceptionally beautiful region of Italy through an intensive series of tours over the course of a busy week (just like it said on the tin).

Our base hotel – an allegedly four-star "Grand Hotel" in Montecatini Terme sadly fell – as reported previously – just a gnat's-cock short of a well-deserved 'Utterly-Crap-No-Star' designation. We were delighted to find it redeemed, however, by our genteel coterie of fellow guests with whom we found ourselves bonding unexpectedly – when a gritty, truly British camaraderie drew us together in the face of our astonished adversity.

In true colonial fashion, we gathered for pre-dinner cocktails in the warmth of a late summer Italian evening on the Hotel patio, where – by dint of our substantial number – we simply took the place by storm. Here, we delighted in rearranging the furniture to create our own ocean-going niche of tables, where The Four-Star Fellowship were to convene thenceforth at every available opportunity. Here, into the late of our expensively upgraded nights, we experimented with cocktails, wines, beers, cigars, contraband brandy, deep joy and pant-wetting laughter alongside the occasional sobering coffee or tea.

We revelled in charging rounds of drinks to fictitious room-numbers and competitively timing the appalling lengths of time it took the poor, bumbling moustachioed bar-tender – immediately nicknamed Guiseppe, after Pinocchio's Dad – to find sufficient ice with which to serve up just a couple of Aperol Spritzers.

And you'll no doubt recall, Observant Readers, that mention was passingly made, in a previous chapter, of a giant penis. This fascinating appendage belonged to a surprising sculpture plonked incongruously in the village square of Greve, Chianti and around which we swirled in admiration. As the appendage attached to the limbless, headless bronze torso became the butt (you may pause here, dear reader, to appreciate that witty, wry, punned juxtaposition) of our puerile jokes, our group felt compelled to arrange themselves for a souvenir photograph.

Sadly, one of our party was unavailable at the moment this compositional masterpiece was conceived (is that a word I can legitimately associate with a giant penis, I wonder?) but was heard to quip thereafter that he'd spent enough time modelling it, so didn't feel the need to appear beside his own representation.

And with that, we bade farewell to our itinerant group of new friends as we went our separate ways at the end of a truly engaging, enjoyable, hospitable and hysterical holiday.

We shall meet again. But probably not there.

PART SEVEN

East to Norfolk, West to Cornwall

"There are four directions:
North, South, East and West.
We are going in the fifth direction,
which is the direction of stories."

Sean Taylor, American NFL Footballer
1983-2007

Spam Wasp Fish

Narborough, Leicestershire, England

We're trundling slowly towards the Norfolk coast, with pleasingly short jaunts between overnight stopovers, mainly because we can and – let's face it – there's no rushing a Knumptywagen.

Tonight finds us in a pub car park in the delightful village of Castle Rising, named (we presume) after a big castle rising above the flint-built eighteenth-century cottages which make up this picturesque and – until we arrived – unspoilt Norfolk settlement.

Now, like a dumped fridge, our incongruous white bulk occupies a corner of the Black Horse car park, where we're anticipative of evening hospitality and overnight shelter, commensurate with an earlier period in English history, when travellers would prevail upon local inns and taverns to refresh both themselves and their horses – provided they plied the landlord with sufficient hard cash.

Whilst plipping a debit-card doesn't have quite the same ring to it, it does serve to at least maintain the same symbiosis betwixt provider and consumer, so we'll let you know how we are received and hopefully file a glowing report on the victuals we shortly plan to consume.

And talking of which, yesterday evening, rather surprisingly, the Navigating Troutess decided to supplement her meagre in-van diet with a wasp. This, she assures me, was totally unintentional and only recognised as a potentially dangerous form of protein when she found an early-evening swig from a bottle of beer to be uncharacteristically 'lumpy'.

Thankfully, both beer and offending wasp were quickly expelled under significant pressure across both herself, myself and the general surroundings as we sat in otherwise calm, contemplative mood, watching two floats bob gently in a peaceful fishing pool. Not really wishing to consider the alarming consequences if the damn thing had actually stung her 'en bouche' or worse, we moved swiftly on to something a little stronger, this time with a stoppered neck, and – utilising a 4-year-old tin of Spam found at the back of a cupboard as bait – successfully caught one perch; one tench and one carp, the majority of which species we had not previously encountered, so some lightness of mood thence thankfully prevailed. All of which contrasted significantly with today's fishing expedition, where we plipped away a small fortune in exchange for a day's fishing for trout – extensive shoals of which had clearly been trained to avoid capture by any means and were also astute enough to recognise a steadily accruing profit-margin if they remained in the water. Which they did.

In conclusion, our departure from an extremely well-maintained and agreeable Narborough Campsite & Fishery was heralded by low-level training runs of two flights of Red Arrow jets overhead, while we refilled our water-tank and poured away the unmentionables. Hopefully, we might return – and unusually, would recommend the site to other Knumpties, who will hopefully be imbued with better fishing and wasp-detection skills than ours.

Black Horse Castle Rising

Castle Rising, Norfolk, England

Observant and committed readers will have clocked a reference in the previous tale to our 'date night' in the Black Horse pub, which we'd discovered was amenable to the occasional Knumptywagen cluttering their car park overnight in exchange for consumption of their victuals. Which we did - and found both to be very good indeed.

But just before that, we enjoyed a wander around this enchanting hamlet, exploring the twelfth-century castle with its vertiginously sloped, grassy, V-shaped moat. An information board explained how the aging residents – 'Sisters' – of the nearby towering-chimneyed Trinity Hospital alms houses – would still attend church services dressed in period costume – scarlet capes and Welsh-style black hats – to honour the patronage of the Howard family, whose preponderance of headstones in the churchyard clearly evidenced their status as Lords of the Manor.

Meanwhile, back at the Black Horse, our evening was nothing short of bloody delightful, made more so, admittedly, by this outing being only our second 'dining out' experience since we were all technically released from Covid lockdown constraints.

As such, we also dressed-up (as much as our limited in-van wardrobe allowed); splashed on a dash of smelly stuff and presented ourselves at the bar of this thriving country pub, sans masks and therefore feeling a little like absconding schoolchildren.

Interestingly, not one person in this thrumming, post-Covid, Wednesday-night bar restaurant was wearing a mask – a fact remarked upon by our welcoming, chatty and jovial barman as we actually leant on the bar to peruse the range of beers on hand-pump.

"We've really missed this" we each admitted, as two customers actually arrived wearing masks –

looking suddenly out-of-place and slightly self-conscious because of it. What strange times we're living through.

Cheery waitresses, chirpy bar-staff and smiley customers created an enjoyable social atmosphere, with difficult menu decisions until we plumped for a halibut-steak special, served on spring onion mash with tender stem broccoli and shrimps in black butter. Unbelieving that such a thing could actually exist, your emaciated author then chose the signature burger which weighed in at a hefty whole ten ounces and took thirty minutes to cook to a perfect pink, if that's OK with you, sir? To while away that intervening half-hour, what else could we do but drink chilled Pinot and enjoy three starters from an imaginative tapas menu which included seared king scallop; feta, mint & beetroot salad and beer-battered king prawn with curry mayo.

Local characters wandered through. One aging rock-star lookalike, on his own in an incongruous white linen jacket and another, a very gentlemanly George (the spitting image of Colin Dexter, creator of Inspector Morse), stopped by our table to recommend the Eton Mess dessert – clearly not realising how overly stuffed our napkin-disguised little tummies had become.

The evening ended with an uplifting post-Covid chat with our NHS-Community-Nurse training waitress (anchored throughout her busy shift by an impossibly heavy-looking pair of big black Doc Martin boots) and a joyously replete stagger across a deeply gravelled car park to the comfort of the Knumptywagen.

In the small, enclosed field next door, a pair of obese and hairy pigs snored in the darkness; a small herd of oversize sheep bleated their good-nights and we were lulled into peaceful sleep by the soft, gentle tolling of the Church tower clock.

Wild Camping Is Royally Preceded

Sandringham, Norfolk, England

Sandringham was the much-loved country retreat of the late Her Majesty, Queen Elizabeth II and has been the private home of four generations of British monarchs since 1862. An unassumingly beautiful architectural building, the House is set in 24 hectares of formal gardens which in turn are surrounded by over ten times that area of Royal Park, much of which is wooded with stately and beguilingly upright conifers, interspersed with the occasional venerable oak of considerable girth and age (a bit like me, then) – thrown in for historic context, aesthetic balance and good measure.

So, that's the blurb bit sorted – what else do you want to know? We surprised ourselves by enjoying our visit to Sandringham – the Royals certainly know how to satisfy their loyal subjects, with typically British quirkiness (evidenced by the occasional pale-green, unoccupied sentry-boxes dotted around the grounds); an historic pedigree the envy of the world – and a presumed army of talented grounds-people imparting a good, stiff upper lip (and a Latin label) to almost everything growing in the landscape at which we cared to cast our eyes.

We didn't do the interior of the Jacobean house – and became smug with that decision as it became clear from our glimpses through ground-floor windows that a shuffling, slow moving, blue-rinsed throng was ambling genteelly amidst Her Majesty's goods and chattels, unable to see much besides the backs of other ticketholders' heads bobbing frustratingly in front. Similarly, we elected to also avoid the queue for the famous Church of St Mary Magdalene which had built-up in anticipation of its sixteenth-century doors being opened on the Royal dot of twelve noon.

Exit through the gift-shop (Sandringham Kitchen Chopping Boards a snip at £99.00) and onwards, in a now Royally endowed Knumptywagen, whence another short jaunt brought us to the padlocked gate of our chosen holiday campsite; sited in a church field just above the large, trendy village of Burnham Market, and with spectacular views towards a very distant North Sea.

An artistically poised windmill draws the eye to the middle ground, presumably to detract from the fact, (soon to become apparent to us newly arrived, naïve visitors) that the sea is bloody miles away ALL ALONG this north Norfolk coast. (Even when we reached a sandy beach after a goodly stretch of strong walking, the actual sea itself appeared to have headed to Norway for a day-out of its own.)

Undaunted, the Chief Pioneering Researcher Of Wild Camping Fields Throughout North Norfolk And Its Environs alighted the vehicle with a lightness of step suggesting that she was in possession of the secret padlock code. In we drove to take up a carefully considered pitch with aforementioned view of picturesque windmill – and a thin grey strip of distant murk iced with a frill of white beyond. The hedgerows trembled as the wind blew through; anoraked children gambolled like lambs through the mown grass and our fellow campers sat out stoically in puffer-jackets and woolly hats, clutching steaming mugs of tea to enjoy the seasonal August Bank Holiday weather.

Here, as we settled into our pitch, we realised that there are bits of the Knumptywagen (mostly slung beneath our wallowing bulk amidst what I assume may be technically referred to as the undercarriage) that we have never, ever had cause to use.

Such was our excitement at the start of our uncharacteristic five-night booking that we felt a burning compunction to Make Ready Our Steadies. A matched pair of these creakingly antiquated, grease-encrusted, rusted stanchions are located beneath the rear of the main body of the Knumptywagen and are designed to be wound-down like mini-jacks to take weight off the rear wheels. As such, they stop the vehicle rolling on its suspension while at rest, as we move about within. A few grunted but otherwise gentle expletives muffled by mouthfuls of cut grass later, our Steadies were successfully deployed – as proven by the Chief Pioneering Researcher cavorting lasciviously in the rear of the vehicle as we declared ourselves pitched and stable for the duration.

Out came our rarely-used windbreak to provide a modicum of shelter for two recliners and pop-up table; down went the doormat; on went the gas and the kettle and into our chairs we proudly slumped – for at least ten minutes – after which we swiftly deployed ourselves back inside the newly-steadied interior to brew tea and get some feeling back into our fingers and toes.

With a prior invitation from family friends to discover how the other half lives and visit them in their static caravan moored at Brancaster, we then decided to reconnoitre the fourmile route and duly unhitched the bicycles from the rear rack; donned as much of the little outerwear we'd thought to bring with us and set off down narrow, high-hedged country lanes in search of the Norfolk Coast Path.

As its name implies, we quickly discovered that – no matter how hard we tried – the narrow flint-studded, potholed and compacted-earth 'Path' stubbornly refused to be misinterpreted as a 'Cycleway' – so we tactically withdrew our shaken coccyges (look it up – I had to) and instead placed our lives and limbs at the mercy of an overwhelming inundation of grey-black, personally-plated Chelsea Tractors as we plied our wobbly way westwards on the scarily narrow A149.

At a peculiar, almost North-American-styled retail development which seemed to have sprung up at Burnham Deepdale, solace from the traffic appeared in the form of a roadside footpath (almost as unnavigable as the Coast Path) which we unashamedly took to, despite the occasional frowning pedestrian, to eventually penetrate an extremely well maintained and discreetly unsigned caravan site facing the marshland which separates sea and civilisation on this stretch of coast.

Unusually for a Bank Holiday Friday, the site was virtually unoccupied – save for a lone and officious resident who appeared highly suspicious of our motives in seeking out our friends' caravan. Since they weren't due to arrive until the Saturday; since we didn't know the specific caravan number and since he'd 'never heard of them' when we provided their names, we were pointed towards to the exit with an imperious finger – which we were pleased to follow and headed homewards, wondering if all our experiences of Norfolkian engagement would be as terse.

Money Money Money

Thornham, Norfolk, England

Let's meet at Thornham Deli at 11:00am enthuse our friends, newly arrived at their static caravan – to find the police knocking on their neighbour's door. (We didn't dob him in after our cycle-based 'conversation' with self-same neighbour the day before, honest!)

OK, sounds like a plan so Chief Navigating Officer checks the map and Thornham is some way distant in a westerly direction from our current position. Cycles? Bit too far on busy, narrow roads solely occupied and wholly dominated by the entire high-end, four-wheel-drive output of Jaguar Land Rover's Solihull plant for the 2020-2021 fiscal year, all finished in a menacing shark grey (with gills down the side for added threatenability) and an entry-level price tag (new – which they all were) just north of £83k. All were sporting the latest line in personalised registration plates neatly affixed below giant, shiny, cyclist-consuming radiator grilles. Maybe not then.

Bus? The Norfolk Coastliner departs nearby Burnham Market every hour, we note – and what a childish thrill if we were to board one of those – kites, buckets, spades, towels all tucked chaotically under our arms. The prospect of a return journey, well after-hours and probably well drunk, minus all our possessions (including the van keys) with little idea of where (or how) to get off – all served to downgrade our sylvan expectations and we pondered some more.

Taxi? Imbued with a lifetime of parental influence, that was certainly not an option for the likes of us – the fares will inevitably cost almost as much as a Range Rover (admittedly pre-loved and in an unattractive colour.) And each way. Move on.

Then, out of a rising transportation despondency, we distil a moment's inspiration: Why don't we just drive there in the Knumptywagen? Well, I'll tell you why.

1) We've paid for our campsite pitch and we're damn well going to get our money's worth.

2) We've already – at some significant effort – already deployed our steadies, for goodness sake. AND plugged in to mains electricity. AND the gas is on.

3) One end of the windbreak is attached to the cycle rack (with a bungee cord, I'll have you know. What do you take us for – idiots?)

4) We'll have to leave possessions such as table and chairs behind, in order to preserve our pitch from the marauding desires of newly arriving piratical caravanners. And finally . . .

5) It's August Bank Holiday Saturday, ferchrissake, it'll be BEDLAM out there and parking will be a NIGHTMARE.

So, up sticks, and off we jolly well go.

Our Thornham Deli brunch was just bloody delightful – fulsome, flavoursome, extensive and smilingly served. A half-empty car park welcomed us, having bowled along a similarly unpopulated A149 as if we owned it. Friends arrived almost simultaneously and – somehow – already knew that a Bank Holiday table for the six of us was ready and waiting, even though the café took no bookings. Mightily impressed, we swept in like royalty, proud of our association with temporary residents, who not only knew a thing or two, but also owned a nearby static caravan that hadn't been visited by the Police.

Yet.

Food, Food, Food

Brancaster, Norfolk, England

It's a pleasing human trait that most of us are driven by our desire and liking for food. Despite the media's continuing interest in the so-called obesity crisis, at least those of us who are enthusiastic about eating stuff don't feel compelled to discuss our fixations in group therapy sessions. So it is that as we trundle our way around Knumptydom, we enjoy the prospect of good breakfasts, lunches or dinners, each of which should preferably not be accompanied by the ubiquitous 'ping' of a microwave.

So where is this taking us? Well, it's taking us to a magnificent seafood paella, expertly home-prepared, cooked and presented in the luxurious open-plan dining area of one large family caravan, moored on a static site on the Norfolk coast with an unimpeded view of the still-distant sea. Following this gastronomic extravaganza (and a surfeit of liquid refreshments, whaddyaknow), we are encouraged to stay the night, yet again in the capacious surroundings of this three-bedroomed, twin-toileted establishment, which – whilst admittedly not enjoying the manoeuvrability of a Knumptywagen – did seem the perfect place to spend quality holiday time.

The following morning, however, despite the previous night's excesses, an anticipated in-house breakfast was withheld, to be replaced instead by a healthy hike along the Coast Path. With this unprecedented activity, we arrived at the White Horse pub at Brancaster, where we were instead proffered a wide choice of breakfast goods, provided they could be contained within the confines of a fresh English muffin. Game on!

More striding the Coast Path ensued, fuelled by our ambition to return to our campsite at Burnham Breck, whence the six seat-belted Knumptywagen would retain and return our entire party back from whence we came.

However, with Burnham Market's Bank Holiday Sunday attractions providing too much interim intrigue, we wandered into the village to find an incongruous party of gentlemen all dressed for the afternoon in black tie, gathered outside the Hoste Arms, apparently awaiting the arrival of their slowly-dressing partners. Successfully attired and clearly well-refreshed, the whole entourage then embarked two double-decker London buses parked on the village green and disappeared eastwards – presumably to a well-dressed wedding celebration in a layby somewhere along the A149.

A nearby pop-up oyster stall proved a further attraction, with one guy busily shucking to a small admiring audience; another guy laying out the freshly opened oysters on an impressively massive bed of ice while the finale was delivered by the salesman of the team, a gentleman of considerable girth. With Dickensian charm, he managed to extol the delights of the raw shellfish, while also freely admitting that they can occasionally cause digestive discomfort; that it normally takes seven years to recover your willingness to try another after a bad episode, and that he himself had been proudly hospitalised after a dodgy session with the otherwise acclaimed bivalve molluscs.

We moved on. As did several other innocent bystanders who – up until that point – had seemed fully willing to partake.

To round off the day, we successfully navigated to a very agreeable parking spot where the Knumptywagen came to rest. We disembarked; ate cake then walked onto Brancaster Beach – a vast expanse of sand with still very little sign of anything sea-like. Our guides (the ones who know stuff) led us some distance along the beach where we were rewarded with a private grandstand view of at least a dozen wild seals, besporting themselves in a small estuary, and seemingly willing to perform a number of circus tricks for our entertainment. (No, alright, they weren't exactly balancing balls; clapping their flippers or blowing a tune on an array of horns, but they did manage a few back-flips and some spectacular leaps from the water.) Watching them transform from seemingly disabled, lumbering grey lumps into sleek, streamlined, sinuous streaks swimming effortlessly at speed through the semi-clear water, we remained transfixed and fulfilled by the experience.

And then, as a final gesture to the day and to herald our return hike along the beach, we launched a rarely used stunt kite which a goodly breeze kept aloft for almost three percent of our walk, gathering sand and marram grass for the other ninety-seven as it crashed, skidded and was dragged ignominiously alongside us, marking the end of a thoroughly wonderful August Bank Holiday Sunday.

Go Placidly Amid The Noise And The Haste

Ely, Cambridgeshire, England

The A14 is a car park. We know this since we can see from afar a tailback of static traffic, thankfully before we join the constipated throng. Frustratingly, satnav is having none of it and no matter which avoidance tactic we try, it resolutely wants us to join that jam and delay our journey home by Lordaloneknows how long. Out comes the map-book and despite no obvious alternative, we plot a route which ultimately adds about ninety minutes to our overall journey time, but – what the hell – at least we keep moving, which always feels better.

We've decamped from Burnham Breck, bang on the 11:30 curfew at which point the site closes until next year, but not before we pay a valedictory visit to Burnham Market. Here, we find the village fully-functioning after its apparent confusion with the Bank Holiday weekend. We observe that even the bookshop is now open, which we'd been keen to visit from the outset but which had been closed (resolutely refusing to display any opening times for the benefit of potential customers such as ourselves) so we voted with our feet and passed by on the other side of the road.

In doing so, our last-ditch lobster hunt was also delightfully fulfilled in Gurney's fishmongers, where freshly cooked, sadly single-clawed lobsters gleamed coral-red from the iced display. Snapping one up (geddit?) and then acquiring holiday-bad breakfast goods from the next-door bakery, we returned to the Knumptywagen, racked the bikes and found to our delight, as we put it into the fridge, that our bargain one-clawed lobster actually sported a full set.

Ely was very pretty and a river ran through it. The imposing and impressive-looking Cathedral – the ship of the Fens – is a delightful amalgam of church architecture through the ages, as the CNO ('O' level in 'Art with Architecture', she'll have you know) was keen to point out. It appears to owe its most lauded feature – the soaring 52m-high octagonal lantern above the main altar – to the fact that this had to be installed after the previous tower collapsed (an indication that cowboy builders were also rife prior to A.D. 1322, or perhaps instead a sublimely ironic act of God's displeasure with the original design?)

Having paid out £8.00 per-head entry fee, we wandered as diligently as we could, craning our necks upwards, downwards, sideways and forwards to marvel at both the power of religion to cause such edifices to be raised to the glory of God – and to the astonishing capabilities of stonemasons throughout history. We lit candles at every opportunity – not from any long-abandoned religious observance but more to feel we were getting our money's worth. Exit without passing through the gift-shop and there we were, back on Ely's pretty, bustling streets.

Onwards to our next port-of-call at Offord d'Arcy to impose (again) upon a long-lost cousin and family, where – in the delightful surroundings of this Domesday Book village – we're assailed by a psychotic, thankfully-muzzled sausage-dog who erratically and without warning, attempts to taste our ankles and calves throughout our visit. Made welcome and immediately anaesthetised through capricious and dedicated applications of wine, we enjoyed a thoroughly sociable evening in the company of family with whom we've remained distant for far too long.

The following morning, we head off towards the aforementioned A14, aiming this time for a friend's art exhibition, close to home and hosted in an isolated, beautifully restored, 18th century Orangery. Dressed with an astounding display of collaged birds of the air, suspended in flocked flight from the ceiling, we enjoyed a show-round in the company of the artist and designer Kate Slater, purchased one of her published, illustrated children's books and headed for home.

As a final delight of the trip, we find that our small flock of self-sustaining hens, three of which are newly acquired, have laid blue-shelled eggs and there's even a few left for tomorrow's breakfast. All in all, not a bad trip.

Canned Heat

Burnham Deepdale, Norfolk, England

Los Angeles, California, 1965. Blues musicians Alan Wilson and Bob Hite's 'hippy' band kick off an offbeat rhythmic harmonica riff accompanied by opening lyrics along the lines of "I'm so tired of cryin' - but I'm out on the road again, I'm on the road again."

Such it is that the tune becomes our gentle earworm as the Knumptywagen trundles out – for the first time this year – on a long-weekend jaunt towards Norfolk to assist in the celebration of a good friend's 60th birthday.

Although bright, sharp sunshine graced us for most of the trip, prevailing winds sadly suppressed the temperature to a shrill, sharp cold – well below the canned heat we would normally expect on jaunts further south – but hell, yes, we're on the road again!

And what roads they are! For almost every mile, extensive surface degradation is riddled with unavoidable potholes which noisily rattle the contents of the cutlery drawer. It's clear that wholly unreported military-grade shelling and strafing with hostile ordnance has been taking place across our fine English counties during our pandemic-induced period of SORN.

Alarmingly, it also seems as if most of Norfolk's fauna has been busy sacrificing itself to the roadside as well. Fully-formed and apparently unsullied deer appear at rest in gutters; shiny-furred foxes lie both intact and – slightly less shiny – flattened across white lines. Matt grey hulks of badgers are slumped like naval shipwrecks; dead rabbits abound (or not, obvs) – along with a singular mad March hare – all are added to our incidental tally, along with a perfectly-preserved iridescently-headed male mallard.

The most unnerving surprise of all this kerbside carnage came with a large, roadside dumped grey-silver sandbag, glistening with reflected sunlight and looking every inch like the hunched back of a small dolphin, incongruous in the extreme given that we were still thirty miles from the nearest coast. The pheasant population had also contributed to the carenage. Suicide-vested in plumes of tan, ochre and bronze they had obligingly sacrificed themselves at regular four-mile intervals by way of macabre milestones marking our journey eastwards.

At some ill-defined point in time, and slightly numbed by the monotony of the road rolling through flat, verdant Norfolk countryside, a rare moment of lucidity intruded into our reveries. When (if at all) had we re-road-taxed the Knumptywagen after its liberation from semi-retirement? The answer was that we hadn't, so with that guilt-ridden anxiety now lodged firmly in mind, every speed-camera was passed at well below the posted limit, with both CNO and Pilot subconsciously hunching and ducking heads in the forlorn hope of avoiding identification – and subsequent criminal proceedings.

And just by-the-by, Wells-next-the-Sea isn't.

It could be argued that it is, sort of – but only in the same way that Pop Tarts could claim to be edible. It is nevertheless a quaintly characterful and agreeable small-town harbouring (geddit?) an upmarket café called Bang, which – as its name thankfully implies – is bang in the middle of town. Except it isn't. Really. But no matter. It still served a damn fine brunch to our famished party of fake seafarers, newly disembarked from a completely unexpected and delightful boat-trip around the inlets and islets which keep the sea at a respectful distance from the town.

And then – what fun, frivolous and joyous sociability ensued! Our continually coalescing party of ten bimbled in nondescript convoy through the Norfolk countryside from visitor-attraction to hospitality and back again, indulging in mass-feeding-frenzies at every opportunity (all at our generous host's considerable expense – and why not?)

Eventually, the Knumptywagen peeled away to make semi-permanent landfall at an impressively well-kept campsite at Burnham Deepdale, where we unfurled a sadly necessary windbreak and settled ourselves in for a good few days of static social activity.

Cornwall Calling

St. Ives, Cornwall, England

The Knumptywagen has sadly lain dormant for the best part of the year so, as autumn begins to colour the scenery, we book ourselves a week somewhere, to be decided almost at the last minute, subject to weather forecasts, all of which turned out to be pretty damp and grey.

However, Cornwall had always been an ambition and – despite the distance from our north Midlands home – off we set, with high hopes and an extremely expensive tankful of diesel.

On a trek of this magnitude (300 miles-ish to first port-of-call) we've previously overnighted with family in Bristol but - having got wind of our planned route - said family had fled the country, leaving the Chief Navigating Officer to find us a half-way point where we might overnight for free.

And what a delightful surprise was Burnham-on-Sea! Come September, according to all the parking signs, no charges were imposed and at the end of the promenade we found a small but friendly cluster of fellow Knumpties gathered roadside behind the shelter of a reassuringly dominant seawall. The walkable Victoria Hotel provided hospitality and sustenance prior to a peaceful overnight and then a sharp start the following morning back onto the M5, next stop St Ives. Here, Ayr Holiday Park found us a pitch overlooking Porthmeor Beach and despite some heftily gusting wind, we then sauntered down the Coast Path on a voyage of exploration and discovery.

Now, maybe our expectations were set a little on the high side, and maybe a blusterous, grey-skied day in mid-October didn't provide the best introduction, but some of the properties backing onto the beach looked a little tired – and the town itself, while still busy with well-wrapped tourists, just seemed a tad jaded, assumedly after an exhaustingly busy post-Covid summer?

Despite the proximity of crashing waves all around us, one surprise was the lack of any obvious fresh-fish shop in the town. Thankfully remedied by our accidental discovery of a harbourside fish & chip shop / restaurant with an almost hidden side-slab of marble, we procured a couple of healthy chunks of fresh hake (along with an obligatory tub of anchovies – a guilty pleasure for at least one of us) and headed back to plugged-in warmth and shelter. A fish-supper was therefore served in-van, rocking like a yacht in the strong winds which – accompanied by always-noisy rain – made for a wakeful night.

The following morning, having felt we'd seen enough of St Ives to satisfy our curiosity, we set sail for Sennen Cove. Still grey-skied and windy, Sennen Cove presented an empty seawall car park; surf dotted with black, seal-skinned surfers and the surprise of a coastal path to Land's End – which we walked with appreciation and enthusiasm. Land's End provided a curiously incongruous mix of commercial tourist attractions so we each availed of the facilities and an enjoyable traditional Cornish pasty before setting our heads down against the still forceful wind and walking back to our point of origin.

Here, despite diligently paying the required fee, we found our ever-so-slightly overlength Knumptywagen had attracted a parking ticket, which we'd naively assumed we'd avoid, forgetting that the days of avuncular and benevolent part-time local council officials had been swallowed wholesale by the malevolent, ever-vigilant, camera-watchful, profit focussed behemoths of private agency.

Downhearted? Of course not! We were on holiday in Cornwall, the sea beckoned and the local surf-shack was knocking out their end-of-season rental wetsuits at twenty-five pounds a pop. To redress our sniffy sense of imbalance, the CNO was even allowed to take a couple back to her private changing room in the now-financially penalised Knumptywagen and pronounced that – hang the expense, I'm having the first one I don't have to squeeze myself into.

Which she did. And then flip-flopped onto the beach, entering the breaking surf with all the confidence, panache and bravery of a cross-channel challenger – and then cavorting like a porpoise for the benefit of her beached photographer, towel- and shoe-holder.

Superstition Mountain

Porthcurno, Cornwall, England

Now. Who knew the likes of us would ever find themselves in the vicinity of the renowned Minack Theatre? This amazing vision and construct had always imparted a mythical impression to those of us Knumpties who live nowhere near the sea, let alone a minimum six hour drive from said attraction. In many respects the Minack had been the stuff of distant dreams when occasionally glimpsed in the pages of newspapers, magazines or on TV. Yet here we were, just a pebble's toss from our current location and no onward plans. So off we went. In fact, we got a bit lost en-route and ended up ditching the van in a car park adjacent to the rather imposing Museum of Global Communications where, with teasingly smirkful irony, we discovered we had absolutely zero mobile-phone signal.

Nevertheless, having checked the car parking terms and conditions for an acceptable vehicle length, we paid the appropriate fee in scrabbled-together and slightly fluffy loose change (being unable to utilise the handily publicised mobile-phone option) and lashed on our walking-boots.

Skirting the breathtakingly stunning Porthcurno Beach, we could then walk the steep and winding road to reach the quaintly rural Minack Theatre entrance. Here we were able to enquire at the Box Office itself if there was any outside chance at all that there might be any form of performance being staged that night, maybe, perhaps, any chance?

Well, of course there was. We're a theatre, don't you know, was the smilingly implied response to our energetic grockle-induced enthusiasm. Great, we say, two tickets please, and can we park the van here overnight? Well, no you can't, sadly, and don't you even want to know what it is you'll be watching, performance-wise, before I sell you these prized and legendary tickets?

So it was we negotiated ourselves into watching a three-man play with a Cornish American theme, alongside a lengthy local-knowledge sort-of conversation about where we could overnight-park the van nearby. Thus it was that a friendly lady at nearby Treen Campsite was pleased to relieve us of twenty-eight fine English pounds for a spot in any of her many empty camping fields, without electric hook-up, no pets and just two adults please – for an overnight stay which we calculated cost us about £1.50 per hour of wet grass and darkness.

Then the challenge of how we might get from Treen Campsite back to the Theatre in time for the 7:30 pm performance? Taxi? What? In this neck of the woods, at this time of year, and those times of night? You must be joking!

Walk the coastal path? What? In the pitch-black, intermittent lashing rain and a wind howling strong enough to blow you down the cliff-side and into the rolling surf? You must be grockles!

So we drove. Yes, it does seem like an obvious solution, but you'd be surprised how your mindset locks down once you've pitched-up and made camp. And not only 'we could drive' but if we time it right, we can enjoy an in-van, pre-theatre dining-experience immediately adjacent to the entrance, then just saunter to our rock-hewn, sea-lashed seats at our leisure.

Somewhat let down by our lack of foresight on the provisions-front, our splendid pre theatre dinner turned out to be hastily-rustled bacon, eggs and beans – the drifting smell of which nevertheless attracted several envious glances from arriving patrons. Thankfully the early-evening rain abated as – wrapped in as many layers as would allow us to exit the Knumptywagen – we made our way into the unique environment of this magically-lit, openair cliff-clinging amphitheatre.

Sitting on our damp stone seats, we thoroughly enjoyed the experience – "part epic adventure, part family saga, at the heart of Carl Grose's black comedy are the emotional ties and trials of three brothers, rubbing along together through thick and thin." Well, yeah, it wasn't Shakespeare but hey, from soundings taken thereafter amongst friends and family, it seems we were lucky to have witnessed a performance at all – since most people seem only to have visited the Minack during daylight hours as a tourist venue – so we felt as if we'd definitely enjoyed the limelight as we drove back in the dark to claim our wet and empty field.

Next Stop Mowzel

Mousehole, Cornwall, England

The morning after our visit to the Minack, we enjoyed a short but fantastic cliff walk from our wet field at Treen. The sky had cleared by chucking drummingly noisy rain onto our roof throughout the night and as a result the clear-aired coastal views were more than breathtaking. From a perilous height we marvelled at the crisp-white rolling surf, an aquamarine sky and wide, wide sea while wild ponies wandered the cliff-top path, indifferent to our apple- or sugar-lump-free presence.

With the open road now calling, we then set off towards nearby Mousehole – another tiny-harboured village within our reach and desire. Wisely, the CNO directed our journey to avoid several lesser, ever-narrowing roads – down which we'd surely have jammed ourselves side-to-side had it not been for her foresight and circumnavigation.

Thus, on a comfortably wide main road we discovered jeopardy-free roadside parking within sight of St Michael's Mount across the bay and - with Penzance to our rear - we pavement-hiked in glorious autumn sunshine the short walk into Mousehole. Despite being half-clad in scaffolding, this charming village was to more-than-fulfil our expectations. (When we'd travelled in Canada, the prevalent joke revolved around the fact that there were ever only two seasons – Winter and Construction, and we guess the same must have applied here, now the summer crowds had departed.)

Nevertheless, with the sun shining warmly, we wandered around the rambling streets; artisan shops; sea-views espied through unlikely stretyns (I know, y'know) and the general sun-blessed ambience of this miniature fishing village. Acquiring old-school postcards, we're directed to the quaint mobile Post Office transit van parked up by the harbour-wall, beyond which we happily witnessed several lady-swimmers taking to the sheltered waters. An artist painted en-plein-air at the water's edge; fishing boats nodded sagely at the wisdom of not being out in the fairly rough, white-capped sea - and archetypal stripy-sweatered, roughly hewn gentlemen smoking pipes clumped about in turned-down wellies.

"Crab Sandwiches" boasted the sign outside the waterfront deli, and – squeezing ourselves onto a sun-washed bench – we availed, as it seemed wholly inappropriate not to. What the sign should have said, had there been sufficient space, was "Absolutely Bloody
Delicious Malted Brown Bread Doorstep Sandwiches Rammed Chock Full of Fresh Crabmeat and Mayo with a Delightful Dressed Side Salad in an Environmentally Friendly and Very Trendy Brown Cardboard Box". Nuff said.

And then we had ice-creams. Because we could.

We Fail To Mount St. Michael

Marazion, Cornwall, England

Executing a swift and rather neat U-turn, we now turn our dirt-splattered rear-end on Mousehole and head back through Newlyn towards Penzance (which we find a little difficult to see clearly, through eyes watering at the cost of refuelling with diesel again.) A pleasing promenade drive fails to distract us as we now have St Michael's Mount (another bucket-list ambition) in our sights.

Standing proud, spectacular and silhouetted in lowering autumn sunlight, this ancient, rugged castle; family home and National Trust garden all set on a tiny tiered island accessed at low tide over a granite causeway (or ferry at high tide) was sadly and disappointingly closed, as we discovered from an amenable car park warden as we heaved-to in the first car park to offer respite from the slightly unnerving traffic-controlling chicanery of the main approach road through Marazion.

"The Mount's closed due to the weather and tides" we're told through our hopefully opened window. "And it's been like that for the last five days" he adds resignedly. "Not even sure it'll be any better tomorrow – but if you're going to park up, you'll need the other car park. You should be alright in there" he concludes, casting an appraising eye along our full 5.5m length. "Yeah, should be, just about."

So we trundle ourselves into the adjacent car park, where Terms and Conditions yet again specify a maximum length of – you guessed it – 5.5m. Made anxious by our ticketed experience at Sennen Cove and aware that, with the rear cycle-rack in use, we were technically a tad over 5.5m – we wander bemusedly on foot in search of directional signs for an overflow car park where we're also advised we can park, having paid the requisite fee based on our pre-anticipated duration-of-stay, thank-you-kindly.

This turns out to be a field on the opposite side of the road to the sea, where we come to rest long enough to get the kettle on, at the same time realising we no longer even have a view of the now unattainable St Michael's Mount. Hey ho! As recompense, out come our lounging chairs as we again risk prosecution and possible incarceration by test-flying a newly acquired birthday-gifted drone, in deliberate contravention of yet more Terms and Conditions, Item 14, sub-clause 3.1, paragraph 2.

Experienced Knumpties will already know that motorhome overnight stops are often available from a network of pubs, which offer safe haven in their car parks at no charge in exchange for custom. Without any formulated onward plan, our research rinses a dose of ragged 3G internet and we get sequentially turned down by several hostelries, all of which were obviously well-entrenched in the Construction season. One friendly voice in the crackling wilderness offers us a spot in their car park, some way inland but at least in our preferred direction, so we wave a mixed-feeling farewell to the Mount of St Michael, and head inland to see what befalls us at The Engine Inn in the slightly-unnervingly named village of Cripplesease. Wish us luck.

A Slippery Field At Padstow

Padstow, Cornwall, England

Who knew? Come on, own up! Who knew that Padstow wasn't a seaside town? We'd never given it a thought as we avidly consumed countless programmes hosted by TV chef and celebrity resident Rick Stein.

But it's the River Camel estuary that flows past Padstow, so as we nudge the Knumptywagen into the safety of the last remaining long-vehicle space in the portside Station car park, we take stock of our surroundings and decide we must explore.

We arrived here following disappointing rejections of our lumbering bulk by both Perranporth and Newquay (where we'd hoped to find opportunity for breakfast, alas unfulfilled by height-restricted car parks in both towns.) As such, we were now feeling a little lunchtime peckish and our purposeful rambling was therefore first towards one of Rick Stein's lauded fish & chip shops, located alongside a neighbouring shoe-store.

Despite anticipative rumblings from below, shoes suddenly became more of a priority as the CNO took it upon herself to be reshod with a pair "she'd been looking for for ages." By which time, Rick's had gathered an off-putting queue to his salt and vinegary portal so we passed by and headed more purposefully into the main town. Which was very pleasant. A bustle of tourists such as ourselves provided the necessary atmosphere as we peeked into gift shops; upmarket fish restaurants; bookshops; gazed across the estuary to Rock; looked in more fish restaurants and generally took in a pleasing selection of independent food and seaside fashion stores.

As the rain abated and raw sunlight made its first tentative appearance of the day, we became captivated by an open-sided fish & chip restaurant overlooking the harbour – and enjoyed a table en plein air but just enough under cover to be sheltered from any further squalls. As it turned out, this particular establishment was not part of the Stein Empire but was just as good as, at half the price, according to an apparently knowledgeable tour-guide who was queuing with her tray alongside our own.

Following our battered haddock lunches, The Tourist Office proved helpfully knowledgeable about local overnight campsite prospects – although we weren't really in need of electric hook-up, let alone swimming pools, childrens' entertainments or onsite (fish!) restaurants and bars. "Ah!" exclaimed our host as if inspiration had suddenly struck, and followed up rhetorically with "I wonder if Jessica's is open at this time of year?"

Passing over a mobile number scribbled onto a Post-it note, she biro'd a vague circle on the top sheet of her pad of tear-off town maps, to denote the field which presumably belonged to Jessica. With grateful thanks we rang the number and left a voicemail, followed up swiftly by a text message to say we'd left a voicemail (I am nothing if not my father's son) and headed back towards the van.

Although we'd undertaken a fair amount of Cornish exploration on our trip, we had sadly discovered virtually no lobster available for consumption, so were naturally curious about the existence of the National Lobster Hatchery, occupying a prominent site almost adjacent to our parked van – and with time still left on the parking ticket, we decided to risk the entry fee and check it out. As semi-interesting static-display panels go, there was plenty to look at, with the walk-though experience punctuated by glimpses through magnifying glass domes to witness the occasional sad, lonely but at least live lobster waving its antenna and chelipeds at us. (See, it was informative!)

Further into the display we encounter an enthusiastic volunteer who talks us through large gently circulating seawater tanks full of minuscule, semi-transparent lobster fry, floating randomly past our gaze as if enjoying an oversized submersible fairground ride. Further on, we witness the development stages of this fascinating marine crustacean, until they become mature enough to be returned to the wild, wild sea – often by the very fishermen who will hopefully harvest their grown-on forms in several years' time.

Without any response from Jessica, we trundle a short distance out of Padstow and – sure enough – at the biro'd spot on our town map, we find an open-gated field clearly laid out for camping. With just one unoccupied vehicle in residence, we park up and get the kettle on. We're then shortly visited by a beslippered lady who we presumptively greet as Jessica, to discover this is in fact Jessica's Mum, looking after the field while Jessica besports herself on holiday in Toronto, so no real surprise that she didn't pick up. (It further turns out that digits had been transposed on our Tourist Office note, so Lord alone knows who received our bizarre phone message and text, or why, out of sheer curiosity, they hadn't called back!)

Anyway, we negotiate for a single overnight stay, skid the van helplessly up the greasy grassed field (in reverse!) to a better viewpoint over the distant River Camel, and not only continue with our tea-brewing activities but launch yet another tentative drone test-flight, from which we discover what a filthy roof we present to the aerialised world. As evening fell, we walked the short distance back into Padstow to conduct a gentle and unremarkable pub crawl in several hostelries before returning to the van for a deserved cheese and wine supper – beneath a very dirty roof.

And no. Despite our best efforts we didn't get to clap eyes on Rick Stein.

A Seaside Swim In Bude

Bude, Cornwall, England

We arrive in Bude full of eager anticipation (on behalf of at least one of us) for a swim in their fascinating beachside, seawater pool.

As a semi-natural amenity, Bude Sea Pool was conceived, built and opened in the 1930's as a semi-natural tidal pool and a safe haven for wild swimming on the edges of the Atlantic Ocean. Free to use and with few restrictions, it's clearly a local amenity which has gained a national reputation.

Created under the natural curve of beachside cliffs, its outer wall protects users from the ferocity of the Atlantic Ocean yet allows the contained water to be regularly refreshed at high-tides to provide a naturally replenished year-round sheltered sea water pool.

Although the day of our visit was grey, overcast and hardly conducive to open air bathing, there were plenty of half-term holidaymakers enjoying both the beach and the adjacent immersive experience. With car parks some distance from the pool, the CNO bravely donned her newly acquired wetsuit in the confined comfort of the Knumptywagen and we flip-flopped our way across a grassy coastal embankment to access the pool from a busy beach.

With water and air temperatures both of similar degree, your bystanding author – again clutching footwear, towel and juggling a phone camera – is informed that the water doesn't feel cold at all (or at least not once you're in, which is the perennial cry from anyone crazed enough to consider that open water swimming is an enjoyable pastime.)

With a throng of variously sized and aged wet-suited bathers all bobbing seal-like in the placid waters, and a backdrop of coloured bathing huts, the whole scene appeared to be a slow-motion, sepia-tinted film, reminiscent of an era when the pool was still only a local attraction.

Sated, (salted maybe?) we return to the Knumptywagen and finding not a lot else of interest to detain us in the immediate vicinity, we up sticks and head north towards the next waypoint on our spontaneously unplanned journey homewards.

The Fuming Raging Storm

Taunton, Devon, England

Holly Bush Farm Campsite had mixed reviews but having already identified the location near Taunton as a good off-the-beaten-track half-way point on the final leg of our journey home, we booked in and turned up mid-afternoon. Brusquely attended to on arrival, we're directed to the lower field, with hard-standing pitches and no need of electric hook-up.

A handful of motorhomes and caravans were dotted around the newly-laid site and – wouldn't you know it – we find ourselves in almost immediate conversation with a purple haired character smoking something presumably exotic on the step of his neighbouring van, which we could see was packed to overflowing with what could best be described as 'a variety of stuff'. He was clearly desirous of an in-depth and subsequently rambling conversation about installing a replacement leisure battery he'd just acquired; the all-consuming benefits of YouTube as the source of all motorhoming know-how on the planet; was it the red or the black lead you took off and replaced first?; how his partner had passed away from cancer only last year; would the installation affect his breaker-switches; did we have any idea how much he might have paid for his bargain van and – by-the-by – did we have a spanner or two (preferably adjustable) he could borrow just so he could fit his new battery?

We swiftly decide that an exploration of the site and the servicing of our own unmentionables had become an urgent priority so managed to disappear towards respite not often enjoyed in the peaceful surroundings of a chemical toilet. On our ramble, we discover that the site is very rural with hilly terrain and a narrow, speedy main road which discouraged demounting the bikes (having diligently lugged them around Cornwall unused) to explore further afield. However, we had previously passed an isolated-looking pub on our way to the site, within walkable distance – so crept back to the van to make a telephone enquiry about their opening hours; likely provision of food and quite possibly drink.

What a find! The Holman Clavell Inn was (and presumably still is) set in the midst of the Blackdown Hills, an Area of Outstanding Natural Beauty and slap bang in the middle of
Devon – where it might conceivably be the furthest you could be from the nearest sea. As such, our first choice from the menu surprised us with its availability – a pint of prawns – unlike our earlier experience in sea-washed St Ives where they unapologetically just didn't have any.

Low ceilings; aged oak beams, whitewashed walls, local Otter Brewery beers on tap and a warm welcome from cheery bar staff and locals alike, we immediately settled in at a scrubbed pine table by the bar. Held in its thrall for the best part of a dark, damp evening, we enjoyed cheerfully noisy groups of dining customers as they mingled with tweedy locals ebbing and flowing around us. Eventually, fully-victualled on starters, mains and puds and with little rosy hamster cheeks, we wrapped ourselves up, strapped on the headtorches and wobbled our way to stealthily regain the sanctuary of the Knumptywagen under cover of darkness.

Despite our replete and semi-comatose states, neither of us could recall any worse maelstrom of a storm which arrived that night. It raged with Shakespearean tempestuosity (is that even a word? Spellcheck seems to think not) around us with a deafening, fuming and alarming ferocity. Thunderous rain lashed onto our roof for almost two hours, amplified by the very nature of the large box in which we were contained. Lightning, seemingly both sheet and forked, crackled down as we peered like frightened children through the bedside window. Around five a.m. it calmed enough to allow us to hear one-another and, come the calm of morning, we were amazed that the site seemed wholly intact – and that we'd only shipped an egg-cup's worth of water which had somehow puddled its way through the main skylight.

Aah, blessed relief, as daylight brightened and we made ready to set off again, until a knock on our door heralded the continued enthusiastic curiosity of our neighbour. Still avidly keen to see if we were absolutely sure we didn't have any adjustable spanners and it was Axminster General his partner had died in, couldn't have been cared for better God bless the NHS and was it really the black lead (or maybe the red one) you took off first? "Sorry," we bustled "but we've an urgent appointment with some trout – must dash" and, with wheels not quite spinning on the newly laid pea-gravel, we took off up the open road, headed still towards home.

Nose Job

Lichfield, Staffordshire, England

Having recently completed over three thousand jeopardy-free miles knumptying around the UK and Europe we eventually came to rest in Chester, outside a family-member's home, where we were due to stay for a couple of nights.

With nothing more effortful than gentle docking into a suitably incongruous pitch on their accommodating drive I did, however, manage to drive the Knumptywagen into a local tree. It wasn't even as if I connected with any force or impact and it didn't really make any impactful noise to speak of – more of a subtle rending, followed by an uncharacteristic silence.

"Oh!"

Slipping surreptitiously from the cab and glancing around like the petty miscreant I now felt myself to be, I was sadly first (but thankfully alone) to witness our beautifully rounded yet eggshell-fragile overcab nosecone now sporting a dent the size of a large baby's head. "Damn!"

Feeling slightly nauseous at my shocking incompetence, I simply walked away and remained in denial for most of the day. Confession and then inspection took place as evening fell, with the Chief Navigating Officer seemingly less perturbed than I was, encouragingly pronouncing that we'd no doubt be able to get it fixed when we got home.

Which we did. After a reassuring phone-call to Martin at our local body shop in Lichfield, we were duly inspected again; enjoyed the shared pleasure of a few considered intakes of breath, a spot of chin-stroking and an estimated solution decided upon.

Thankfully the dent hadn't penetrated to the interior, so the repair was in essence superficial, apparently involving a spot of judicious hammering and then trowelfuls of grey filler, to be sanded, smoothed and rounded to baby's-bottom silkiness.

The follow-on dilemma – thankfully transparently identified by Martin at the outset – was the cost of then respraying the filled dent, necessitating full-width front-end coverage at a substantial supplement which we didn't feel was worth it just for appearance's sake.

"Get a sticker" Martin suggests as we stroke our chins again and mull over the creative possibilities this opens up. "I know a bloke – Liam – who does bloody big stickers" we're confidently told. And indeed he does. Thus, the outcome was our brash new front-end, colour-keyed and now sporting – in a very large font – a very large graphic proclaiming a very large "Knaus" as conspicuous alert to any oncoming traffic that there are Knumpties on board.

Such is the unexpected and entertaining outcome of witnessing occasional smiles creasing the faces of pedestrians as they spot this overstated, self-effacing brand rolling towards them that we've now decided to stick one on the back too!

So, many thanks Martin. And Liam? How're you fixed for a rear-end anytime soon?

A Day On The Water

Keswick, Cumbria, England

On 5th December 2015, Storm Desmond inundated much of Cumbria with widespread flooding. Over the course of just two days, somewhere in the region of 180 miles of roads and 800 bridges were significantly damaged or destroyed, with an estimated 1.15 trillion litres of rain falling in Cumbria alone.

So it was with some concern that we received a phone call from Keswick Camp Site, two days before our three-night booking, to inform us that flood alerts had again been issued for the area. With its northern perimeter defined by the rising River Greta, we were advised that if we still wanted a pitch, we must – for the duration of our stay – remain within 20 minutes of the site and be in a fit state to drive at all times.

Given that our plan was to spend a day in a boat on Derwentwater and the rest of the time drunk, this wasn't an ideal option. Thankfully, old friend; fishing guide extraordinaire; TV personality; local resident; published author and itinerant musician Eric Hope (he of hemmingwaysfish.co.uk – is that enough of a plug for you, Eric?) came swiftly to our rescue and pointed us towards higher ground at Castlerigg Farm campsite, a safe distance above Keswick and its turbulent river.

From here, as a long-planned birthday treat, we'd be able to ramble down to the landing stages at Keswick and board The Beagle, Eric's trusty fishing boat for a day on – and hopefully not in – the water.

Childhood memories of holidays in the Lake District are still accompanied by the sound of the incessant swoosh of windscreen wipers as my parents, two brothers and myself would park-up for our picnic lunch in a scenic beauty-spot somewhere – and view it through gradually-steamed-up windows as summer rain continued to lash down unabated.

So it was with surprise and excited delight that we found ourselves gazing out over a brightly-lit scene of tranquil beauty, as a warming autumnal sun threw highlights and shadows over distant Catbells and shimmered invitingly in the wake from the first passenger launch of the day. Shading our eyes, we could also just make out an approaching boat, headed toward us with all the promise of either Swallow or Amazon, we cared not which, for behold, here was Eric, our Captain and Mentor for the day.

And so we fished. We scoured the depths of Derwentwater, paying heed to the sonar powered fish-finder screen displayed in the boat's small cabin to guide us to apparently fish-populous locations. And we fished. And we fished. And we fished.

On previous excursions, we'd enjoyed the thrill of meeting with goodly catches of decent-sized pike and perch, lured to the net by Eric's skilful deployment of trundled worms; exotic spinners, plugs and – when the need arose – his own unpleasant concoction of 'snurge' (don't ask) to attract piscatorial denizens. Evidential photos abound on Eric's website and indeed in our own extensive digital albums, of sharp-eyed, vividly-coloured fish, safely caught, admired and returned to the water unharmed.

But not today.

Today, although the early October weather was amenable, we barely troubled the fish. Don't be downhearted on our behalf, gentle reader, for we did at least net a few obliging perch and one rather startled-looking jack pike (which we neglected to photograph) so we can't chalk-up the day as a rip-roaring paean to angling. But, as Spike Milligan and many others who fail to comprehend the angling fraternity would say, 'Fishing is complete and utter madness' even at the best of times.

And regardless of this shortfall against our Key Performance Indicators, we had a fabulous day, made more so with the added dimension of a spot of bird-stalking in the wetlands at the southern end of Derwentwater. Here, the gin-clear River Derwent meanders into a marshy delta where our attention is momentarily caught by sight of a tall, snow-white bird, lurking amidst the waving rushes. It gives every impression of being a heron, were it not for the astonishing Persil-like brightness of its all-white plumage and – on closer inspection – its elongated yellow pointed beak. "It's an egret" we surmise "except it's poised like a heron" and indeed, as we gently motor quietly closer and it takes flight, its arced wing profile and span are also pure heron. Even in this comparatively isolated location, Google comes to our aid and after much debate fuelled by zoomed and grainy phone-photos; kindergarten binoculars and a tricky manoeuvre upriver, we conclude it's a surprisingly rare Great Egret, more commonly found in southern climes and definitely not at the marshy end of Derwentwater on an early October Monday.

We are content. What on earth could improve on being afloat on reflected and unrivalled scenic nature; being piloted around beautiful Derwentwater in a private boat; a picnic lunch without the swoosh of windscreen wipers; a risky but successful boat-launched drone-flight; spotting fighter-jets screaming down the valley below the height of the surrounding hills; waving idiotically at launch-passengers; sniggering at still-damp wild-swimmers struggling to get changed onshore and generally, in the way of fisherpersons the world over, just talking absolute bollocks to each other for most of a perfect day.

Piscatorial Peace

Bromyard, Herefordshire, England

We'd visited Kingfisher Trout Fishery and Campsite at Bromyard, Herefordshire on a couple of pre-Covid occasions and thus managed to convince ourselves – having suffered a dearth of fishing opportunities on the trip so far – that it was on our route home. Having tweaked the journey plan to accommodate just a slight diversion from the tedium of the northbound M5, we phoned ahead and – enjoying a frisson of friendly recognition on answer - booked ourselves a half-days' worth of fluff-chucking in this agreeably rural spot.

So it was, in the pouring rain, we reacquainted ourselves with the on-site owners, parked the Knumptywagen waterside and began to pick over the remaining contents of the fridge while we waited for the rain to stop. Which it did, and the sun came out, lighting an autumnal crown of colour which surrounded the naturalised fishing pool as we expectantly tackled up the fly-rods and donned our fishing greens, tucking trousers firmly down into welly tops.

And then we fished.

On almost her second cast, the CNO experienced what's known in the trade as a knock, which thrilled and stimulated her – thinking this presaged an enjoyable and productive session. Sadly, it was not to be as this isolated, inquisitive sub-surface tasting of the artificial fly represented the only contact with anything piscatorial during the entire afternoon. Obviously, anglers around the world can always draw on a reliable and seemingly bottomless supply of anecdotal evidence as to why no fish were caught during any particular session, and with the preceding storms, heavy rain and associated atmospheric pressure all contributing to the fish just being ‘off it’ for the day, we justifiably drew our session to a close.

With dusk drawing in around us, we retired to the van – listening to yet more rain beginning to drum a repetitive paradiddle on the roof – and slowly cobbled what was left of our provisions into an evening meal, our last van-based supper of the trip. Wine was taken and obviously would need to be finished, so we repaired to our over-cab bed with our senses comfortably numbed enough to attempt sleep – despite the fact that it was probably only nine-o-clock.

And finally, as a fitting epilogue to a weeks-worth of our Cornish trip, I’m delighted to reproduce here the final uncharacteristically brief note I find scribbled into our dog-eared travel journal: "Awoke, breakfasted and travelled home to unpack and settle back in."

Ulysses

Lichfield, Staffordshire, England

I hadn't fully appreciated what an efficient postcode system we have in the UK. Travelling in Europe, especially guided by satnav, leaves us struggling on occasions to identify a location to which we might want to head. Easy enough to key-in 'Fréjus' or 'Bologna' which obviously gets us into the vicinity, but for more specific locations such as campsites (or even more remote Agricamper locations), finding our way to them can be a challenge.

Our go-to travelling reference tool for this trip has been a moderately hefty hard-copy Camping Card ACSI Guide which lists (along with a handy fold out locator-map and accompanying app) over 1,800 inspected campsites in mainland Europe and beyond.

But rural areas of France, for instance, are vast and don't conform to our own familiar postcode protocols. So ACSI instead use globally recognised geographical Longitude and Latitude references. These marvels of navigational ingenuity may enjoy a long history but are sadly cumbersomely numerical; prone to mistyping and – as far as our own otherwise excellent Garmin Camper 770 satnav is concerned – can only be keyed-in to a well-hidden and completely counter-intuitive sub-menu of a sub-menu, so are a complete pain to load-up before we depart for our next destination.

Enter, stage left, What Three Words. Avid readers will recognise that I've applauded this application of genius to the planet's surface in previous posts but really, it's such a delightfully simple proposition. So easy to understand, so easy to use and so easy to navigate that the inventors really do need a Very Big Award, Heartfelt Thanks and A Pat On The Back. Accurate to any 3m square patch in the whole-wide-world including the oceans, (should you be enthusiastic enough to be crossing the Atlantic in a solo rowing boat) the W3W app generates a unique 3-word code for any 3m square, so you can locate – in our case – the exact entrance to a large rambling campsite, or indeed – as the inventors proclaim – the specific access gate to a football stadium or concert hall where you've agreed to meet your pals.

As such it should surely be adopted by organisations such as ACSI, to replace the cumbersome degrees, minutes and seconds of their current locators and provide the world with a simple, memorable, easily communicated and uniform method of finding our way around the planet.

In tribute to the effectiveness of W3W, and with lip-service paid to the often impenetrable nature of James Joyce's classic novel, Ulysses, here follows a complete list of our trip through the UK, France, Italy and back through France again, which identifies every single location of the Knumptywagen's main door, where it came to rest in each of the overnight locations of our 2,360-mile trip.

Not only does the list throw up some interesting literary and maybe even poetic connotations, but for us it provides a simple reference tool should we feel the need to retrace any part of our trip in the future.

And if you really don't have anything better to do, you can always download the app and trace our trek . . .

sober.ties.sadly
developed.trudges.message
adopts.spray.wiggly
sketch.dogfight.horseback
rosemary.ices.roamed
qualify.curated.describe
marquees.mouth.vowing
fall.handy.warnings
pruning.messaging.speech

reach.wiggles.adjust
forecaster.incidentally.soda
gumdrops.quashing.talent
drifting.greed.closeness
cheerfully.squids.eggshells
reminders.copy.compete
solos.heartbreak.quoted
shawl.moistens.shrewd
smarten.audition.polkas
fees.sector.harmless
sober.ties.sadly

About the Author

As the co-owner of a used motorhome (acquired on impulse through an early pension payment in 2015) Andy Paterson initially commenced an online blog to record early travels as he and his wife – the Knumptywagen's Chief Navigating Officer - set about learning the challenging demands and responsibilities of motorhome ownership.

In a previous existence, the author enjoyed a career as a graphic designer, including an early stint at Oxford University Press, from where he retains agreeable memories of the rarified world of book publishing.

Currently living in Lichfield, Staffordshire, the author is retired and married with three adult children and five grandchildren. Pastimes include leisure travel; the occasional spot of fly-fishing; an immersive role in a local (and now officially renowned) Gospel choir; shed-based Dad-DIY and relearning how to bottle-feed small grandchildren.

He is generally well-behaved, presentable and no doubt wildly overconfident about the commercial success of book publication.

Given that the author's blog still exists online, you can catch up with more recent tales of derring-do – and indeed (should you so wish) message him direct using the Contact page at *Knumptytravel.com*

Acknowledgements

This book would not exist without the encouragement, support, enthusiasm and cajoling of my wife, the Knumptywagen's Chief Navigating Officer, alongside the rest of my immediate and extended family (of which there are many) as well as dear friends, of which there are fewer but who have been no less vociferous with their chivvying.

My heartfelt and emotional thanks to you all – you know who you are – and if you don't already own a copy of this delightfully entertaining book, then do feel free to take a few of *your* family and friends to your local bookshop – and buy several copies!

Thank you.